C000024983

To Barbara
With best wishes,
Sonia Waterfall
29th August 2021

A Pacifist's War:

Sid's story

*

by

Sonia Waterfall

Published in 2021 by FeedARead Publishing

Copyright © Sonia Waterfall.

The author asserts the moral right under the Copyright, Designs and Patents Act 1988 to be identified as the author of this work.

All Rights reserved. No part of this publication may be reproduced, stored in a retrieval system, or transmitted, in any form or by any means without the prior written consent of the publisher, nor be otherwise circulated in any form of binding or cover other than that in which it is published and without a similar condition being imposed on the subsequent purchaser.

British Library C.I.P.

A CIP catalogue record for this title is available from the British Library.

For my generation of the Waterfall family:
Tony, Hazel, Roger, Brendalyn, Anthony, Jane,
my brother, John, and sister, Fran

Other publications by Sonia Waterfall:

Escape to Auschwitz: Hulda's story
Choices and Opportunities: memories of a Baby Boomer

All available from the publisher FeedARead at
www.feedaread.com

Cover design by Duncan Elson

Background cover photo: Sid's Long March map, 1945

Front cover photo: Sid in uniform outside 'Lyndhurst', Embsay,
1940

Back cover photo: 'Wednesday Nighters', a painting by Helen
Handley, c.2000. L-R: David Handley, Arthur Smith, Sid, John
Wilson

9

CONTENTS

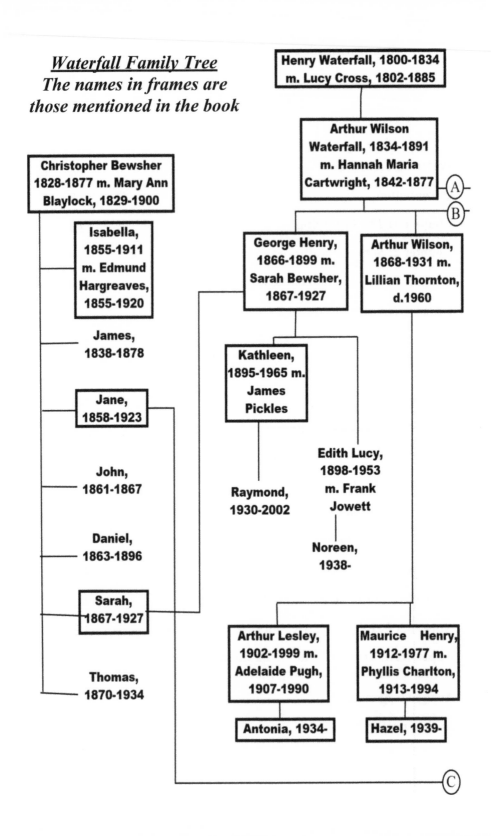

Waterfall Family Tree
The names in frames are
those mentioned in the book

Henry Waterfall, 1800-1834
m. Lucy Cross, 1802-1885

Arthur Wilson
Waterfall, 1834-1891
m. Hannah Maria
Cartwright, 1842-1877 (A)
(B)

Christopher Bewsher
1828-1877 m. Mary Ann
Blaylock, 1829-1900

Isabella,
1855-1911
m. Edmund
Hargreaves,
1855-1920

James,
1838-1878

Jane,
1858-1923

John,
1861-1867

Daniel,
1863-1896

Sarah,
1867-1927

Thomas,
1870-1934

George Henry,
1866-1899 m.
Sarah Bewsher,
1867-1927

Arthur Wilson,
1868-1931 m.
Lillian Thornton,
d.1960

Kathleen,
1895-1965 m.
James
Pickles

Edith Lucy,
1898-1953
m. Frank
Jowett

Raymond,
1930-2002

Noreen,
1938-

Arthur Lesley,
1902-1999 m.
Adelaide Pugh,
1907-1990

Maurice   Henry,
1912-1977 m.
Phyllis Charlton,
1913-1994

Antonia, 1934-

Hazel, 1939-

(C)

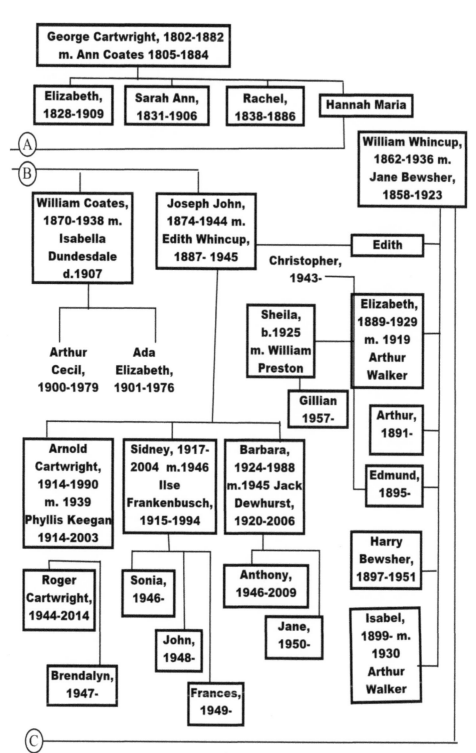

George Cartwright, 1802-1882 m. Ann Coates 1805-1884

Elizabeth, 1828-1909

Sarah Ann, 1831-1906

Rachel, 1838-1886

Hannah Maria

A

B

William Whincup, 1862-1936 m. Jane Bewsher, 1858-1923

William Coates, 1870-1938 m. Isabella Dundesdale d.1907

Joseph John, 1874-1944 m. Edith Whincup, 1887- 1945

Edith

Christopher, 1943-

Arthur Cecil, 1900-1979

Ada Elizabeth, 1901-1976

Sheila, b.1925 m. William Preston

Elizabeth, 1889-1929 m. 1919 Arthur Walker

Gillian 1957-

Arthur, 1891-

Arnold Cartwright, 1914-1990 m. 1939 Phyllis Keegan 1914-2003

Sidney, 1917-2004 m.1946 Ilse Frankenbusch, 1915-1994

Barbara, 1924-1988 m.1945 Jack Dewhurst, 1920-2006

Edmund, 1895-

Roger Cartwright, 1944-2014

Sonia, 1946-

Anthony, 1946-2009

Harry Bewsher, 1897-1951

Jane, 1950-

Isabel, 1899- m. 1930 Arthur Walker

John, 1948-

Brendalyn, 1947-

Frances, 1949-

C

Introduction

In 2002, two years before our father died, my sister Fran and her husband Duncan sat down with our father, Sid to record some of his memories.

It was this interview that first sparked an interest in Sid's life story and in particular his war story. The interview introduced to the next generation facts that had never before been revealed.

Then came the clearing of the house after his death in 2004 and the discovery of letters, documents and photos from Sid's early life. These were put to one side because our grandmother, Hulda's letters had also been discovered at the same time and these took precedence. All these documents had found their way into my niece, Nicola's possession and she did the original sort, preservation and scanning of them.

Once Hulda's story had been told and while I was still sidetracked by my own memoir, I started work on gathering together and organising the documents relating to Sid's story. A large part of 2017 was spent in Skipton Library in Yorkshire following up references to the pre- and post-war part of the story. Meanwhile, Nicola had sent me scanned copies of the documents she had and I had organised them onto my computer. The memoir was finally published in 2019 and it was October of that year when I finally started writing 'Sid's story'. Thanks to the COVID pandemic I continued right through 2020 finally finishing before Christmas that year.

Apart from the interview and the original letters, my most valued and interesting resources were the Waterfall family tree (online at www.waterfall.name), Arnold Waterfall's unpublished autobiography, the Craven Pothole Club (CPC) publications and the Stalag VIIIB/344 Lamsdorf Prisoner of War Facebook Group and website www.lamsdorf.com .

*

When I began writing there were a number of decisions to be made including whether our father should be called Sid or Sidney. He had been called both during his lifetime – Sidney by his parents, his teachers, many of his business colleagues and, surprisingly, by his wife. His siblings, his peer group and other friends knew him as Sid.

In the end I used both, depending on which part of his story I was writing about. It's interesting to note that when he was writing to his parents he signed himself as Sidney and when he wrote to his siblings, he was Sid.

*

The other issue was place names. Many had changed their spelling over time and in some cases had gone through several versions before the modern spelling came into general use.

Once again I went for the easy way out, chose one version and tried to be consistent although sometimes putting another version in brackets if I thought clarification was needed.

*

The maps might also need a word of introduction. They started with place names on them but this made them look crowded and fussy so then I moved to numerical indicators, explaining them in captions and using the same numbers against the place names in the text.

The only exception to this is the map of Crete with alphabetical indicators being used for place names and numerical ones to show the movement of the medical units during the Battle of Crete.

*

All these were my decisions and hopefully they're acceptable to my readers.

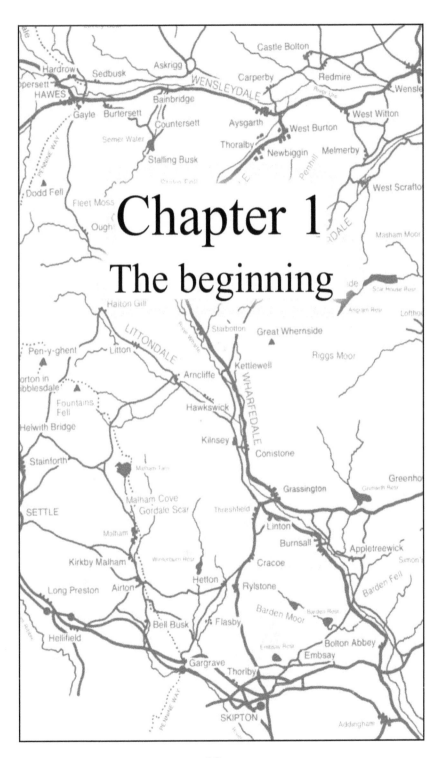

Chapter 1
The beginning

Chapter 1

2002

It was May 2002 and Sidney Waterfall and his younger daughter Fran sat down in the living room of his Park Home near Embsay with a voice recorder. Fran's husband, Duncan, provided the technical support.

Sidney and Frankie had moved into the Park Home 12 years previously as the family home at 'Lyndhurst', 26 Skipton Road, Embsay had become too difficult to maintain as they grew older.
Even though they weren't in the house that he and Frankie had lived in for almost 50 years, he still felt the memories crowding in as he looked around. Most of the furniture had been brought from the old house and was as familiar to him as the clothes he was wearing.

His mother's old desk was in one corner and was the oldest piece in the house – a davenport with compartments and secret drawers. The extendable dining room table, the setting for endless Sunday dinners and games of Monopoly was in the dining alcove. Nowadays it was mainly used when he was working on his stamp collection or when the grand children visited and a jigsaw puzzle was spread out on it.

With a bit of prompting from Fran he began to talk.

He talked about his childhood with Arnold and, later, with Barbara. He talked about his father, Joseph John, who was a big influence in his life and his mother Edith who provided the comforts of home as well as being thoroughly involved in the business. He talked about the Uncles and Aunts of which there were many and of his grandparents on his mother's side – his father's parents having died long before he was born

*

1917-1923

The beginning and the family

In world history terms, 1917 was a hugely important year. It was the year of the Russian Revolution when the Tsar abdicated and he and his family were sent to Siberia, then the Bolsheviks assumed power in the name of the Soviets. The war on the Western Front was not going well for the Allies until, in May that year, the US officially entered the war and a huge influx of new troops decisively tipped the balance in favour of the Allies and against Germany. It was the year that Churchill returned as Minister for Munitions and the year that both the artist Edgar Degas and W.F Cody 'Buffalo Bill' died.[i]

*

It was also the year that Sidney was born on 25 June 1917 at 10 Sheep Street, Skipton in the room at the top of the first flight of stairs that Edith, his mother, used as a birthing room for each of her three children.[ii] Sidney was the second son of Joseph John and Edith Waterfall, their eldest, Arnold, having been born three years earlier in 1914. Barbara, their daughter, arrived seven years later in 1924.

*

Skipton was a small market town in, what was then, the West Riding of Yorkshire.

Little is known about the origins of the town but it is likely that there was a small settlement there from the seventh century onwards. In the *Domesday Book* it was referred to as Sciptone and other early charters used Sceptone and Scepetone from the Saxon *scep,* a sheep. So it is likely that the early inhabitants kept sheep.[iii]

After the Battle of Hastings and the Norman invasion, Skipton Castle was built in 1090 as a wooden motte and bailey, by Robert de

Romille, a Norman baron. In the twelfth century it was strengthened with a stone keep and this elevated Skipton from a village to a *burgh* administered by a *reeve*. The Middle Ages saw the growth of the town surrounding the castle and during times of threat and disorder the town attracted an influx of families who saw it as a means of protection.[iv]

During the English Civil War, the castle was held for the king and was the last royalist stronghold in northern England before it was forced to surrender on 20 December 1645 after a three year siege[v]

It was in 1204 that the first charter was granted allowing a weekly market trading in sheep and woollen goods and this contributed to Skipton's prosperity. A cattle market was held regularly in the High Street until 1906 when it was moved to a site off Gargrave Road. A market in the High Street continues the tradition to the present day.

In the nineteenth century Skipton emerged as a small town, connected to major cities by the Leeds and Liverpool Canal and a railway line. It was at this stage in its development that Sidney was born.[vi]

*

His parents, Joseph John and Edith (nee Whincup) had married five years earlier on 25 March 1912 at Belmont Baptist Chapel in Skipton. Joseph John was thirty-eight years of age and Edith was twenty-five. Once they were married, they moved into 10 Sheep Street, above and behind the bookshop that Joseph John had bought from Edmund Hargreaves in 1907. Edmund was Edith's uncle by . marriage to Isobella Bewsher, her mother's sister [vii]

*

Edmund had previously run the business from 12 Sheep Street for five years until 1885 when he moved into Number 10. When Joseph John took over the business in 1907, the goodwill and fixtures were valued at £450, the stock at £956. Of the total, £500 had to be paid immediately, the rest later. The rent to the Hallam Estate was £100 per annum. viii

The property at 10 Sheep Street has an interesting history and was mentioned as the freehold of one Marmaduke Hodgson as early as 1631. By 1710, ownership had passed to Peter Holgate and his wife Mary. Peter died soon after his marriage and Mary remarried in 1713, this time to George Chamberlain, an ironmonger.

The Chamberlain family were now to occupy the property for one hundred and forty years. One thing the Chamberlain family left behind were their ghosts as three members of the family had the reputation of walking after death. In 1900 the Craven Herald reported that the three ghosts "lived and died where Mr Edmund Hargreaves now has his shop and there is to my knowledge some alive who have seen them". Towards the end of the period of the Chamberlain's residence it seems that part of the building was converted into a house and a shop and let to Christopher Demaine, a joiner. ix

From 1854 until 1885 when Edmund Hargreaves moved his stationery business into the property, it was a drapers establishment passing through five different owners.

*

The family lived above and behind the shop which had a double frontage, a balcony above and a good sized warehouse. The ground floor had a sitting room directly behind the shop, a living room behind that so that with all the doors open the family could be in the living area having a snack and could, at the same time, watch out for customers entering the shop. Adjoining the living room was the scullery, known as the Black Hole of Calcutta. It housed a set-pan for heating water at the back, a gas stove and the only water tap in the building dripping into a shallow sandstone trough. Whatever light existed came from a temperamental gas jet.

For the first seven years of Sid's life, the only toilet was wooden-seated and out in the backyard. According to Arnold's description, it was a luxury model as it was connected to the mains sewage system and there was a bucket of water which was used to flush it. To get out to the backyard you had to go through a lean-to washhouse which was open to the wind at each end and housed the zinc bath, a cast-iron, wooden roller mangle and a washing tub with a wooden posse and scrubbing board.

In 1924, after Barbara's birth, the family partitioned off a bathroom from the warehouse area on the first floor and this was the first time they had hot running water and an inside toilet.

The kitchen had a black range with an oven on one side and a set pan on the other. This, however, wasn't a luxury model as the user had to scoop the hot water out of the top with a ladling can. However, it soon got hot and it was easy to fill the zinc bath and have a bath in front of the fire. The problem came with emptying it into the shallow sink in the scullery – a bucketful at a time. [x]

Upstairs on the first floor was a tiny room known as 'The Snug'. It had a fireplace and was used if it was really cold because it was easily and economically kept warm. It was also a good drying room for Edith's Coltsfoot heads prior to wine-making.

Next to the Snug was the visitors bedroom and it was this room that Edith moved into when it was time to give birth to the children so it was in this room that Sidney was born.

Back on the landing and two steps led to double glass doors leading onto the balcony or Minstrel's Gallery as it was known. At the time of Sidney's birth, this was used to store stock. The other door from the landing led into the warehouse and it was here that the new bathroom was installed in 1924.

Also from the landing, the steps that had led from the ground floor up to the first floor, continued up two flights to the second floor. At each turn of the stairs was a lovely large arched window, the lower one edged in stained glass, and these allowed plenty of light to stream in and made climbing the stairs a pleasure.

The second floor had two large bedrooms and one small one, the latter being the maid's room. Up another four steps to one side was another large room which was at first used as a large junk room. Later, as Barbara grew old enough to need a bedroom of her own, it was divided into two, the far one as a billiard room, the near one as a bedroom with two single beds for the two boys. [xi]

*

One of Arnold's memories from the 1920s was of the Gas Lamplighter going along Craven Terrace behind 10 Sheep Street each evening. He was also the 'getter-upperer' in the morning. His hook with which he lit and extinguished the gas flame, was on a long pole and he was able to knock on the bedroom windows to wake the mill workers – *'by prior arrangement and for a consideration of course'.* [xii]

*

Sidney's father, Joseph John was born in 1874 at Kirby Malham, Yorkshire. He was the fifth out of six children of Arthur Waterfall and his wife, Hannah Maria (nee Cartwright). Of the six children, two died in childhood. All four of the surviving brothers were educated at Ackworth School for four or five years each. Hannah Maria died in 1877 and Arthur in 1891 so none of Joseph John's children knew their grandparents on their father's side of the family.

George Henry, Joseph John's eldest brother, born in 1866, married Sarah, one of the Bewsher sisters all three of whom were connected to the Waterfall/Whincup family. He died in 1899, seven years after his marriage.

Arthur Wilson, the second eldest brother born in 1868, was apprenticed to Rowntree's the grocer and became a grocer himself for twenty years after which he became a hotelier, finally owning the Hotel Metropole at Morecombe. He married Lillian Thornton and they had two sons, Lesley and Maurice, both of whom grew up to be close friends of Arnold and Sidney. He died on Striding Edge on Helvellyn, of a heart attack aged 63 in 1931.

William Coates, the next in line, born in 1870, and closest in age to Joseph John, married twice. His first wife, Isobella (nee Dunderdale) bore him three children, and died in 1907 aged twenty-nine and his second wife, Mary Martha (nee Haygarth) married him in 1908 and both she and William died in the same year, 1938.

*

Joseph John was born into a Quaker family and went to the Friends School at Rawdon in 1886, followed by Ackworth in 1888. Arnold, in his autobiography, mentions a letter signed by two elders stating that *'Joseph John should be accepted by the school at £15 per annum'*.

Arnold writes that his father was happy at Ackworth but never spoke of the years after leaving the school. In effect, he and his brothers were orphans after their mother died in 1877 and Quaker records show he moved around various Leeds addresses as well as Airton where his Cartwright aunts lived.[xiii]

His first employment was with Hotham and Whitings, in those days the equivalent of a wholesale supermarket. Here he was happy, working for a Quaker firm. In his spare time of an evening he would go round trying to sell insurance for the Friends Provident Company. In the early 1900s he moved on to Myers and Co, a cap manufacturer, possibly because they offered a better wage.

The years in Leeds introduced him to what became his favourite indoor game, chess, and he joined a local chess club. At the same time he became a member of the Leeds Friends Horsforth Cycling Club and according to the meets card of 1898 they had fourteen meets between 2 April and 8 October on Saturdays visiting such places as Ackworth, Ripley, Harrogate, Blubberhouses and many others. On Tuesdays they had an evening run – all this for one shilling per year subscription.

He and his brother Arthur, had cycling holidays together during this period of his life and into the early years of the twentieth century However, he never ventured north of Carlisle, nor south of Barmouth

28

in his life, being perfectly content exploring the Yorkshire Dales and the Lake District.[xiv]

After the death of his mother and the years in Leeds with his father, Joseph John moved to Airton and was brought up by his three Cartwright Aunts, Elizabeth, Sarah and Mary, Rachel being away in service at the time.[xv] During the Leeds years he had always kept in touch with his aunts and on one visit to them he dangled a five year old girl on his knee, little suspecting that one day she would become his wife.

When he moved to Skipton after buying the property at 10 Sheep Street in 1907, he was instrumental in re-opening the Quaker Meeting which had been closed for several years. For the first few years there was only an average attendance of eight but many visiting Quakers, whether passing through or staying for the weekend, added to the number and ensured the survival of the Meeting. In his autobiography, Arnold mentions that although Skipton was only a small Meeting, it was also part of a strong monthly Meeting which included Keighley, Salterforth, Cowling, Settle and Bentham.[xvi]

When World War I started Joseph John had to attend both Military and Medical Tribunals because of his Quaker convictions. The fact of him being a Conscientious Objector didn't please some of his customers but because he had become well-known and highly respected during the seven years he had owned the shop, the majority of customers tolerated his beliefs and continued to support the business.[xvii]

*

On the Waterfall side of the family, Arthur Waterfall, Sidney's grandfather, was an only child born to Henry Waterfall and his wife Lucy (nee Cross).

Lucy is notable because, on leaving Ackworth school, where she was educated, she became a teacher in the school of Hannah Kilham at Leavy Greave near Sheffield. Both she and Hannah went to work in Sierra Leone and were the first teaching missionaries to teach in an African language[xviii]. After her return from Africa she became a

29

governess in several households before she met and then married Henry Waterfall in the Friends Meeting House at Brighouse, Leeds in March 1833.

Unfortunately, Henry died in October 1834, six months after the birth of his son. Arthur lived in Leeds with his mother until he was sent to Ackworth School in 1845, followed by Bootham School in York from 1848 to 1850.

*

Arthur married Hannah Maria Carwright at the Friends Meeting House, Airton, in October 1865 and it was in this part of Yorkshire that their six children, including Joseph John, were born. After His wife's death in 1877, he moved to Leeds and is listed in the 1881 and 1884 Friends members book as living at at Woodlands Cottage, Far Headingly, with five other Waterfalls, including Joseph John, who was only seven (1881) and ten (1884) years old respectively at these points in time[xix].

Three years later and ten years after Hannah Maria's death, Arthur found himself in prison. Early in 1887 he was charged with two offences of indecent assault. The court documents from Leeds Assizes records them as follows:

4 May 1887 Arthur Waterfall, aged 52 years, Gardener, was taken into custody on the 27th April 1887 and charged with unlawfully and indecently assaulting Mary Ellen Ellis at Leeds Assizes on 7th March 1887 ... He pleaded guilty of indecent assault ... and was sentenced to 12 months hard labour.

3 Aug 1887 Arthur Waterfall, 52 years, Gardener, Was received into custody on the 27 April 1887 and charged with unlawfully and carnally knowing one Margaret Ann Wilkinson, aged 15 years at Leeds on 14th February 1887. He was tried on the 3rd of August 1887 .... pleaded guilty ... and was sentenced to 8 calendar months but to be concurrent with the sentence he is at present undergoing.

It was after this period of his life that he moved to Skipton where he died in October 1891.

Cartwright family c.1860. Rear L-R: Sarah Anne, Hannah Maria (Sidney's grandmother on his father's side). Middle L-R: Rachel, George Cartwright and Anne Cartwright. Front L-R: Elizabeth and Mary.

Edith and Joseph John Waterfall's wedding photos, 1912

Waterfall family portrait, 1917. L-R: Sidney, Edith, Arnold, Joseph John

Arnold and Sidney, 1923/4.

Whincup family c.1905. Rear L-R: Elizabeth, Jane (Sidney's grandmother on his mother's side) with Isabel, William (Sidney's grandfather) Edith (Sidney's mother). Front L-R: Arthur , Harry and Edward.

Sidney's grandmother on his father's side, Hannah Maria Cartwright, was the youngest of six daughters born to George Cartwright and his wife Ann (nee Coates). One daughter died in childhood but the other five grew to adulthood and remained living in their parent's home. Hannah Maria was the only one to marry.

A photo exists, probably dated around 1860, of George and Ann Cartwright and their five adult daughters posed outside their home in Airton, just across the road from the Friends Meeting House there.

An obituary of Hannah Maria, written soon after her death in January 1877, says:

She was a dutiful and obedient child, loving and affectionate to her parents, and was fond of reading, choosing such books as were most likely to improve her mind. She was also ... very fond of learning poetry ... which she would often repeat after retiring to rest, to those who shared her room. After leaving Ackworth, where she was at school three years, she lived with her parents at Airton, and while still in her teens, commenced a bible class for young women, which she continued until her marriage

In 1867 she married Arthur Waterfall, to whom she was a true help mate, always encouraging him to yield obedience to the pointings of duty. To her children she was a loving and affectionate mother ... though not of strong health. Her health, during the last year of her life became more delicate and consumption was feared. Various remedies were tried but in vain.

The birth of her last child, Edmund, on 9 October 1876 was the final straw for Hannah Maria. He died three weeks after his birth, closely followed by his mother three months later on 20 January, 1877, aged 34 years of age. Joseph John was three years of age when his mother died.

*

Edith, Sidney's mother, was born Edith Whincup in 1887 at Saltaire in Yorkshire but in her early years the family moved to Skipton. By 1911 the family was living at 13 Keighley Road, Skipton and a year later she married Joseph John, aged twenty-five.

She was the third out of eight children and she was the first to survive into adulthood, as did her five younger siblings. In Arnold's account he thinks that it would have been a relief for Edith to move into 10 Sheep Street and get away from a crowded household with two younger sisters and three brothers. [xx]

Sidney's grandfather on his mother's side, William Whincup, was born at Kirk Deighton, Yorkshire in 1862 and his grandmother Jane Bewsher was born at Carlisle, Cumberland in 1858. They were married at Bradford in 1883 and both died at Skipton, Jane in 1923 and William in 1936.

It's interesting to see that an Arthur Walker married Edith's sister, Elizabeth Whincup, in 1919. She died ten years later and Arthur then married her youngest sister, Isabel, in 1932. The Whincup girls obviously had something about them

*

As well as Jane Bewsher marrying William Whincup in 1883, her younger sister, Sarah also married into the family when she married George Henry Waterfall, Joseph John's eldest brother, in 1892. George Henry was also linked with 10 Sheep Street for in its early years he worked there and indeed died there in 1899 when it was still owned by Edmund Hargreaves.

George Henry and Sarah were the parents of Kathleen, and Edith Lucy who, after their father's death, looked upon Uncle Joe (Joseph John) as their new father. He got them into Rawdon School and both helped in the shop each Christmas.

Isabella Bewsher, Jane and Sarah's eldest sister, had already (in 1881 at Kirby Malham) married Edmund Hargreaves, from whom Joseph

John bought the shop in 1907. ^{xxi}

And so, the families of Waterfall, Whincup and Bewsher were inextricably entwined with three Bewsher women in the mix.

*

After their wedding in 1912 Joseph John and Edith had two years working together until Arnold and then Sidney were born. They had a honeymoon at Grange-over-Sands for five days before returning to 10 Sheep Street and after this they didn't have another holiday together until their Silver Wedding anniversary in 1935.

The shop needed two people to look after it but instead of getting extra staff they felt it was better to employ a housemaid to look after the house and the children with Edith doing the cooking (which she loved) and shop work.

Edith became a Quaker when she married Joseph John, though she still liked to go to the Baptist Chapel for a good sing-along. In later years, on Sundays, the boys would often go with her in the evening as well as to Meeting in the morning. So Sundays, the only full day when the shop was closed, were usually taken up with church-going.

J.J.Waterfall's only sold books as a side-line in the early days as the bread and butter came from the news agency which meant a hard slog beginning at 5.30am. Joseph John would take the handcart down to the station and collect the papers. Many would then be individually rolled, addressed and put on the horse-drawn mail coach for delivery up the Dales. Then the paper rounds would be got ready for the newsboys and the shop would be opened.

All this meant that family holidays were not possible as either Joseph John or Edith had to stay at 10 Sheep Street to keep the business going – there were only three days in the year without newspapers.

*

Two of Arnold's earliest memories are of Sidney as part of his life. He remembered being piggy-backed down from his bedroom on the second floor to see his baby brother in the best bedroom on the first floor. Much to his surprise he wasn't allowed to play with him but Edith promised that he could help to splash him when he had a bath.[xxii]

He also remembered helping the maid, Dora, push Sidney in his pram up Raikes Road and past the German Prisoner of War camp. He remembered the German POWs being fascinated by Sidney's rosy-red cheeks, many of them stepping out of line to pat his cheeks. [xxiii]

It's obvious that the extended Whincup family played a big part in both Arnold and Sidney's childhood. Arnold remembered Sundays at Grannies and sing-alongs around the piano.

Towards the end of World War I he remembered his uncles coming home on leave from the army and the fascination that the leather shoulder straps had for him. He was allowed to explore all their pockets and strut around wearing one of their leather-brimmed khaki hats - *'the nearest I ever got to wearing a uniform'* he said. He remembered the postcards they sent to him (their first nephew) from France (Edmund), Egypt (Harry) and Italy (Arthur).

His grandfather William had hens on an allotment near Sandylands Cricket ground – a long way for a little boy to walk but an exciting excursion every time. His job was to collect the eggs, smash up pottery for grit for the hens and, sometimes, to hold the hens after their necks had been wrung – a job he wasn't so keen on.

There was also an Uncle Mike who had a farm at Saltaire that Arnold and Sid loved to explore and an Uncle Tom who had a pigeon loft – another exciting excursion for little boys. [xxiv]

*

In the early years of the twentieth century it was common for traders and their families to live on the premises and this meant that the

Left: Sidney and Arnold, 1918/19

Sidney as a baby, 1917

Joseph John in the doorway of J.J. Waterfall's, 1920s.

37

hide and seek and cowboys and indians. The town's streets and ginnels were their playground. Bikes for children were too expensive in those days but scooters were used instead and woe betide any pedestrians who didn't see them coming down Sheep Street and round the corner to the Post Office. Skipton Castle was another great playground for the children of the town centre – the grandfather of one of them was the castle custodian, living in the Gatehouse, and he let them have the run of the place.[xxv]

*

Both Arnold and Sid used to love going to the pictures and once Arnold turned ten he and Sid were allowed to go on their own. Arnold remembers going with a shilling for them to go into the half-price nine-penny seats. They weren't allowed to go into the cheaper seats but one Saturday afternoon there was a picture that they both wanted to see and the only ones left were the one and halfpenny seats – right at the front on wooden benches. This was in the silent days with a piano playing the appropriate music. They had to sit there and look up at the screen from that front row for over an hour and it gave them neck ache for the rest of the week. They didn't do that again.

*

From 1922 onwards Joseph John and his two sons would go away for a week each year at the end of April/beginning of May

Grange-over Sands was their base several times from where they visited the Lakes, doing the Lakeside to Ambleside steamer trip and once having to come home early when Grannie Whincup died – Arnold remembers asking his father why she had to die when they were on holiday.

Also popular was Scarborough where Uncle Arthur and Auntie Lillie had the Waverley Hotel opposite the railway station.

North Wales was also visited several times. In 1923 Sid, aged just six years old, climbed Snowden for the first time and the previous year the three of them had stayed at Colwyn Bay visiting castles at Conway and Caernarvon and the Penmon Priory on Anglesea. [xxvi]

Edith was not a walker and so missed a lot of the companionship her men-folk shared. She was the provider and always ready to look after the shop while the men-folk went off to a cricket match, on a walk or away for a few days. She always had a hot meal ready for them when they returned.

If Edith wasn't a walker, she certainly enjoyed the thrill of a drive in a car. Her best friend was Mrs Boothman who, with her husband, had a haberdashery shop at the corner of Otley Street. Mrs Boothman was an excellent saleswoman travelling the Dales selling her goods and on these trips Edith was often invited along for company.

On one occasion Mrs Boothman invited Edith and her sons to go on holiday to Walney Isle in Morecombe Bay with her and her three children – all in her T Ford. Arnold noted that when they reached the unmetalled Buckhaw Brow the car refused to go up in first gear so they had to turn it round and reverse the whole way up. It was on this trip to Walney that Arnold accidentally hit Sidney on the head with a stone, whilst they were '*shying*' at piles of loose rocks they had built up. After this incident Edith blamed Arnold as the cause of Sidney having to wear glasses from an early age.

Arnold denied this of course, saying that Sidney was accident prone which often resulted in egg-like lumps on his head. Once he fell out of the shop window and twice he fell out of an armchair, his head hitting the hard iron fender around the hearth.[xxvii]

*

In the wider world, 1923 was the year when the Duke of York married Elizabeth Bowes-Lyon, and the year when Hitler's attempt to overthrow the Republican government of Germany in his beer-hall *Putsch* failed. Prohibition was in full swing in the US and it was the year that Sergei Eisenstein's film *Battleship Potempkin* was released.[xxviii]

It was also the year that Sidney first started school.

*

i   The Twentieth century: a chronicle in pictures, Hamlyn, 1989. p79.
ii   Waterfall, Arnold. Life at 10 Sheep Street. [unpublished] c.1978. p2
iii Hatfield, Ella. Skipton. Otley, Smith Settle, 1991. p15
iv   Op cit endnote ii. p16
v   Op cit endnote ii p17
vi   Op cit endnote ii p18
vii Waterfall, Nicola. Sidney Waterfall, 1917-2004. [unpublished] p1
viii Waterfall, Arnold. Op cit endnote ii, p2
ix   Ibid, endnote viii, p1
x   Ibid, endnote viii, p2
xi   Ibid, endnote viii, pp2-3
xii Waterfall, Arnold. Autobiography [unpublished] c.1987 p22
xiii Ibid endnote xii. p9
xiv Ibid, endnote xii p11
xv   Ibid, endnote xii, p7-8
xvi Ibid endnote xii p15
xvii Waterfall, Arnold. Op cit endnote ii p7
xviii Waterfall, Arnold. Op cit endnote xii. p2
xix Ibid, endnote xii, p4
xx   Waterfall, Arnold. Op cit, endnote ii, p6
xxi Waterfall, Arnold. Op cit, endnote xii.
xxii Waterfall, Arnold. Op cit endnote ii, p8

xxiii Ibid, endnote ii, p8
xxiv Ibid, endnote ii, p7
xxv Waterfall, Arnold Op cit endnote xii p27
xxvi ibid, endnote xii, p5
xxvii Ibid endnote xii p30
xxviii The Twentieth century: a chronicle in pictures. Hamlyn, 1989.p114.

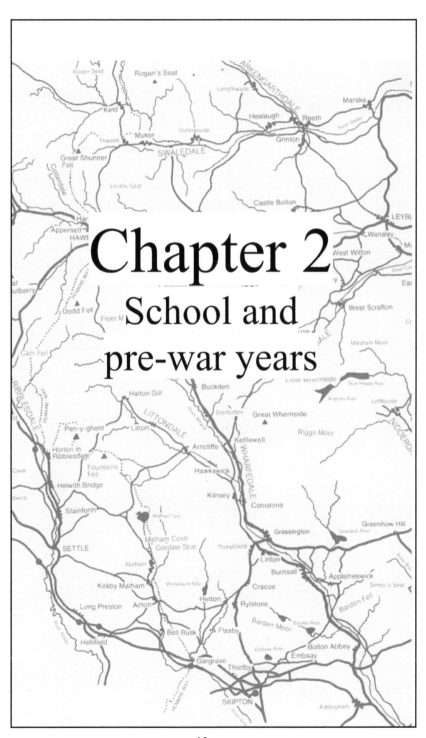

Chapter 2

School and
pre-war years

Chapter 2

2002

In May 2002, Sid and his younger daughter Fran sat down together with a voice recorder, Fran's husband, Duncan, providing the technical support.

After an hour of recording Sid's memories, it was coffee time so Duncan switched off the recorder, Fran made the coffee and the three of them took the opportunity to get up and move around for a few minutes. They stood at the kitchen window and looked out at the view over to the next door park home with the weeping ash tree Sid and Frankie had planted on that side of the house and the rock garden at the end of the garden path.

Sid smiled to himself as he recalled the trip up to his friend Albert's house at the base of Whernside where the larger of the stones for the rock garden were loaded into a trailer to be transported back to their new home. Frankie had so enjoyed choosing the plants for that area.

Wherever he looked there were more memories of his and Frankie's life together.

Fran brought him back to the present and suggested they continued with the recording. She asked him about his teenage years and got him talking again.

He didn't mention school but talked instead about walks with his father and Arnold and camping every summer with his friend Geoff up Pigeon Ghyll . He talked about pot-holing and rock climbing during the summer months and football, skating, skiing and billiards in winter.

*

School and Pre-war years

1923-1939

Sid started school aged six – Edith, his mother was adamant that none of her children were going to school before they were six and she got into trouble with the educational authorities on more than one occasion. However, her will prevailed as it so often did where family issues were concerned and six it was.

Sid's first school was a kindergarten at Skipton Girls' High School where boys were allowed until they were nine years old. In his memoir, Arnold remembers Miss Broadbent, the head, as a real dragon of a headmistress to the kindergartners but otherwise a well liked and respected headmistress. In 1925 when Sid was eight years old, the cost for a term's fee at the Girls High School was £3-19-10.

For the two boys, the best thing about going to school there was Botherby Wood which surrounded the school at that time. This was a wonderful wild stretch of woodland with a stream running through it and a small pond and it was here that they used to play after school, climbing trees, building tree houses and playing around the pond.[i]

*

After kindergarten at the Girls High School, came Ermysteds Grammar School for boys in 1927. For Sid this was only for a year and the most interesting thing for him was that he learned to play rugby. A year at the school at that time cost £14-2-10.[ii]

*

Then it was on to Ackworth in 1928 for the rest of his school

47

years. The school, at Ackworth, near Pontefract in Yorkshire, was, and still is, a Quaker boarding school, founded in 1779. Sidney and his siblings were there between 1925 and 1940 and were the fifth generation of Waterfalls in a direct line to be educated there. Financially, Joseph John and Edith found it difficult to send their children to Ackworth despite the generous bursaries that Arnold, Sidney and Barbara each received.[iii]

To get to Ackworth, they had to travel by train – Skipton to Leeds, change trains, then on to Pontefract Monkshill where they were met by coaches for the final short trip to the school. When Arnold first started he was lucky that his Uncle Arthur and Aunt Lillie had taken over the School Inn and he could stay there with Joseph John for a few days to get the feel of the school. His cousin Maurice was already a student there.

When Sid started three years later, Arnold was still there and could keep an eye on him until he settled in. From an Ackworth Old Scholars' Association Report of 1929, when both Arnold and Sidney were students there, we learn that there were more girls than boys at this time. Also that the *Great Frost in February* resulted in *days skating under sunny skies on Mill Dam, Hemsworth Dam and Pontefract Lake* and that June that year was dull and July *presented us with a Heat Wave.*

Unfortunately for Sid, Uncle Arthur and Aunt Lillie had, by that time, moved on to the Hotel Metropole at Morecombe and Maurice had gone on to Bootham school at York. Uncle Arthur and Aunt Lillie were only at Morecambe for three years when Arthur died in 1931. The Ackworth Old Scholars Association Report for that year published his obituary which ends

During the Easter holidays this year he set off to climb Helvellyn by way of Striding Edge; he reached the top and there among the nature he loved so well, he died on 9 April, 1931, aged nearly 63.

*

Sidney was at Ackworth for five years and his diaries from this period show a definite inclination towards History and Geography but also Poetry.[iv]

His two poetry diaries cover four years from 1928 to 1932 and comprise stanzas or complete poems, often with illustrations. The illustrations are sometimes cut out from magazines etc and other times are either copied or drawn freehand by Sid. The poems cover a vast array of subjects and writers, some well known, others not. The occasional poem written in Sid's handwriting lead me to think that these may be his own choices and of particular importance to him. One of these he passed on to his children many years later:

Leisure
by W.H.Davies

What is this life if, full of care,
We have no time to stand and stare

No time to stand beneath the boughs
And stare as long as sheep or cows

No time to see when woods we pass
Where squirrels hide their nuts in grass

No time to see in broad daylight
Streams full of stars like skies at night

No time to turn at beauty's glance
And watch her feet how they can dance

No time to wait til her mouth can
Enrich that smile her eyes began

A poor life this if, full of care,
We have no time to stand and stare

Both volumes have numbered pages and an index as well as a

Ackworth Corinthians, 1930-31 League of Champions Knockout Winners. Sid, middle row, far right

ACKWORTH SCHOOL.
TIME TABLE.

Left: Ackworth timetable, c.1930

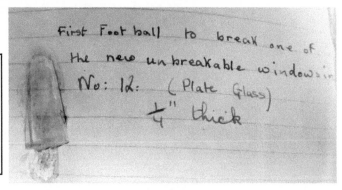

First Foot ball to break one of the new unbreakable windows in No: 12: (Plate Glass) ¼" thick

Right: A piece of broken glass from Sid's Ackworth Scrapbook, c.1930

Picture Gallery identifying the illustrations. Very well organised and typical Sidney. The second volume has a loose leaf page on which he had practised his signature – a normal teenage occupation.[v]

*

The archaeology workbooks, dating from 19 October 1927 to 8 June 1932, show a fascination with the detail of history and architecture. The buildings described range from small local churches (Hubberholme, Coniston and Kirby Malham) and isolated Welsh churches (Llangelynin, Llanbedr and Penman Priory), to castles (Carnarvon and Conway) and cathedrals (Ripon).

It seems that the school ran excursions to the various sites and some must have been extended trips necessitating overnight stays allowing enough time to visit six sites in some places.

Each account is illustrated with postcards, illustrations from leaflets, cut out and glued into the workbook and, in most cases, hand drawn plans.

In each volume there is an index of places visited and on what date and at the end of volume 1 is an Appendix of the shading used on the plans and the dates of the different architectural periods[vi]

*

The Mapping and Survey notebook shows Sid's early introduction to the love of maps. In later life one of his friends said he could *read a map like a book* and this love of maps was passed on to his children. During his working life he managed the map section at *J.J.Waterfall's,* the family business, and also had his own considerable collection of maps from the various periods of his life.

The notebook lists topographical and technical definitions, some illustrated by the signs as they would appear on a map and a number of hand-drawn maps obviously set as exercises. [vii]

*

There also exists a scrapbook that Sid kept for the last three years of his time at Ackworth, the earliest entries starting with the Autumn term of 1930. From this we discover that his school number was 131 and he was in Chalfont House.

Football played a large part in his school life. In 1931 he was playing for the Ackworth 2nd XI but by 1933 he was playing for the 1st XI, the Masters XI and the House XI, often being listed as Captain for the latter. He mentions that he broke his arm at one point and had to make do with umpiring rather than playing until it was fully healed.

Amongst the more unusual items is a piece of glass from a broken window (broken by a football) and a piece of candle wax as a reminder of *when the electric light went in the 3rd bedroom*. There's also a list of Masters' nick-names. From this we discover that in 1930 Mr Cooper was 'Stylo', Mr Lidbitter was 'Jumbo, Mr Bibby was 'Ferret and Mr Westwood was 'Tramp' or 'Snipe'

There were the results of a History exam in November 1930 with a 'B' for Sid and a note that he was *'Top all term at History'*. But he only got 25% for Algebra and a note says *'my only 'E' in Autumn term 1930'*. In the Sixth Form he got an A (76%) for History and a 'B' for Geography in exams held in March 1933.

Where the non-academic side of his school years are concerned, there are Putting score cards from 1932, the results of the Ping Pong League matches – won by S.Waterfall - and notes about the formation of a Stamp Society, both from 1931. There is a members card from the Skipton Amateur Swimming Club from 1932, a programme from the Craven Naturalist and Scientific Association for the winter of 1933-34 and a flyer about a Disarmament Meeting to be addressed by Gerald Bailey, from the National Peace Council and a Representative at Geneva.

On a lighter note there is a ticket (Row I, No. 6, at a cost of 2/4) for 'Princess Ida' at Skipton Town Hall and another Matinee ticket and programme for 'White Horse Inn (seat B 2 at a cost of 3/6) at Leeds Grand. All of which give us some idea of the extent of Sid's interests during this period of his life.[viii]

Sid took his School Certificate in 1933 and passed with a credit in History and a distinction in Geography.[ix]

*

While at Ackworth he kept in touch with friends in Skipton. There exists a collection of around fifteen letters from girlfriends who all wrote to him passing on the news of what was happening at home: who was going out with whom; who wanted to go out with whom; who was writing to whom; who danced with whom at different events and encouraging him to write back to them. Whether he did or not is not known but he was obviously popular with the girls – particularly Jessie, Nelly, Dora, Dot/Dorothy, Amy, Maggie, Evelyn and Polly.

*

Outside of school hours, walking with Joseph John was the most popular pastime for the two boys. During the periods at Ackworth this would have been restricted to the few weekends they were allowed home during term time and the school holidays.

Their favourite walks were Skipton Moors (7) with a stop at Rankins Well for a drink, Sharphaw (2) and Flasby Fell (1) with the view from the former being a highlight. There were occasional trips to the Valley of Desolation (9), where Dippers built their mossy nest behind the waterfall and up Pinhaw Beacon (12) which at that time housed a large colony of Blackheaded Gulls. The walk up past Norton Towers, Rylstone Cross (4) and Cracoe Memorial (5) to the hidden village of Thorpe (6) was a favourite

Below: Sid and Arnold's walks with their father in Wharfedale

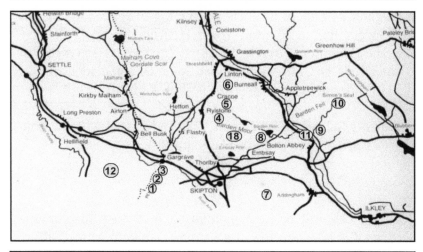

1: Flasby Fell. 2: Sharpaw. 3: Sugar Loaf. 4: Rylstone Cross 5: Cracoe Memorial 6: Thorpe 7: Skipton Moor 8: Queen's View 9:Valley of Desolation 10: Simon' Seat 11: The Strid 12: Pinhaw Beacon 18: Embsay Crag

Below: Sid and Arnold's walks with their father in Ribblesdale and Bishopdale

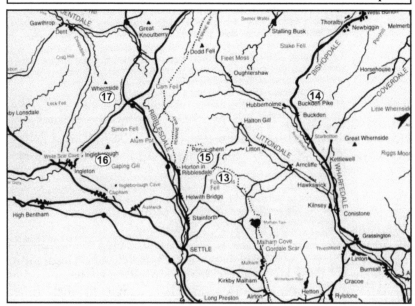

13: Fountain's Fell 14: Buckden Pike 15: Penyghent 16: Ingleborough 17: Whernside

one . On this walk there were Nightjars to hear, Merlins to watch and often Pied Flycatchers as well, more common here than many other places.

An annual trip was the walk through the fields from Eastby to Bolton Abbey to see the arrival of King George V and Queen Mary at Bolton Abbey Railway Station for their annual holiday with the Duke and Duchess of Devonshire. The King went grouse shooting while the Queen explored the area in her car. Her favourite view was from the top of the moors on the Eastby to Barden road and she declared it one of the finest views in their kingdom. It was known as the Queen's View **(8)** from that time onwards.[x]

A popular short evening stroll in summer was up Park Hill, from the top of which it was said the Parliamentarians shelled the Castle. Turning right over the stile at the top, the three men-folk would play ball between the three large trees in the corner of the field and then return through the woods past the regular nesting place of the Long tailed Tits.

Joseph John was interested in natural history in all its aspects. He knew where to find mushrooms, blackberries, cloudberries, bilberries, raspberries, hazelnuts and watercress and there were regular picking trips with the boys towards the end of each summer.

Another 'fruit of the forest' that was collected annually was Coltsfoot heads for Edith's homemade Cleat Wine, their main source of supply being the old quarry up Skibeden Road. Edith's Cleat, or Coltsfoot Wine was an anomaly as she strongly supported the White Ribboners, the Ladies Temperance Organisation. A Quaker friend, knowing Edith was a professed teetotaller, asked if he might take a sample home to test it for alcohol content. When the result came back noting a very high content, Edith wouldn't accept it and continued making it though she never drank it herself. She usually made about six litres a year with a maturing cycle of seven years.[xi]

There was many a search for the Lady's Slipper Orchid though it was never found. It was the searching that was the pleasure, any findings were a bonus.

There was generally an annual pilgrimage with the boys to see how the Mountain Avens were flourishing; the beautiful Grass of Parnassus; the Bird's Eye Primroses; the insect-eating plants like the Butterwort and Sundew; the Globe Flowers and the Lilies of the Valley.

When the two boys and Joseph John went away walking on longer trips, they usually stayed in Quaker hostels. It was while they were staying in a hostel that Sid first picked up a billiard cue and started playing billiards, taught by his father.[xii]

*

If summer days were blissful for a budding naturalist, winters were memorable for skating. Joseph John was an old style skater with wood blocks, heel screw, leather straps and a plain steel blade to skate on. He fitted the boys up with a pair each and took them out on the ice. Arnold notes

In the 1920's there hardly seemed a winter without two or three weekends skating. The finest setting was the round dam in Castle Woods lit by flares. For a long skate the Canal was excellent as long as you remembered that the ice is often thin under the bridges. Coniston Hall lake was another lovely setting.

Skiing also became a part of their lives during the 1930s and when the weather turned wintry and walking, rock climbing or pot holing were no longer possible they got the skis out. Arnold managed to borrow three pairs with sticks for himself, Sidney and Bill Bowler. He describes them:

They were of ash with irons pierced through the middle and turned up on either side of the ski. A toe strap was then put across and one's toe forced in between the iron and the toe

strap. Then a long strap was threaded through the hole in the ski and brought round to the heel where each end was fastened to a tightening clasp. Primitive but they served their purpose, for us to get the feel of the skis and learn the rudiments...[xiii]

Before the war Arnold remembers the threesome always getting two or three weekends skiing, generally above Cray but otherwise it was Thorpe or Park Hill, Skipton.

Another winter activity, indoors this time, was billiards. In the late twenties Joseph John bought a half-sized Riley's slate-bottomed billiard table. There was a large unused room on the top floor of 10 Sheep Street and their Uncle Harry (Whincup) divided it up to create an extra bedroom as well as a Billiard Room. It was at this time that Barbara got her own bedroom downstairs and the two boys moved up into the newly created bedroom next to the Billiard Room.

As well as providing an indoor activity for the boys it was also a boon for Joseph John and gave him the opportunity to turn off from the worries of the business even though he was still on the premises. It was used during the mid-day break as well as in the evenings. Having the use of a billiard table also gave the boys extra kudos with their friends who couldn't get enough of it.

*

Arnold would have finished his education at Ackworth in 1930 after which he started working with his parents at 10 Sheep Street. From 1931 onwards he kept a diary of walks he did in the Dales. Some that are dated during school holidays or at weekends would have been taken with Sid and their father, others with his father or on his own or with friends as he would have been sixteen by this time.

Between 1933 and 1936, Arnold walked the Yorkshire Three Peaks (Penyghent **(15)**, Whernside **(17)** and Ingleborough **(16)**) three times and kept very precise notes of the times taken. In July 1933, with Sid, it took them 10 hours and 20 minutes including resting time. The second time was a Craven Pothole Club walk which was undated and his notes were scribbled on the back of a letter inserted into the diary. This one took 9 hours and 30 minutes. The third time, with Bill Bowler and J. Smith was on 29 March 1936 and took 9 hours 16 minutes including resting time.

Other walks mentioned in Arnold's diary were Sharphaw **(2)**, Buckden Pike **(14)**, Thorpe Fell **(6)**, Pinhaw Beacon **(12)**, Great Whernside, Fountains Fell **(13)** and Penyghent **(15)**.[xiv]

*

Other interesting notes in Arnold's diary are the results of Table Tennis games between the two brothers (12 August 1931), Miniature Golf games between Sid, Arnold and Joseph John (undated), Billiards between the three of them (1930 to 1936) and Mahjongg between the three of them. They were obviously a very close threesome who spent a lot of their free time together.[xv]

*

Also dating from this period (1930) is an account, written by Sid, of two walks taken with his father, Joseph John. They were staying in Arnside and both walks started and ended there. As well as describing the route and vegetation the account tells what they ate for lunch, how they watched ants for fifteen minutes, watched '*the interesting occupations of half a dozen guinea fowl*', watched golfers on the golf links and talked to a tame dove. They missed the bus home on one walk and had to walk an extra two or three miles to Milnthorpe '*where we were lucky in finding a fair where we spent some of our money*'. It sounds like an idyllic time spent with his father when he was thirteen years old.[xvi]

Arnold remembers he and Sid spending a holiday in 1930 at the Young Friends' Camp at Scar House Farm above Hubberholme. There were about twenty young Quakers there and Arthur and Lill Raistrick were their leaders. They *walked, becked and swam in wonderful weather and a new experience was picking Cloudberries on Buckden Pike, an alpine plant which only grows above 2,000ft. This was the holiday when the two of us crossed the bridge over the top fall at Gordale and got a mighty ticking off for doing so.*[xvii]

Arnold notes that the following year was their last Young Friends' holiday, this time at Tenby. After that the annual pot-holing camps at Gaping Gill took precedence.

*

After Sidney left school in 1933 he went to work as a solicitor's clerk at Knowles & Harrison at 15 High Street, Skipton. Now that he was living once again at 10 Sheep Street, his life was divided into two seasons, summer and winter. For him summer began at Easter and ended on a bank holiday in September.

For the five summers that he worked at Knowles & Harrison, he and his friend Geoff Holmes, who was a Deputy Sanitary Inspector, camped out at Pigeon Ghyll at Close House Farm on the outskirts of Skipton. Otley Road runs east out of Skipton and about a mile out of town is the turn off to the farm. Mr Wilman, the farmer, allowed them to use the land free of charge but each year they bought him a bottle of whiskey and his wife a box of chocolates.

They had a two-man tent but it had high walls so they could stand up in it and a wooden floor covered with carpet. They had a wireless and a chest of drawers. Sidney called it '*a real luxury job*' and '*home-from-home*'.[xviii]

They cooked their evening meals there after work but had breakfast at home each morning. They either cycled into town and back or ran across the fields to come out at the junction of Otley Road and Moor Road where the old Grammar School was. From there it was only five minutes to 10 Sheep Street where they got washed and changed, had breakfast and went to work.

During the day the tent was left open and Mr Wilman kept an eye on it but they never had anything stolen. During winter they cleared the campsite and stored their gear at Mr Wilman's.

At weekends they had a lot of visitors – all their friends used to go up, both boys and girls. One time they were all up there having fun and acting the fool and a dog appeared – it was their family dog, Jim, closely followed by Sid's father. Joseph John didn't say anything at the time but Sid felt obliged to go and talk to him next time he went home and explain that they were just having fun.

One other time, he and Geoff were late for work and were cycling *'hell for leather'* down the farm road to Otley Road when they came off their bikes. There'd been a circus in Skipton and the two boys ran head on into a big pile of elephant poo which brought them down.[xix] The washing and changing for work took longer than usual that day.

*

There exists detailed notes in Sid's handwriting of an eight-day trek undertaken around this time. Unfortunately, the notes aren't dated, nor do they mention the participants but they seem to belong to the period post-Ackworth but pre-war. The numbers in the following description relate to the map showing the route.

They began by taking a bus from Skipton to Grassington **(1)**, heading up to the lead mines, then over Great Whernside and Little Whernside to an overnight stop at West Burton **(2)**. This was a day of twenty-one miles and described as *'Energetic'* From there they walked via Thoralby and Aysgarth, across the moors to Semerwater and the next overnight at Coutersett **(3)** - a day of eleven miles and *'Non Energetic'*. The next day was to Gayle then cross country to Dent **(4)** where they stayed the night – a day of seventeen miles and *'Mid Energetic'*. Then it was over Whernside to the Hill Inn on to Gaping Gill and ending the day

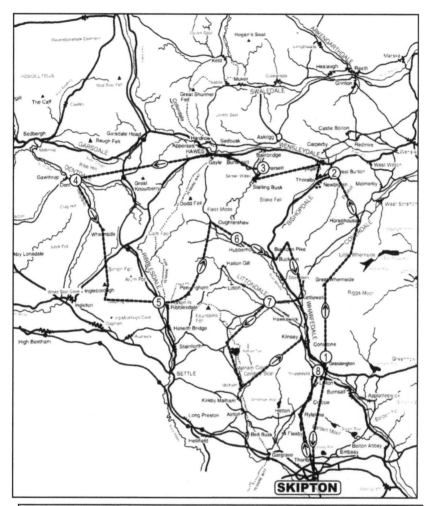

Sid's Yorkshire Dales 8-day trek, 1930s. Key: 1- Grassington; 2 - West Burton; 3- Countersett; 4 - Dent; 5 - Horton-in-Ribblesdale; 6 - Beckermonds; 7 - Arncliffe; 8 - Grassington. Beginning and ending in Skipton.

Left: Sid in camp, Gaping Ghyll, 1930s

61

at Horton in Ribblesdale **(5)** twenty-six miles and *'Very Energetic'*. From there it was over Penyghent, cross country to Oughtershaw with an overnight at Beckermonds **(6)** eleven miles and *'Non Energetic'*. The next day was thirteen miles and *'Mid Energetic'* when they followed the river Wharfe down to Buckden, continuing over Buckden Pike, descending to Kettlewell and over the tops to Arncliffe **(7)**. The penultimate day, seventeen miles and *'Mid Energetic'* was from Arncliffe over the moors to Malham, up Gordale Scar, on to Mastiles Lane, down to Kilnsey and on to Grassington **(8)** where they spent their last night. The last day was twelve miles through Thorpe, up onto the tops and back to Skipton via the Cracoe Memorial, Rylstone Cross and Norton Towers.

In eight days they'd covered 127 miles with an average of sixteen miles per day. It was the first of several long-distance treks Sid was to complete during his lifetime.

*

If the summers were spent camping and walking, the winters were spent playing football. Sidney had started playing at Ackworth and in 1932-33 he played for the first XI.[xx]

On leaving school he played for Christ Church Association Football Club from 1933 to 1936 and then for Sutton United Association Football Club from 1936 to 1939. The season started mid September and continued until the end of April with a match practically every weekend.[xxi]

Sidney kept a record of the fixtures for each season, noting the date, their opponents, which ground they played at (home or away), the result, goals scored for and against, the names of the scorers, which competition the match was part of, and whether he'd played or not. Sid himself usually played at Half Back, was usually in the top three where numbers of games played was concerned and occasionally scored a goal (two or three each season). The main competitions they played in were the League, the Hospital Cup and the Victory Shield and the teams they played were mainly Aire Valley teams but also a few Wharfedale teams.

The last match noted was played on May 6th 1939 and by this time most of the men would have known that war was approaching and that this would be the last season of football for most of them.

*

Pot-holing and rock climbing also played a large part in Sid's life during those pre-war years. In the following descriptions the numbers in the text relate to the two maps on the previous page.

Arnold remembers that his first interest in the Yorkshire underground was aroused during a holiday with Joseph John and Sid at the Hill Inn, Chapel-le-Dale, in 1924 when he was ten years old and Sid was seven. In his autobiography he recalls

Our equipment was two hand torches and we had a tremendous time exploring Great Douk (11), Gatekirk (9), Ivescar (8), Bruntescar and, after those, Weathercote (7) wasn't so exciting. That holiday was the first contact with the Three Peaks, for we climbed both Ingleborough and Whernside, seeing the large colony of gulls on the latter's tarns.

The same year saw us at Douk, Kettlewell, Sleets (2) and Scoska (4) the latter two in Littondale. It should have included Doukerbottom (3) but we couldn't find it. We found it the following year by climbing the ridge above and looking down upon it.[xxii]

He mentions that while he was at Ackworth, his father would send him any cuttings from the papers concerning caves, potholing and the activities of the Craven Pothole Club and the Yorkshire Ramblers Club. As soon as he left Ackworth in 1930 he joined the Craven Pothole Club and his first active meet was in February 1931.

Arnold was the keener of the two brothers where pot-holing was

Below: Pot-holes in Wharfedale and at Greenhow

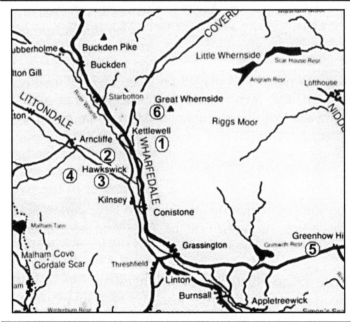

(1) Langcliffe Pot (2) Sleets Gill Cave (3) Dowkerbottom (4) Skoska (5) Stump Cross (6) Kettlewell Caves (Dow Cave)

Below: Pot-holes in Ribblesdale

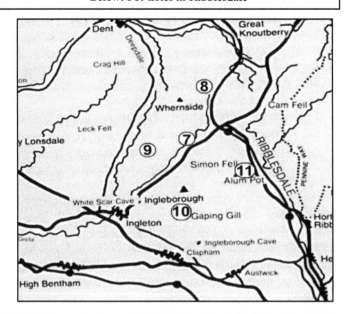

(7)Weathercote (8) Ivescar (9) Gatekirk (10) Gaping Gill (11) Great Douk

concerned. He was one of the founder members of the Craven Pothole Club and would go off potholing most weekends. Sid used to go with him because a lot of his friends went. They used to hire a Pennine bus plus a driver for the Pothole Club trips. Everyone would meet in the High Street, get on the bus and go off for the day, then get back on the bus to come home, stopping off in Stainforth for ham and eggs for 2/6.[xxiii]

Both Arnold and Sid joined the Craven Pothole Club when they were sixteen, Arnold in 1931 and Sid in 1934.

It's difficult to write of their separate achievements because so many were shared. The Craven Pothole Club played an important part in their lives from the 1930s onwards. Arnold was on the Committee 1933-34, Secretary 1935-1954, Vice President 1955-56 and President 1957. He was a member for 59 years. Sidney was Librarian 1936-1958, Trustee 1937-1968, Vice President 1961- 1963 and President 1964. He was a member for 70 years and, at his death, was the oldest living member of the club.[xxiv]

Where pot-holing was concerned, Arnold was a leader – his name was etched in the club's archives as a 'CPC Great' and he has many pioneering explorations to his name. The most notable was the conquering of the Rat-Hole, a succession of tortuous passages between two chambers in the Gaping Ghyll complex of caves. It took three well-planned attempts over three years for a team of six to accomplish this and it has become a legend in CPC history.[xxv]

Sidney was also described as a pre-war pioneer, being more a member of the support team during underground explorations; his skills providing backup both underground and above ground.

Pot holing was a Sunday activity for the boys and this came in conflict with their Quaker upbringing as Joseph John liked his family, whenever possible, to attend the weekly Sunday Meeting down the Ginnel in Skipton. As a compromise they agreed not to miss three meetings in a row. This allowed them to go pot holing on two consecutive weekends - important because some of the caves being explored needed more than just one day. At this time, in the early thirties and just out of school and in their first jobs, they were both working full time. Sid got weekends off but Arnold didn't as he was working in the family shop at 10 Sheep Street and Saturday was their busiest day.[xxvi]

*

Sidney was a good pot-holer but rock climbing was his real strength. He and Arnold pioneered many new routes on local Millstone Grit crags and in his later years Sid featured in a television documentary with Chris Bonnington.

A lot of the climbs were on the Bolton Abbey Estate and they had to dodge the gamekeepers who were very protective of the grouse being raised for the shooting season starting in August. However, Joseph John knew the Estate Agent at Bolton Abbey and had a word with him – telling him that his boys just wanted to climb and weren't doing any damage. The result was a permanent pass on to estate land for Mr Waterfall and his two sons. After that there were no more problems with the gamekeepers.[xxvii]

In his autobiography, Arnold writes that

At a very early age, Sid and I found a way of climbing onto our kitchen roof, via an open Midden door, onto the scullery roof and then traversing onto either the washhouse or kitchen roofs. Then it was possible to traverse along our high yard wall, cross over to the stairs window and down to the ground again via the sitting room windows.

That was many years before we ever knew anything about rock-climbing he says, *but obviously there were hidden talents there!*

Arnold goes on to describe how they became a threesome in their teenage climbing exploits:

Stump Cross (5) exploration team, 1935. Sid, back row, fourth right. Arnold, front row, second right

Sid at the start of the 85 foot entrance pitch of Langcliffe Pot (1), Upper Wharfedale, 1936

Sid at Waterford Ghyll, 1930s

Left: CPC Easter climbing meet in Langdale, 1935. L-R: Harry Pearcey, George Gill, Mabel Greenwood, Bevis Wilkinson, Sidney Waterfall, Bill Bowler, Jack Clough.

A young man by the name of Bill Bowler started working in Skipton and learnt of the existence of the Craven Pothole Club. We heard of his interest in rock climbing and teamed up and went climbing on a Tuesday afternoon.[xxviii] [Tuesday was half-day closing in Skipton at the time]. The threesome became well-known for pioneering climbs on both local gritstone and in the Lake District.

In the book *'Yorkshire Gritstone'* edited by Graham Desroy Sidney and Arnold (and friends) are described as *THE team of the era in this area* [xxix] – this area being the gritstone crags of Wharfedale and Airedale, especially Crookrise **(4)**, Rylstone **(5)**, Simon's Seat **(8)** and Eastby Crag **(2)**.

This book provides a detailed account of the brothers' rock climbing activities for the six years between school and the outbreak of the war.

About Brandreth **(11)** on Blubberhouse Moor, it says *'activity undoubtably took place pre-war, possibly at the hands of Sidney Waterfall and friends from the CPC'*
About Crookrise **(4)**, it talks about *'route-thirsty locals in the guise of the CPC. While everybody thought they were crawling along on hands and knees in some trogloditic paradise, they were actually picking off the plum lines with youthful agility. Hemp ropes and plimsolls were the standard kit. The main activists were Arnold and Sidney Waterfall and Bill Bowler'*.
Of Route 2 on Crookrise, it says: *'This was an exceptional lead for the time, being both delicate and bold it showed a move away from the traditional style of route.'*
About Deer Gallows **(3)**, it says *'The Waterfall brothers, Sidney and Arnold and their friends were hyper-active during the pre-war years in the area and left their mark – but no records – on Deer Gallows as they did almost everywhere else on Barden Moor'*
In the list of first ascents at the end of the book it says of Deer Gallows: *'First ascents unknown, but more than likely the work of the ubiquitous Waterfall brothers, Sidney and Arnold, and their friends'*.
About Eastby Crag **(2)**: *'The earliest recorded climbing at Eastby*

dates back to the early 1930s when Sidney Waterfall and friends pioneered a number of routes, as they did on almost every crag in the area.'

About Great Wolfrey **(9)** on Appletreewick Moor, *'Great Wolfrey has enjoyed the unique position of being left to a few hardy climbers with an exploratory nature ... sited as it is in splendid isolation, six kilometres from nowhere ... a superb lonely setting giving one the feel of being a real pioneer. Sidney Waterfall and friends visited the crag during the 1930s.*

Rolling Gate **(6)** on Barden Moor was first visited in 1934 *'when Sidney Waterfall and his friends of the CPC made their appearance.'*

About Rylstone **(5)**, also on Barden Moor, it says:

'In 1933, Sidney Waterfall, his brother Arnold and their friend Bill Bowler, all members of the CPC, began climbing regularly on the crags in the Skipton area, including Rylstone, and within a couple of years produced a host of new routes. The best climb of this period was undoubtably Dental Slab, an all-time classic severe, which required novel cleaning methods involving a pothole ladder and trenching tools to strip it of heather and turf. Sidney Waterfall, who was still living at Embsay in 1988, had the original ladder in his bedroom "to throw out the window in case of fire"'.

Talking about the history of the climbs on Simon's Seat **(8)**, it says:

'the next stage of the development belongs, as with many of the crags in this area, to the Waterfall brothers, Sidney and Arnold and their friend Bill Bowler. They climbed Arete Wall, Layback Crack and the impressive Chockstone Chimney in the mid-30s. [xxx]

In a book published in 2010, Ron Fawcett, a rock climber of a later generation, said, when talking about pioneering the Dental Slab route on Rylstone *'they must have been bold lads because the route looks a lot harder than it is. It must have been a real step in the dark.* [xxxi]

*

The threesome always looked forward to the Lake District meets

Gritstone rock climbing sites pioneered by Sid and Arnold

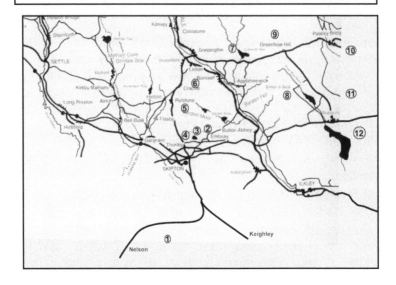

1. Widdop. 2. Eastby Crag. 3. Deer Gallows 4. Crookrise 5. Rylstone
6. Rolling Gate 7. Hebden Ghyll 8. Simon's Seat 9. Great Wolfrey
10. Brimham Rocks   11. Brandrith 12. Almscliff

Sid on rock in Devon

70

whether they were day trips or weekends. Their main venues were Dow Crags on Coniston Old Man or Gimmer Crag in Langdale.

In his autobiography Arnold describes two climbs they did:

On one memorable day the threesome decided to try 'A' route on Dow Crag. It was classed as a Severe route which was a class of climb we enjoyed. Unfortunately Bill took the wrong route somewhere, got under an overhang and brought me up. Fortunately there was a good belay to give us some confidence before tackling the next move. Bill disappeared round the corner and the rope kept moving up. He shouted down that he'd got over the overhang, but 'there's a slab that's a bit thin'. That I presumed was just to encourage me - or did he mean it, for the exposure was great. He took in 50 foot of rope and then I brought up Sid, and he belayed himself. Then it was my turn to negotiate the overhang which you could not see from the belay, though it might not have helped me to see how Bill had tackled it. The technique of a low-centred gravity climber like Bill and a lanky six footer like me, with a higher centre of gravity, can be quite different.. Bill often had to make two moves to my one, but when reach didn't count, his balance was better. It seemed to take me ages to surmount that overhang and there was no denying the slab was 'a bit thin', especially when the occasional sly remark floated down from above. We felt pleased we had done the climb, but I for one rest on my laurels and am glad to leave Very Severe climbs to others.

The other was on Gimmer Crag in Langdale:

We'd climbed Middle Fell Buttress, a nice Very Difficult climb to warm up on before reaching Gimmer itself ... We decided to climb 'B' Buttress on Gimmer. Half way up is the crux of the climb, a technical problem called a double lay-back. A normal lay-back is inching up a crack, by pulling on the nearside edge of the crack with one's hands and at the same time pushing on the far side of the crack with one's feet. In this case , one has to change over half way up, and pull on the side you were pushing on, and push on the side you were pulling on, far easier writing it down than actually doing it.. We were lucky in the fact that lay-backs are common on the Dales Crags, so that we spent little time on the problem and proceeded on our ascent of the climb, and descended down another climb to Bilberry Shute for our lunch. Whilst we were eating, an old craggy faced elderly climber approached us and greetings were exchanged. What club were we from? Craven Pothole Club. Never heard of them. Then we had to explain that we were really a pot-holing club but did a little climbing. How many times have you done this climb? This is our first time. He didn't believe us. It's true we said in unison. Well, said he, I've seen dozens of parties climb it, but I've never seen a party climb it as efficiently as you three have just done. We explained to him that the Yorkshire Gritstone climbs have many such laybacks and he replied, Well that is why they're known as a wonderful training ground for climbers.[xxii]

*

Meanwhile, change was in the air.

Sidney turned 21 in 1938 and it was then that he received a pocket watch from his grandfather, William Whincup, who had died in 1936. It was engraved *'From grandpa to Sidney March 1936'* and remains in the family to this day. Also by this time, he was seriously involved with Amy Wilkinson, a young local girl.

Arnold married Phyllis Keegan in May of 1939. Arnold describes his wedding day, saying he still had to get up at 5.30am to collect and prepare the daily newspapers for delivery. Then he could get changed and join the rest of the family for the train trip to Leeds where they were married at the Leeds Meeting House, Sid acting as best man for his brother.

Also in 1939 the family bought a house at 'Lyndhurst', 26 Skipton Road, in Embsay, a small village just outside Skipton. The house had been built originally in 1922 and had been owned by one family since then. Joseph John bought it for £930 and it was to remain in the family for the next fifty years.

Sutton United Association Football team. Sid, back row, fourth from left

Edith washing Jim, the dog, in the backyard behind 10, Sheep Street,

Right: Sid and Amy, Bridlington, c.1939

'The family home, 'Lyndhurst', Skipton Road, Embsay, when first bought by Joseph John and Edith Waterfall in 1939. Front row, far left.

Once married, Arnold and Phyllis moved into the living accommodation above 10 Sheep Street, Skipton and Joseph John, Edith, Sid and Barbara moved to Embsay.

Sid no doubt felt the wrench of leaving 10 Sheep Street, Skipton where he'd been born and had grown up. However, the family was increasing and as Joseph John and Edith got older, their health was deteriorating and they had already handed over part of the running of the business to Arnold. Neither of them retired completely but the new house provided them with a bit more comfort as they got older.

*

Meanwhile, the outside world was intruding on normal life. The threat from Germany was increasing daily, the *Anschluss* of Austria had happened in March 1938, 'Peace in our time' was declared by Chamberlain in September, 1938, closely followed in October by Germany's annexation of the Sudetenland and *Kristallnacht* in November. There was no doubting Hitler's intentions and by the beginning of 1939 the population of Britain began to prepare for war. National Service for 20 and 21 year olds was introduced and gas masks were made available.[xxxiii] The clouds were gathering and young men like Sid and Arnold must have felt they were living on borrowed time despite being Quakers.

For the two boys the years of their youth were coming to an end. War was finally declared on 3 September 1939 on what everyone remembers as a glorious late-summer's day. On the same day, conscription was introduced for all males between 18 and 41, with the passing of The National Service (Armed Forces) Act 1939.[xxxiv]

Men could be rejected for medical reasons and those engaged in vital industries or occupations could be 'reserved'. Provision was also made for conscientious objectors and both Arnold and Sidney, as Quakers, fitted into this category. They were required

74

to justify their position to a tribunal which had the power to allocate the applicants to one of three categories: unconditional exemption; exemption conditional upon performing specified civilian work; exemption from combatant service meaning that the objector had to serve in specially created Non Combatant Corps or other units such as the Royal Army Medical Corps.[xxxv]

From now on the future, for both Sidney and Arnold, would be in the hands of government officials.

*

i   Waterfall, Arnold. Life at 10 Sheep Street. [unpublished] p6.
ii   Ibid endnote i. p8.
iii Waterfall, Nicola. Sidney Waterfall 1917-2004. [unpublished] p4.
iv   Waterfall, Sidney. Ackworth School notebooks. 5 volumes. [unpublished]
v   Waterfall, Sidney. Ackworth School poetry workbooks. 2 vols. [unpublished] 1928-1932.
vi   Waterfall, Sidney. Ackworth School archaeology diary. 2 vols. [unpublished] 1927-1932.
vii Sidney Waterfall. Mapping and Survey workbook. [unpublished & undated]
viii Waterfall, Sidney. Ackworth School Rembuk. [unpublished] 1930-1933.
ix   Op cit endnote iii. p5
x   Waterfall Arnold. Autobiography. [unpublished] c.1987 p109
xi   Ibid endnote x p120
xii Transcription of an interview with Sidney Waterfall conducted by Duncan and Fran Elson, c.2002.
xiii Op cit endnote x p235
xiv Waterfall, Arnold. Unofficial records. [unpublished] 1931-1936
xv   Ibid endnote xiv
xvi Waterfall, Sidney. Arnside diary. [unpublished] 1930.
xvii Waterfall, Arnold .Op cit endnote x p243
xviii Op cit endnote xii
xix Op cit endnote xii
xx   Waterfall Nicola. Op cit endnote iii. p5.
xxi Waterfall, Sidney. Football Association Club records. [unpublished]. 1933-1939.
xxii Waterfall, Arnold. Op cit endnote x p181
xxiii Op cit endnote xii
xxiv Bottomley, Hugh. Vale – Sidney Waterfall. Craven Pothole Club Record. Number 75, July 2004.
xxv Smith, E. The rat-Hole conquered. Journal of the Craven Pothole Club vol 2(1), 1950. pp30-32.
xxvi Waterfall, Arnold. Op cit endnote x p210
xxvii Op cit endnote xii.
xxviii Waterfall, Arnold. Op cit endnote x p223
xxix Yorkshire Gritstone. Edited by Graham Desroy. Yorkshire Mountaineering Club, 1989. p627.
xxx Ibid endnote xxix. Pp80, 202, 204, 243, 273, 340, 438, 445, 500, 599, 602.
xxxi Fawcett, Ron with Ed Douglas. Ron Fawcett: rock athlete. Vertebrate Publishing, 2010.
xxxii Waterfall, Arnold. Op cit endnote x p225-6
xxxiii The Twntieth century: a chronicle in pictures. Hamlyn, 1989. pp189-95
xxxiv
     https://en.wikipedia.org/wiki/National_Service_(Armed_Forces)_Act_19 39 . Accessed 25 January 2020.

xxxv

https://en.wikipedia.org/wiki/Conscription_in_the_United_Kingdom#Second_World_War .Accessed 25 January 2020.

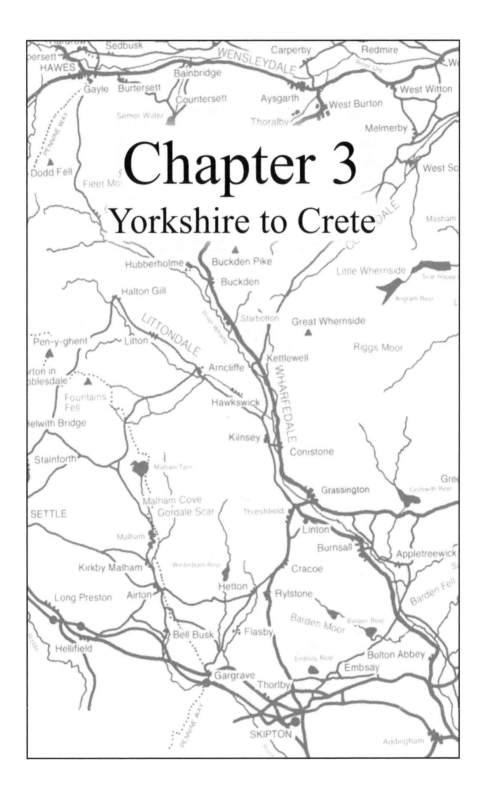

Chapter 3
Yorkshire to Crete

Chapter 3

2002

The three of them sat down to continue recording, Sidney was in his usual recliner and Fran sat next to the fireplace in the chair that had been Frankie's while she had been alive. Duncan sat on the small two-seater sofa, from where he could reach the recorder which was on the coffee table.

The coffee table, made out of a single slab of wood, highly polished and with wrought iron legs had been Frankie's pride and joy during their years at 'Lyndhurst'. It had been an obvious choice to bring with them when they moved to their Park Home.

Wherever Sid looked, memories appeared in his mind and he smiled in gratitude at the good life he had lived.

Back in the present, Fran took charge and asked a question to get Sidney talking again.

This time Sid talked about his experience as a Conscientious Objector, the tribunal he had to attend, being assigned to the Royal Army Medical Corps and the training he had to undergo. He talked about the journey to Egypt, his arrival on Crete, the Battle of Crete, the retreat over the mountains to the south coast and his capture.

*

1939 - 1941

Yorkshire to Crete

At the start of the war in September 1939, both Sidney and his brother, Arnold, had to make life-changing decisions for the first time in their lives. As young men born into a Quaker family they had to register as Conscientious Objectors at their Local Employment Exchange.

At the local tribunal, held in Leeds on 23 December 1939, Sidney appeared before a judge and a number of other officials. He had to produce references supporting his claim and made the following statement:

My objection is based on religious grounds. I am a birthright member of the Society of Friends, I have regularly attended Quaker meetings since I was about seven years old. I was educated at the Friends School at Ackworth, Nr Pontefract, Yorkshire and I have been a member of the Skipton meeting all my life.

I wish to state, however, that I am quite willing to undertake non-combatant duties.

The decision of the tribunal on 28 February 1940 was that Sidney should be placed in the Royal Army Medical Corps (RAMC).[i]

Arnold, meanwhile had not opted for non-combatant duties and had been sent to work on the land for a period of time before being released to manage the business as both Joseph John and Edith grew older and their health began to fail.

*

For Sidney, nothing more happened until 16 May 1940 when he had to report to Beckett Park College in Leeds for a two month course of training.

The No 11 Depot and Training Establishment had opened at Beckett Park in December 1939 and this was where recruits undertook a special intensive course of training in technical subjects.

Sid wrote home the day after he arrived saying

Well I arrived here about 2.20pm yesterday and so far_I have nothing to grumble at. We have spent most of the time having our kit doled out.

They give a room to four chappies and of my room mates, one comes from Birmingham and the other two from Northampton.

I should think there were about 300 or so of us arrived yesterday. Beckett Park is a very nice place, but of course it is not as nice as Lyndhurst, and it has ample sports facilities having its own football and cricket pitches, tennis courts, gymnasiums and even a swimming bath. We are allowed to bathe everyday between 6pm and 7pm, and on Sundays in the morning.

He goes on to say that he has no problem with the food and that he was unlikely to get any leave soon. At the end of the letter he listed the equipment that the Army had provided.[ii]

*

In a second letter from Beckett Park he tells his parents that

I have packed my civvies and addressed them to Sheep Street, and that he is settling down and has now got all his kit.

He continues;

On Saturday night we had our first inoculations and I am glad to say I had no after effects although one or two of the Company fainted or went dizzy. We have another one which they say is worse but I hope I will be alright.

He goes on to say that Sunday

is more or less a full day's holiday and we were allowed out of the Park for the first time. I only went for a little walk in the afternoon and in the evening I went out and laid on the cricket pitch and wrote to Amy. It was grand lying in the evening sun.

The next day they had to present themselves before the chief instructor

to get ourselves sorted out in accordance with our civil occupations and I was put down for a Clerk so I might get an office job. I do hope so as I will probably fit in better there.

The same day they had their dental examinations and Sid was glad to report he didn't have to have any extractions. He also tells his parents that he still does the Daily Express crosswords as the four of them in the room buy the paper every day and share the cost. He says he has met a boy who was at Ackworth with him called Tomkinson but he left the same day – destination unknown. He tells them that he is missing them both and Amy a great deal and

I am always hoping I will soon be back for good.

He comments

Things do not look very good at present do they, although I think he [Hitler] *is slowing up a bit don't you. I do think however that if we beat him back or even hold him for a month or two he has shot his bolt. I sincerely hope so.*

He ends the letter *Your loving Son, Sidney[iii]*

Beckett Park Leeds, where Sid did his training, 1940

NATIONAL SERVICE (ARMED FORCES) ACT, 1939

Local Tribunal for the Registration
of Conscientious Objectors,

To Mr. *S. Waterfall* *County Court.* *Albion Place. Leeds.1.*
Skipton Road.
Embsay
Skipton.

28. 2. 40 (date)

Case No. *NE 859*

NOTIFICATION OF RESULT OF APPLICATION

At the hearing of the above Tribunal on ....your application for registration in the Register of Conscientious Objectors was considered and it was decided :—

* (a) That you shall, without conditions, be registered in the Register of Conscientious Objectors.

* (b) That you shall be conditionally registered in the Register of Conscientious Objectors until the end of the present emergency, the condition being that you must until that event undertake the work specified below (being work of a civil character and under civilian control) and, if directed by the Minister of Labour and National Service, undergo training provided or approved by the Minister to fit you for such work :—

....

....

....

....

* (c) That your name shall be removed from the Register of Conscientious Objectors and that you shall be registered as a person liable under the Act to be called up for service but to be employed only in non-combatant duties.
A Quaker — should be put into the R.A.M.C

* (d) That your name shall, without qualification, be removed from the Register of Conscientious Objectors.

A copy of the evidence before the Tribunal and their findings is enclosed.

An appeal may be made to the Appellate Tribunal within twenty-one days of the date of decision by forwarding a formal application on form N.S. 24, which may be obtained on application at the above address.

Signed..

Clerk to Tribunal.

N.S. 19

(4937. Wt. 29766—5810 10,000 . 9/39 T.S. 677

Strike out inappropriate items before issue.

**The result of Sid's Conscientious Objector application, 1940, with the note
'A Quaker - should be put into the RAMC'**

Right: Group of trainees at Beckett Park, 1940. Sid standing on the back row third left.

Left: Sid, his sister Barbara and Jim the dog in the garden at 'Lyndhurst', Embsay, 1940

Below: Form of consent for Sidney to marry Amy, January 1941. Sidney was shipped out before the marriage could take place.

CONSENT TO THE MARRIAGE OF A MINOR.

District.............. **SKIPTON**

Proposed Marriage of.............. SIDNEY WATERFALL

residing at.......10, Sheep Street, Skipton

with.............. AMY WILKINSON.

residing at.......7, Brougham Street, Skipton.

I, (a).......WILLIAM WILKINSON...............being the (b) Father......and

I, (a).......JENNIE WILKINSON...............being the (b) Mother......of the above

(a) State Name in full.   (b) Insert "Father," "Mother," "Adoptive Father," "Adoptive Mother," etc., as the case may be.

named.............. AMY WILKINSON...............who is 20 years
of age, and being the PERSONS WHOSE CONSENT TO HER MARRIAGE IS
BY LAW REQUIRED, do hereby give our Consent to the above Marriage.

Witness my hand this....3rd....day of.......January............1941.

(Signature of person }
giving consent) }

(Address)..............7, Brougham Street, Skipton.

(Witness to the }
above Signature) }

(Address)..............7, Brougham Street, Skipton.

Witness my hand this....3rd....day of.......January............1941.

(Signature of person }
giving consent) }

(Address)..............7, Brougham Street, Skipton.

(Witness to the }
above Signature) }

(Address)..............

[SEE BACK.

Other descriptions of what happened at Beckett Park tell us that there were a new batch of recruits every two months, all of them coming straight from civilian life and having to become trained troops by the end of the course. They came from all walks of life and from all parts of the country and so were a real mixed bunch in ability and attitude.

There were 30 men in each platoon and they were housed in a block where they slept and ate. On their first day they were issued mattress covers which they filled with straw and hay and this was their bed for the duration of their stay.

Each day, as future possible medics, they went off to the main building where they were taught basic dentistry and the rudiments of nursing including bandaging, treatment of various types of wounds, burns and bites, the use of antiseptics and the sterilising of instruments for surgery. They were also taken through a gas chamber where they had to ease off on the respirator in order to take a sniff of the gas for recognition purposes. The swimming pool was used to teach the men how to take casualties over water.

There was a daily drill session and at the end of the training period there was a route march of around 20 miles.

All the men were fitted out with their uniforms and there were tailors on site for the sewing on of insignia.[iv] They were also given their service number, in Sid's case it was 7380174.

*

While Sid was at Beckett Park, the evacuation from Dunkirk, code-named 'Operation Dynamo' was set in motion. On 26 May 1940 men were crowding the beaches waiting to be evacuated and over the coming seven days 338,226 men were taken off those beaches and brought back to England. In all, 222 naval vessels and 665 civilian craft had continuously ferried across the English Channel between Dunkirk and the British coast. The most remarkable feat of all was that performed by the little ships: trawlers, coasters, tug-boats, open boats, ship's lifeboats, fishing vessels, river cruisers, paddle steamers and more than six hundred small pleasure craft. Between them they evacuated over 80,000 men in small groups varying in size from several hundred to half a dozen.[v] It was an event that was to become part of British folk lore.

*

After the two months training at Beckett Park, Sid was sent home on leave for a long weekend and then was stationed with No 11 Depot as a Clerk CIII with the 7th General Hospital which was situated in Leeds until 6 January 1941.[vi] During this period Sid managed to get home on leave at regular intervals. He was granted seven days leave at the beginning of October, another seven at the end of the same month, two days at the end of November, and a further six days during December.[vii]

It was during this period that he obtained a marriage licence in order to marry his girlfriend, Amy Wilkinson. However, it was never to be used.

*

The Battle for Britain began in earnest that summer. During July and the early days of August 1940, aerial dogfights had become a daily occurrence over Britain as had British bombing raids on German industrial targets.

On 13 August, the 'Day of the Eagle' launched Germany's air attack on Britain as a precursor to the invasion. On that day wave after wave of German aircraft, 1,485 in all, flew in search of aerodromes and aircraft factories which now had to be destroyed if invasion were to follow. Over the next five nights the air battle continued but by 18 August Hitler had failed to fulfil his one condition of invasion, the breaking of Britain's air-power.

89

Through the decoding of Enigma messages, the powers-that-be in London knew that there would be no invasion if the RAF maintained control of the air space and it was on 18 August that Churchill made his famous speech, saying *'Never in the field of human conflict was so much owed by so many to so few.'*

Air raids continued for the rest of the month but in September the target widened with Hitler announcing on 4 September *'we will raze their cities to the ground'* and the bombing of London started. This srpead later to Liverpool, Swansea and Bristol on 12 September and Southampton, Cardiff and Manchester on 15 September. The *Luftwaffe* were taking huge losses and on 17 September, Hitler postponed the invasion of Britain *'until further notice'.*

The Blitz would continue, the British people would suffer but to all intents and purposes Hitler's battle for Britain had been lost.[viii]

*

On 5 January 1941, Sid and the rest of his corps were moved up to Glasgow, from where they embarked and left Britain for the Middle East. Because of the Axis (Germany and its Allies) domination in the Mediterranean, the convoy had to slip down one side of Africa and up the other to reach their destination, a voyage lasting over eight hot and tedious weeks. They docked at several places for supplies, including Freetown in Sierra Leone, **(1)** and Cape Town **(2)** and Durban **(3)** in South Africa[ix] and whenever he was allowed Sid went ashore to stretch his legs and explore new places.

In a later letter to his mother he says:

I know when I was in Durban it seemed so pleasant to walk down fully lit streets after England's "black-out". [x]

The men's quarters during the voyage were in the space

90

normally used for cargo. They all slept in hammocks which had to be taken down when not in use to enable the men to move about. Washing, toilets and food were basic but the men got used to it and made the best of it.[xi]

The it was on to Aden **(4)** and through the Red Sea, known as 'The Sweat Sea' because of its intense heat. The men disembarked at Suez **(5)** on 9 March 1941. After being confined to ship for so long they were given a few days' leave in Cairo **(6)** where they were billetted in a compound on the banks of the Nile. While here, Sid managed to get out into the desert to see the Sphinx and the Pyramids.

After their leave period, they were moved back to camp in the Suez Canal zone **(7)** and the 7th General Hospital was stationed here for the next month.

*

Egypt had long been viewed by the British as a strategic link to India. They had first occupied the country in 1882 following the Orabi Revolt against the Egyptian Khedive. Though never formally a British colony, the Kingdom of Egypt was essentially under British control, even after the formal recognition of Egyptian independence in 1922, with British troops remaining around the Suez Canal zone

During World War II, Alexandria was the HQ of the Royal Navy's Mediterranean Fleet after having been moved there from Malta in the mid-1930s. The British Army forces continued to be stationed in the Suez Canal zone.[xii]

*

On 13 April 1941 the men of the 7th General Hospital re-embarked at Alexandria **(8)** and moved on to Crete **(9)**, arriving at Suda Bay on 19 April 1941.[xiii]

*

From the deck of the ship Sid would have seen a township

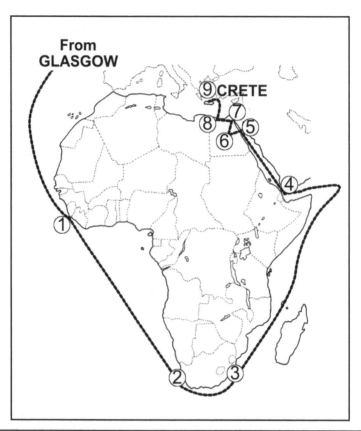

Map showing Sid's route by sea to Crete from the UK. Jan - Mar, 1941,
1 - Freetown, Sierra Leone. 2 - Capetown, South Africa. 3 - Durban, South
Africa. 4 - Aden. 5- Suez, Egypt. 6 - Cairo, Egypt. 7 - Suez Canal Zone,
Egypt. 8 - Alexandria, Egypt. 9 - Crete.

Left:
Egypt,
Mar -
April
1941.
Sid far
left

Right:
Egypt,
1941.
Sid
second
left.

(Suda) nestling amongst a rolling countryside of vineyards, olive and citrus groves which rose to the massive White Mountains still crested in snow in early spring. Crete is 160 miles long and 40 miles wide at its broadest point. Most of its population is spread along the northern coastline while the southern coastline consists of mainly fishing villages, nestling beneath the mountain ranges.

From the single quay in the harbour at Suda the men would have probably marched a few miles to the site set aside for the establishment of the hospital west of Chania and close to the beach.

*

On the same day as Sid arrived on Crete, British troops in Greece were moving back to the southern ports to prepare for embarkation for Crete, their evacuation made possible by the determined defence of Thermopylae by British, Australian and New Zealand units.[xiv] Two days earlier, Yugoslavia had surrendered in Belgrade and the writing was on the wall for the troops in Greece.[xv]

*

In his first letter from Crete on 4 May, Sid describes the place:

We have at last reached our destination and set up hospital and as you will no doubt have gathered from the past week's events we have been very busy. In fact, for the last eight days I have not been to bed before midnight at all and on one night we worked right through and never went to bed at all. However, I made up some sleep the following afternoon as I took my blankets and went out to one of the headlands and found a quiet sheltered corner and slept in the open.

We have got an absolutely marvellous camp here – we are right on the beach on a sort of headland with two glorious little bays either side and, as you will imagine, I have done as much bathing as possible although I have not had much spare time

93

since arriving. To make the scene perfect we are backed by a range of snow-capped mountains rising to about 7,750 ft and one of these weekends when things quieten down a bit I am going to do a lot of exploring.

He goes on to tell his family about how he met up with two Skipton boys he used to go to grammar school with, Rusty Fell from Earby, and Brian Hoe from Gargrave. The rest of the letter concerns letters he has received, hopes that they are all healthy, that business is brisk, that they are receiving his allotment OK and reassurances that he is *keeping very fit apart from being a little tired from this past week's work.*[xvi]

*

The work Sid talked about initially involved building wooden huts and erecting marquees and tents of various sizes covering a large area of almost treeless ground at Galatos **(4)**

The main building, used as the officer's mess, was on a slight rise on the middle of the three promontories and just a few yards from the sea. Leading to the officer's mess was a track and to the west of it was the cookhouse with another building to the east. The marquees to be used as hospital wards were mostly grouped near the cookhouse and a large Red Cross of cloth was laid out on the ground amongst them.

Red crosses were painted on the roofs of three of the buildings and a large one was marked out on the ground near the sea. A Red Cross flag also flew at the entrance to the hospital where the track joined the coast road.[xvii] So there was no ignoring the fact that it was a hospital compound.

*

On 23 April 1941 Greece had surrendered and the Greek king and government had been evacuated to Crete. The next day saw the beginning of Operation Demon, the evacuation of 50,000 Allied and Greek troops from the south coast of Greece by the Royal Navy, some to Crete and some to Egypt. [xviii]

The 25,000 troops landing in Crete at the end of April had very little in the way of arms or personal equipment, and they were dirty, ill-organised, conscious of their recent defeat and with no proper chain of command existing.[xix] No accommodation had been organised for them and they bivvied in olive groves, sleeping in their clothes and under their greatcoats during the crisp spring nights.

Many walking wounded from the final days on the mainland also arrived on Crete during those final days of April together with other casualties suffered during the voyage from Greece when they had found themselves under air attack.

It was probably this influx of battle-weary and wounded soldiers that accounted for how busy Sid had found himself during the eight days prior to his letter home on 4 May 1941.

With the combat soldiers evacuated from Greece came the Field Ambulance Units, notably the No.5 and No.6 (New Zealand) Ambulance Units that were to work closely with the 7th (British) General Hospital, that Sid belonged to, during their time on Crete.

The No.6 Unit was set up near Galatos **(5)** in the same area as the 7th General Hospital while the No.5 Unit was established initially at Ay Marina **(2)**, west of Chania before moving closer to Maleme for a few days as the battle for the airfield continued **(1)**.

A Field Ambulance Unit was not a vehicle despite its name but was rather a front-line unit of up to 250 personnel which treated men injured in battle.

To enable the NZ units to become operational as quickly as possible, the British Hospital supplied tents, dressings and stretchers and by the end of 27 April over a thousand men had been given essential treatment in the dressing station and the more serious cases had been transferred to the 7th British General Hospital.

*

With the expulsion of Allied forces from mainland Greece, Hitler was keen to complete the campaign by capturing Crete which otherwise could have provided a base for air attacks on the German flank or against oil resources in Romania. He ordered Operation Mercury, the invasion of Crete, to be prepared immediately. This was based around the deployment of Germany's elite paratroop force, the *XI Fliegerkorps,* heavily protected by the German air force.[xx]

Due to Enigma intercepts, the Allies were expecting an attack on the island and had almost three weeks to prepare. Churchill had sent a message to his commanders on Crete warning them of the possibility:

It seems clear from our information that a heavy air-borne attack by German troops and bombers will soon be made on Crete ...The island must be stubbornly defended.[xxi]

The defenders of Crete were a mixed force of British, Australian, New Zealand and Greek troops, numbering around 35,000, many more than the attacking force. They were commanded by Lt. General Bernard Freyberg, a British-born New Zealander. He was the first field commander to have the advantage of receiving ULTRA intelligence information (obtained by breaking high-level encrypted enemy radio and tele-printer communications at Bletchley Park[xxii]) which gave him the precise date of the attack.

Though large in numbers, the Allied force lacked adequate artillery, tanks or communications equipment and was spread very thinly along the north coast at Maleme, Chania, Rethymnon and Heraklion. As well as this there seems to have been a certain amount of infighting at the top with commanders disagreeing on tactics, strategy and defence planning during the three weeks before the fighting began.

*

Left: On the boat to Crete, April 1941. Sid far left.

Right: Chania town centre before the bombing May 1941

Left: Chania buildings after the bombing, May 1941

Right: Site of 7th (British) General Hospital near Galatos before the invasion. Crete, May 1941

Invasion of Crete, May 1941, showing the four main areas of the German Airborne Landings

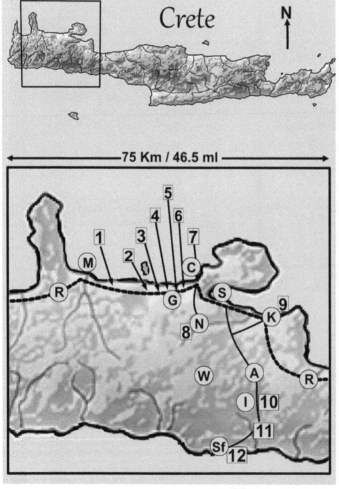

Crete

75 Km / 46.5 ml

Left: Movement of the medical units along the north coast of Crete and then south to Sfakia, May 1941. Placenames identificaton: A = Askafou, C = Chania, G = Galatos, I = Imvros, K = Kalivia, M = Maleme N = Nerekouru, R = Main North Coast road, S = Suda Bay, Sf = Sfakia, W = White Mountains

Until 12 May 1941 the *Luftwaffe* had concentrated its attacks on shipping to and from Crete and in Suda Bay. From 13 May onwards, with the completion of new airfields in Greece and on the island of Melos, it transferred its attention to the airfields of Heraklion and Maleme. Fighter aircraft carried out low-flying attacks or provided escorts for bombers and dive-bombers.

At the 7th (British) General Hospital, the first hint of what was to come was on 18 May when a bomber pilot released his bombs on the hospital area even though it was clearly marked with Red Crosses. Three RAMC officers and two orderlies were killed and a third orderly was wounded.

By 19 May, following the destruction of 29 of the 35 British fighter aircraft on Crete, the six remaining fighters were transferred to Egypt. It was felt that there was no point in sacrificing them in view of Germany's overwhelming air superiority. If Crete was to be held, it would have to be held without air support.[xxiii]

On 20 May 1941 the attack began at 8am. The enemy air attack was heavier than anything previously experienced. Wave after wave of bombers came in, escorted by scores of fighters. Stuka dive-bombers, with screaming sirens and swift Messerschmitts bombed and methodically strafed the countryside from Suda to the valley running south-west of Maleme, around Chania, over the rolling hills of Galatos and down to the sea. The staff of the 7th Hospital and the No 6 Ambulance Unit had to survive almost an hour of a continuous attack despite the Red Crosses on display. First came a line of bombs which sent up great spouts of earth and then came a deadly hail of gun fire, setting alight hospital wards and tents.

Since the hospital area was well marked with Red Crosses, these attacks were regarded as intentional breaches of the Geneva Convention that had been signed in 1929 and ratified by Germany in 1934.

Then, as the bombers withdrew to Greece, from the west, in groups of three, came the big Junkers 52s – group after group of them; and from underneath appeared white specks which fluttered down to earth over the olive groves.[xxiv] They were paratroopers, three thousand of them, descending along the north coast.

The 7th (British) General Hospital was then overrun by German paratroopers of III Batallion, 3rd Parachute Regiment. They drove out patients able to walk, herded them and hospital staff into the nearby area of 6th (NZ) Field Ambulance and later marched their 500 captives towards Galatos.

Later in the afternoon, the group of guards and prisoners were picked up by a NZ Battalion patrol and, after about an hour and a half of action, the Germans were encircled and defeated and the party of medics and patients were released to return to base.

By 22 May 1941, the 7th (British) General Hospital was functioning in caves on the sea coast **(7)** and the 6th (NZ) Field Ambulance Unit had established an operating theatre in a concrete culvert running underneath the main north coast road **(6)**.

During this time on the north coast, all Allied medical units were treating wounded German prisoners as well as their own troops. Sid's friends in later life always maintained that Sid had told them that he had treated Max Schnelling, the world famous German boxer, while he was working in caves on Crete.[xxv]

*

As they landed, the paratroopers were met with fierce resistance and suffered heavy casualties. However, on 21 May, a second parachute battalion landed on either side of the Maleme airfield and once the airfield was taken it gave the German air force a foothold on the island and they were able to land transport aircraft carrying large numbers of troops. At this point the 5th (NZ) Field Ambulance Unit moved east to operate in the same area as the other two medical units **(3)**

The battle hung in the balance for several days. A German

convoy bringing reinforcements was sunk by the Royal Navy with the loss of 5,000 men. However, German superiority in the air was gradually established and the Royal Navy lost three cruisers and six destroyers almost all from air attack.

By 23 May 1941 German forces on Crete had increased to 17,500 and Freyberg's forces were being pushed back to the south of the island with only small pockets still holding out at Rethymnon and Heraklion.

On 25 May it was decided that both the 5th (NZ) Field Ambulance, which had been evacuated from its more westerly position the day before, and the 7th (British) General Hospital should be moved to Nerokourou **(8)**, south-east of Chania where a site had already been prepared for the reception of casualties. This was done overnight with the seriously wounded being moved by truck and the walking wounded and staff walking the seven miles to the new site. The 6th (NZ) Field Ambulance then joined them, evacuating 250 walking wounded to Nerokourou.

On 26 May Freyberg reported that he could no longer hold the island and front-line troops were steadily falling back and a general move was being made towards the south coast from where evacuation was possible.

On the same day it was decided to move the medical units to Kalivia **(9)**, 15 miles to the south-east along the north coast. Once more, trucks carried the seriously wounded in two trips but again, the walking wounded and staff all walked, arriving shortly before daybreak on 27 May.

One of the staff of the 5th (NZ) Field Ambulance described the move:

Another night's march – this time past the stone walls of the Suda base, past the scattered dumps whose bombing had been witnessed from the higher slopes earlier in the day – and from the slopes of Nerokourou, the systematic destruction of the old city of Chania. On along the coast road, over the promontory demolitions were being prepared; on past the embarkation point for those who were being evacuated by sea; on through the deserted and echoing streets of Kalivia into another olive-studded dispersal area.[xxvi]

Shortly before midnight on 27 May, leaving only a minimum of Australian staff with the patients, the men of the medical units set out on the first stage of the long march south across the island to the south coast. Passing through burning villages, they had 10 weary miles of winding hill road before reaching the pass above Askifou.

*

By 28[h] May the bulk of the Allied forces on Crete had disengaged from the enemy and were making their way through the defile in the ridge of the central mountainous area that separated the north coast from the port of Sfakia on the south coast.

The retreat was not an orderly one and discipline had disintegrated to a large degree. Men discarded heavier items that might have slowed them down and ditches alongside the road were strewn with abandoned arms, equipment, kitbags, packs and gas masks as well as tins of food and ammunition. The road was one long stream of men – walking wounded with bloody bandages, airmen, sailors from the ships in Suda and ambulance men.

In the first days of the retreat the soldiers on foot would often be passed by trucks laden to capacity with wounded and hangers on. However, as they climbed higher, the lorries would run out of petrol and be abandoned and the foot columns would push them off the road to clear the way so that the bottom of the gorge was littered with shattered upturned trucks.

In the neck of the pass the fighting troops executed a leap-frog action, keeping the Germans at arms length while protecting the mass of the retreating garrison. They toiled their way higher and higher then across the flat plateau of the plain of Askifou, then down again through endless hairpin bends as the steep dusty road wound its way down to the coast.

The columns moved at night as there was a belief that the Germans did not fight at night. During the day the men got what rest they could, sleep being almost impossible because of the continuous air activity by the *Luftwaffe*. They bedded down amongst the boulders of the rocky countryside, in ditches or in caves. Many went without food or water as the only rations were whatever they could carry with them and the wells along the route soon ran dry.[xxvii] Everyone suffered from fatigue, hunger and thirst.

It was during the day, while the men were attempting to keep under cover, that German planes strafed the road to try and halt the retreat.

It was at this point that Sid decided he'd had enough. He told his mates that he wasn't going to stop there to be shot at – he was going to climb down into the gorge. To him it was just another crag to be climbed and he was used to that as he'd spent his youth climbing the limestone and gritstone cliffs of the Yorkshire Dales. This is how he told the tale:

I said I'm not stopping here, I'm going down into this gorge. They said 'You can't go down there – it's all cliff faces'.

'Well,' I said, 'I don't care what it is, I'm going down and if you want to come, I'll lead you the way down.' And I did just that.

I had about eight or nine lads and a couple of officers following me down this climb into a limestone gorge. When we got down to the bottom we came across a cave with a lot of English squaddies in it – it was one of the first group of soldiers to be sent in to go behind enemy lines. They called them Layforce before they became SAS.

They were all sat in this cave at the bottom of the gorge and didn't know what to think of us coming down the crags. We dropped in on them accidentally and they treated us like lords – they thought it was marvellous that we'd managed to get down.

Well, when we were marching on the route we were all lying flat on the ground while they were machine-gunning us.[xxviii]

It was typical of Sid that he found what was to him an obvious way out of an unpleasant situation.

*

Layforce was an ad hoc military formation of the British Army consisting of a number of commando units formed in February 1941 and under the command of Colonel Robert Laycock after whom the force was named. It consisted of around 2,000 men and was originally tasked with conducting raiding operations to disrupt enemy lines of communications.[xxix]

They landed on Crete on the night of 26/27 May and it was decided that they would not be used in an offensive role but would instead be used to cover the withdrawal route towards Sfakia. This was a role they were poorly equipped for but nevertheless they took up defensive positions along the road over the mountains. From then until 31 May, together with two Australian and one New Zealand infantry battalions, they carried out a number of rearguard actions to enable the main body of troops to be taken off the beaches by the navy.

Lt Col.George Young was the last commander of Layforce left on Crete and he had his HQ in a cave in the Sfakia ravine. It was his job, as the most senior officer left on the island, to offer the surrender to the Germans.[xxx] Could this have been the group of Layforce troops that Sid and his mates found in the gorge after their climb down the crags?

*

After a period of rest with the Layforce group, Sid's little group of men continued moving down the gorge until they hit the south coast near Sfakia from where they joined up with the rest of the force who were waiting to be evacuated off the island.

A dressing station had been established in a church at Imvros **(10)** and as more of the men of the medical units arrived, they were added to the staff. One medic describes the scene as they arrived:

The stone floor of the church was covered with wounded on blankets and ambulance stretchers ranged all round the walls and down the centre. The altar, in an alcove at one end, was covered with shell and field dressings and a little food – cocoa, tinned milk, sugar and biscuits. There were quite a number of medical officers and personnel there and we set to work bandaging, applying splints and making the patients as comfortable as possible. Some were walking cases, but many appeared to be more severely wounded and could not be moved.[xxxi]

*

Moving on from the church at Imvros, 7th General Hospital set up their operations in caves situated on a ledge above the beach at Sfakia **(11)**.

Crete Force Headquarters (the HQ for all Allied forces on Crete) shared the caves and had set up a radio transmitter there and it was from here that they were trying to organise the embarkation of the troops and their transport to Egypt.

Embarkation of the wounded started on the night of 28/29 May 1941 and continued over the next three nights. The walking wounded were led in three columns down the steep slope, through the scattered boulders and oleander bushes to a halt within sight of the boats at Sfakia **(12)**. From here parties of 50 proceeded to the boats and were taken off. However, the going was rough and the pace slow and not all could embark before dawn despite the assistance from medical personnel.

It was becoming obvious that the more seriously wounded would have to be left behind with a small number of staff to stay with them. Straws were drawn amongst the unmarried medical personnel to decide who would stay.

The night of 30/31 May was the last night for evacuation as the losses (2,265 sailors killed at sea) sustained by the Royal Navy in their efforts to evacuate Crete were unsustainable. In five nights, 17,000 men had been taken off Crete, most of them from open beaches during the few short hours of darkness. 5,000 men, separated from their units and scattered about the island, had to be left behind.[xxxii] Sid was amongst them and this was to be the beginning of Sid's life in captivity.

Happenings on Crete were just one small part of the total war effort on both sides.

The last 11 days of May had seen a defeat for Britain on Crete, a disaster for Germany (the sinking of the *Bismark)* at sea, a victory for Germany in the Western Desert (at Bir Hakeim in Libya), and the surrender of Iraq to the British.

On May 25 King George of the Hellenes who had been evacuated from Greece to Crete, was evacuated again, with his Ministers, from Crete to Egypt. In Egypt, for the British Command, the defence of the Suez Canal was once more a matter of urgency.

On May 27 Roosevelt announced that 'the delivery of needed supplies to Britain was imperative. *This can be done, it must be done, it will be done,'* he said, and added the inspirational words that would be quoted for the duration of the Western campaign: *'The only thing we have to fear is fear itself.'*

From every corner of German-occupied Europe, German troops were now being moved to the East. In all, between the end of January and the beginning of June 1941, 17,000 trains had conveyed German troops to the borders of Russia – an average of more than 100 trains per day. The preparations for the invasion of Russia continued into June 1941.[xxxiii]

*

i   Waterfall, Nicola. Sidney Waterfall, 1917-2004. [unpublished] p8

ii   Ibid endnote i p8

iii Waterfall, Sidney. Letter to Joseph John and Edith Waterfall [undated]

iv   Far Eastern Heroes. To Leeds.
     www.far-eastern-heroes.org.uk/alberts_warhtml/to_leeds.htm . Accessed 11
     December 2019

v   Gilbert, Martin. The Second world War: a complete history. Phoenix,
     1989. pp75-83.

vi   www.scarletfinders.co.uk/112.html Accessed 12 December 2019

vii Army service record for Sdney Waterfall.

viii Gilbert Martin. Op cit endnote iv. Pp115-125.

ix   Www.commandoveterans.org/files/Layforce.pdf .Accessed 22 December
     2019

x   Letter from Sidney Waterfall to Edith Waterfall, dated 12 November 1944

xi   Op cit endnote v. p13

xii https://en.wikipedia.org/wiki/Egypt_during_World_War_II . Accessed 12
     December 2019

xiii Army service record for Sidney Waterfall

xiv Gilbert, Martin. Op cit endnote v. p175

xv   Ibid endnote v p174

xvi Letter from Sidney Waterfall to his family, dated 4 May 1941.

xvii Www.nzhistory.govt.nz/media/photo/attack-on-the-7th-general-hospital-
     in-crete . p2. Accessed 15 December 2019.

xviii Gilbert Martin. Op cit endnote v. p175

xix Clark, Alan. The fall of Crete. Athens, Efstathiadis Group, 1962. p27

xx   Overy, Richard. The second world war: the complete illustrated history.
     London, Carlton books, 2010. p66.

xxi Churchill, Winston. The Grand Alliance. (The Second World War, volume
     III) Penguin Classics, 2005.p241

xxii Https://en.wikipedia.org/wiki/ULTRA . Accessed 15 December 2019.

xxiii McKinney, J.B. Medical units of 2NZEF in Middle East and Italy.
     Chapter 6: Crete. www.ourstory.info/library/4-ww2/NZmed/nzmed.html .
     Accessed 23 December 2019.

xxiv Ibid endnote xvii

xxv Wilson, John. Personal reminiscences of Sidney Waterfall, told in an
     interview with Fran Elson and Sonia Waterfall, August 2017.

xxvi McKinney, J.B. Op cit endnote xxiii

xxvii Clark, Alan. Op cit endnote xix. p158-9.

xxviii Transcription of an interview conducted by Fran and Duncan Elson
     with Sdney Waterfall. [unpublished] 2002.

xxix Https://en.wikipedia/wiki/Layforce . Accessed 24 December 2019.

xxx www.commandoveterans.org/files/Layforce.pdf . Accessed 24 December
     2019

xxxi McKinney, J.B. Op cit endnote xxiii

xxxii Gilbert Martin. Op cit endnote v. p187

xxxiii Ibid endnote v pp186-188.

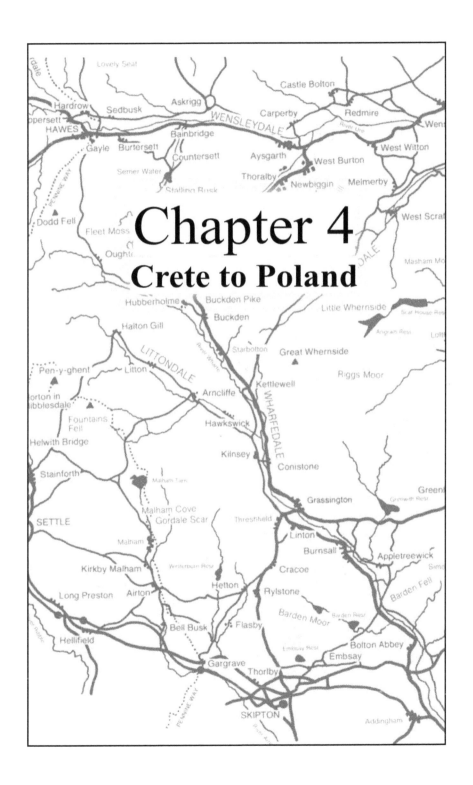

Chapter 4
Crete to Poland

Chapter 4

2002

In the living room of the Park Home at Overdale, Sidney, Fran and Duncan continued with the recording. The room they were in contained many items from the family home at 'Lyndhurst' which they'd had to leave as Frankie became more disabled and was unable to cope with stairs.

The small table under the window and close to Sidney's recliner, had curved legs, a wooden scalloped edge and an inlaid surface. In the Park home it had now become a memorial to Frankie. On top of it was a wooden tray with brass handles and a glass base and behind the glass was a particularly lovely piece of Frankie's lace. On the tray was a pot of Afican Violets and a photo of Frankie taken amongst the rhododendrons at Cragside on one of her last visits to Rothbury in 1994.

Sidney was surrounded by familiar items that reminded him of times past.

He was brought back to the present by a question from Fran and he carried on talking.

He talked about his capture, the five months he spent as a POW on Crete, the journey by sea to the hell-hole that was Salonika and then the onward journey by rail to Stalag VIIIB in Silesia, now Poland.

*

Crete to Poland

1941

Twelve thousand Allied soldiers and thousands of Greeks were left behind on Crete after the surrender on 1 June 1941, Five thousand of them at Sfakia where Sid found himself.[i]

For those captured at Sfakia, their first experience of captivity was a forced march back up the route they had taken as they'd retreated from Chania, with very little to eat except what Cretan villagers offered them along the way.[ii]

Like the other prisoners, the medical officers and wounded were marched back across the island on 1 June and herded together overnight in a field without food or water. On the evening of 2 June the wounded were taken to Maleme and given a meal. Orderlies cleaned out several shops and bedded down the wounded in them. Here they were to remain until 12 June when they were transferred to the camp hospital in the main POW camp near Galatos.[iii]

It would have been during this period, until the new POW hospital was established, that Sid found himself in the hands of the Alpine Corps, mainly Austrians, with whom he had a lot in common – namely climbing and soccer. These troops put their prisoners to work, in the first instance, stripping the orchards of fruit which was sent back to the Reich to feed the civilians there. So, for several days, Sid was working in the outdoors, eating well and being treated humanely by his captors.[iv]

*

There was no interest in the prisoners from the German victors as their focus was on maintaining their hold on the island and the Cretan population. They had sustained huge losses during their airborne invasion and their first priority was to their own survivors, not to the prisoners in their care. The guards were mainly paratroopers who weren't interested in the prisoners' plight and considered guard duty beneath them. This made them careless and many prisoners took advantage of this and found ways of leaving the camp under cover of darkness and making contact with friendly Cretans who provided them with food to take back to camp.

*

The main prisoner of war camp was established near Galatos and Chania on the site previously occupied by the 7th (British) General Hospital where Sid had been stationed when he first arrived on Crete and during the invasion. Here about seven thousand prisoners were herded into a very small area. There was no water supply and no sanitation arrangements to begin with and rations were in short supply. The men possessed only what they were wearing and most slept out in the open, without greatcoats or blankets.[v]

To begin with, a medical inspection room was set up in a marquee and medicines, dressings and surgical equipment were collected from the ruined tents that had formerly been wards of the 7th General Hospital. Up to seven hundred men were treated daily. The number of patients and staff increased as POWs came across the island from Sfakia. Another marquee was erected and patients were accommodated on hospital beds and on the ground.[vi]

There is no evidence to tell us when Sid arrived back in the Chania/Galatos area but, as a medical orderly, there is no doubt he would have been immediately put to work in the hospital section of the main POW transit camp.

The senior medical officer remaining on the island (Lieutenant-Colonel Bull of the New Zealand Medical Corps) arrived at the camp on 8 June and immediately set about improving medical facilities. A two hundred bed camp reception hospital was set up with a staff of eight British Medical Officers, four NCOs and eighty-nine other ranks. As during the first few days, accommodation was supplied from salvaged 7th General Hospital furniture including beds and mattresses but blankets were in short supply and continued to be so.

After another week, a surgical ward with an improvised operating theatre and sleeping accommodation for Medical Officers was established in a building formerly used as the officers' mess of 7th General Hospital.

Overcrowding continued and rations were short – eight to ten men often sharing one can of bully beef. By the beginning of July the Germans were beginning to plan for the onward movement of prisoners, first to mainland Greece and then on to established POW camps in eastern Europe. This would certainly have eased the overcrowding and the shortage of rations.[vii]

*

It was probably during this first period of captivity that Sid wrote the following poem entitled *The Cretan Prisoners' Song*:

This is my story, this is my song,
We've been on this island too blooming long.

When we came here 'Old Crete' to defend,
We hadn't the faintest how it would end.

Another withdrawal, strategic retreat,
Our officers leading the race to the fleet.

And just as they left us at Spakhia [sic] *Bay,*
They gave us this message as they sailed away.

Now boys do not panic, things will turn out alright,
The Navy will come back on Sunday night.

But they needn't have worried, 'Jerry' knew of our plan,
And by noon on Sunday, had got each single man.

Now here we all are, right in the mire,
Studying the Germans from behind the barbed wire.

We've been living on rumours, a new kind of food,
If you go to the   [unreadable word], you'll see how it's brewed.

The 'Jerry' is busy, or so they say,
Over in Europe, keeping Russia away.

Here is a new one, it's just come to hand,
We're being 'repatted' to Old Gyppo Land.

It can't be too soon, don't delay it too long,
And fulfill the wish of this Prison Song. [viii]

*

In verse three '*the officers leading the race to the fleet*' refers to the commonly held belief that the officers looked after their own safety before that of their men during the evacuation from Sfakia.

The men left behind on the beach had been told that the ships would return for them but naval losses in the Mediterranean meant that this became impossible – as verses four, five and six say.

The mention of Russia in verse nine probably refers to Operation Barbarosa, the code name for the Nazi invasion of the Soviet Union which began on 22 June when German tanks crossed the Meml River into Soviet-controlled Lithuania. The build-up for this was a primary objective for the Germans during the early months of 1941 and continued to keep them '*busy*' for weeks and months to come.

The hope of being 'repatted' expressed here in verse ten was the first mention of repatriation that arose frequently in Sid's letters home over the next three years. Repatriation was a system of exchanging wounded/sick Allied POWs for German POWs which occurred at irregular intervals during the war years. Each repatriation required medics to travel with the wounded to care for them. This stemmed from the Third Geneva Convention which listed *Protected Personnel* as a) civilians not taking part in hostilities b) military personnel placed *hors de combat* by sickness, wounds or detention and c) military medical or religious personnel. The possibility of repatriation gave the sick/wounded and their carers ongoing hope that they could be sent home.[ix]

*

Meanwhile, back in Yorkshire, the first that Sidney's family knew of his whereabouts was on 21 July when they received a letter from the War Office notifying them that Sidney had been posted as 'missing' on 2 June.

The letter continues:

The report that he is missing does not necessarily mean that he has been killed, as he may be a prisoner of war or temporarily separated from his regiment.

Official reports that men are prisoners of war take some time to reach this country, and if he has been captured by the enemy it is probable that unofficial news will reach you first. In that case I am to ask you to forward any postcard or letter received at once to this Office, and it will be returned to you as soon as possible.

On the 25 June (his 24th birthday) Sid had sent a pre-printed postcard to his family saying:

Dear All,
I am a prisoner of war in German custody.
I am unwounded and quite well. Please do not write to me until you hear from me again as I am at present only in a Transit Camp.[x]

However, this did not arrive until much later than the War Office notification and the period between the two letters must have been one of extreme anxiety for the family.

*

On Crete, the invasion was soon followed by German reprisals. The Wehrmacht had just suffered its heaviest losses so far in the war and someone had to pay. They vented their anger on the armed resistance fighters of the Cretan civilian population. Soon after the surrender of 1 June, stories started circulating about Cretans joining in the fighting against the German paratroopers and assisting British and Commonwealth troops by hiding them, feeding them and helping them escape.

An order was issued naming the reprisals to be taken:

1) *Shooting*
2) *Fines*
3) *Total destruction of villages by burning*
4) *Extermination of the male population of the territory in question*

And, it continued *all these measures must be taken rapidly and omitting all formalities.*[xi]

By 10 June at least nine villages had been destroyed and 550 men shot before the British became aware of what was happening and started to send Special Operations Executive (SOE) officers to Crete to help organise the resistance. The SOE were small groups of irregular forces operating behind enemy lines

Cretan resistance, starting with isolated acts of revenge and minor skirmishes, gradually became more organised. Cretans welcomed the British officers, certain that another Allied army would return to throw out the German occupiers.

One SOE officer paid tribute to their Cretan allies, saying '*We depended on their magnificent loyalty. Without their help as guides, informants, suppliers of food and so on, not a single one of us would have lasted twenty-four hours.* [xii]

The Allied army never returned but the last Germans eventually left Crete in October 1944 after over three years of continuous resistance from the Cretan civilian population.

*

Back in the main POW camp at Chania/Galatos, the 15 July saw the first batch of POWs, medical officers and orderlies shipped from Chania to Salonika. Then on 20 July another two thousand were moved to Suda Bay for embarkation followed by a further one thousand, two hundred on 25 July.

This alleviated the overcrowding somewhat but it was reported that although sanitation was improved and there were fewer flies, there was no improvement in rations, clothing, drugs or dressings. Cricket matches in the camp and swimming in the sea helped to allay the boredom of the men. Dysentery was still rife and malaria increasing. POWs were becoming pot-bellied and obviously suffering from malnutrition. During June, July and August it was estimated that every POW had at least one attack of Sonne dysentery – a particularly nasty version of the disease. [xiii]

By the beginning of September most of the occupants of the camps except for the main one at Galatos, had been evacuated to mainland Greece. By mid September, most of the remaining POWs from the main camp and the sick from the hospital, some three hundred British and one thousand Greeks, embarked for transport onwards. It is highly likely that this was when Sid was shipped out as 13 September was the date on the first record of him as a POW. Also he mentioned that they disembarked near Athens and then re-embarked next day for the trip up through the islands to Salonika which was the northernmost town and port in Greece. [xiv]

119

A New Zealand report mentions that this mid-September transport called in at Piraeus **(1)** where the remaining staff and patients from the Kokkina hospital embarked – this would account for the men from Crete disembarking and then reboarding the next day.[xv] A similar report mentioned that all British prisoners of war had typhoid inoculations before entering Germany and those passing through Athens in 1941 were inoculated there – this could be another reason for the overnight stop before continuing to Salonika **(2)**.

*

By all accounts Dulag 183 (sometimes called Frontstalag 183), Salonika Transit Camp, was a terrible place holding thousands of prisoners in appalling inhuman conditions. All who passed through it, whether they stayed for a few months or a few days, remember this camp for its starvation diet, filthy conditions, frequent beatings, heavy labour under strict German guards and the badly equipped hospital.

The diet for both men and patients was the same: for breakfast, three-quarters of a five inch biscuit and mint tea; for lunch, a pint of barley, bean or lentil soup (three quarters of this being water); for tea, one-sixteenth of a loaf of bread and mint tea. This did not do much for the sick or wounded and even less for those prisoners being expected to do heavy labour.[xvi]

One Medical Officer who was there said:

Men died from medical neglect and others were murdered. The commandant is, of course, a war criminal. He was a gross individual who was known to our troops by the technically appropriate name of 'Swing-belly'.[xvii]

What Sid remembered most were the bed bugs. He said:

it was a terrible place – a big army camp – it was full of bed bugs. You used to stand the bed that you had in tins full of petrol to prevent them climbing up from the floor but instead the bugs used to climb up onto the roof and drop on you from there.

He remembered being there for '*a few weeks*' before being moved on in October.[xviii]

During the six months it was in operation, the camp hospital handled over three thousand patients, most of them moving through to camps in Germany. Half of these were wounded from the conflicts in Greece and Crete and the remainder were suffering from various illnesses caused by the conditions the men were forced to live in since their capture.

As the sick and wounded moved on, the medical personnel moved on with them. For most patients, moving on meant first of all being moved by truck from the hospital barracks to the railway trucks. Once in the trucks, most lay for ten or eleven days with just straw for a bed, no blankets, very little food and minimal medical treatment. The only toilet was a bucket that was soon full and for many of the injured it was too difficult to get to and they just had to lie in their own filth for the duration of the trip.[xix]

*

The various accounts of the trip across Europe to the camps in the Reich tell us that the usual route from Salonika **(2)** was via Belgrade **(3)** in Yugoslavia (now Serbia), Szombathely **(4)** in Hungary, Vienna **(5)** in Austria, over the border into Germany to Augsburg **(6)**, Nuremburg **(7)**, Chemnitz **(8)**, Dresden **(9)** Breslau **(10)** (now Wroclaw in Poland) and finally to Stalag VIIIB in Silesia. These stops were where the men were given food and drink and the opportunity to clean out their trucks as much as was possible.[xx]

For the 'healthy' men, the numbers in each cattle truck varied from forty to seventy according to different accounts. They were all crushed in together with no room to move – all they could do was stand or perhaps sit down with their knees drawn up to their chests.

STALAG VIIIB

Crete

Sid's route after capture from Crete to Stalag VIIIB, Sept/Oct 1941.
1 - Piraeus, Greece; 2 - Dulag 183, Salonika, Greece; 3 - Belgrade, Yugoslavia
(now Serbia); 4 - Szombathely, Hungary; 5 - Vienna, Austria; 6 - Augsburg,
Germany; 7 - Nuremburg, Germany; 8 - Chemnitz, Germany; 9 - Dresden,
Germany; 10 = Breslau, Germany (now Wroclaw, Poland);

SKIPTON FOOTBALLERS

Mr. and Mrs. J. J. Waterfall, of Sheep Street, Skipton, have received official notification that their younger son, Private Sidney Waterfall, R.A.M.C., serving in the Middle East, has been posted as missing. Aged 24, he was previously employed by Messrs. Knowles and Harrison, solicitors, Skipton. He has played half-back for Skipton Christ Church and Sutton United football clubs.

Missing in Action notice, Craven Herald (Skipton)
newspaper, 1941

ADVICE TO THE RELATIVE OF A MAN WHO IS MISSING

In view of the official notification that your relative is missing, you will naturally wish to hear what is being done to trace him.

The Service Departments make every endeavour to discover the fate of missing men, and draw upon all likely sources of information about them.

A man who is missing after an engagement may possibly be a prisoner of war. Continuous efforts are made to speed up the machinery whereby the names and camp addresses of prisoners of war can reach this country. The official means is by lists of names prepared by the enemy Government. These lists take some time to compile, especially if there is a long journey from the place of capture to a prisoners of war camp. Consequently " capture cards " filled in by the prisoners themselves soon after capture and sent home to their relatives are often the first news received in this country that a man is a prisoner of war. That is why you are asked in the accompanying letter to forward at once any card or letter you may receive, if it is the first news you have had.

Even if no news is received that a missing man is a prisoner of war, endeavours to trace him do not cease. Enquiries are pursued not only among those who were serving with him, but also through diplomatic channels and the International Red Cross Committee at Geneva.

Further, foreign broadcasts which include names of prisoners of war are listened to by official listeners working continuously day and night.

The moment reliable news is obtained from any of these sources it is sent to the Service Department concerned. They will pass the news on to you at once, if they are satisfied that it is reliable.

There is, therefore, a complete official service designed to secure for you and to tell you all discoverable news about your relative. This official service is also a very human service, which well understands the anxiety of relatives and will spare no effort to relieve it.

Officail advice to relatives of a man listed as Missing in Action

123

Whatever they had been used for before, whether transporting men or animals, there was dirty straw on the floor and a smell of excrement and urine from previous passengers. As well as that there was the stink of unwashed bodies and their filthy, shitty, lice-infested uniforms. The doors and windows were boarded up and the only light was what came through the gaps in the wooden slats of the sides. When night fell it was pitch black. They had no idea where they were going or how long it would take. All they could do was survive.[xxi]

With his usual laconic understatement, Sid described his experience:

There were about forty people in these cattle trucks lying on straw which was used as a mattress. It wasn't a nice journey wasn't that. But it was what you made it. If you went with the idea of going against the grain all you had to realise was that the people with the guns were the Germans and if you behaved yourself you were alright.[xxii]

There wasn't much talking on that journey. Some men were so exhausted, sick or demoralised that they never said a word. Others exchanged experiences but not for long. Everyone was afraid, wondering what was going to happen to them and talking seemed to make it worse. There wasn't much that could be said to help people so silence became a kind of refuge.

It was impossible to sleep in more than short bursts because of the noise of the rails, the constant battering the men got bouncing off each other and against the sides of the truck and the cramps in their joints. Some were afraid to sleep for the fear of lapsing into unconsciousness and never waking up – the feeling of suffocation was intense what with being crammed into the truck and up against other men's stinking bodies. Some men kept themselves awake by watching the rail tracks pass by through the cracks in the floorboards.

The journey passed slowly, travelling through hilly country, sometimes slowing down even more to allowing for passing trains. The competition for the rail lines meant that often they were stopped for long periods before setting off again, usually, it seems, traveling at night and stopping during the day. When they stopped, the trucks were opened, the slop buckets were emptied and the rations and water for the next stage of the journey were distributed.[xxiii]

Some accounts say that the men were allowed off the trains occasionally, others that they spent the entire journey in the truck crammed in with their fellow prisoners.

One prisoner (an officer) recorded the rations they were given. On leaving Salonika, they were given enough to last four to six days: four small four ounce tins of pork and two-and-a-half loaves of bread. Four days later at Belgrade each received a cup of ersatz coffee and the Serbian Red Cross left bread on the train to be divided up. Three days later, after a stop in Hungary, they arrived in Vienna and received a pint of hot, thick pea soup, served in cartons and later that day, a sixteenth of a loaf of bread per man, a small tin of pork and a cup of ersatz coffee. The next day at Nuremburg, it was mint tea and a sixteenth of a loaf of bread per man. Then Dresden brought a loaf of bread per seventeen men and Breslau brought more soup and ersatz coffee, issued by the German Red Cross.[xxiv]

*

Once again the train came to a halt. It was ten days since they'd left Salonika and the men on board were beginning to wonder if their journey would ever end. This time the halt was followed by banging and clattering, shouting and the sound of marching boots. One by one the doors were unbolted, pushed back and light streamed in illustrating the sorry state that the men were in.

Dirty and dishevelled, weak from illness and in pain from the continuous confinement, some of the men managed to stagger out of the door and lower themselves to the ground. Others just fell out of the train and lay there where they fell. Sid crawled to the door and managed to get out, landing on legs that nearly buckled under him. Fresh air at last and space to move about.

They had arrived at the station of Annahof (today's Sowin) located about three kilometres from the POW camp and they had to walk the last part of the route on foot. The track was partly cobbled like an old farm road and ran through pine forests before emerging into flat, bleak and desolate countryside, bitterly cold in late October.[xxv]

Arriving at the camp, they were first deloused and shaven clean. The clothes and kit they had travelled in were taken away to be deloused in cyanide gas chambers while the men were stripped and passed through a shower room. Then they went on to a dressing room where they waited until their kit had been aired and was ready to wear again. One man described the experience:

We were sitting in chairs, naked, getting our hair cut off with shears. When we came out we had to pick our clothes up and grabbed anything we could get. I got myself a pair of trousers, no underwear of course, just my khaki and a blouse.[xxvi]

During the following days the men had their photos taken, were given their POW numbers and had their personal files completed. The data gathered was sent to the International Committee of the Red Cross (ICRC).[xxvii]

Finally, everyone received a card to be sent to their family informing them of their capture and where they were. Each card said exactly the same:

I am a German War Prisoner.
I am well.
With very best wishes.

All the POW had to do was add his full name, his POW number and the address to which the card was to be delivered.#

*

Sid completed his card on 2 November 1941 and it arrived in Skipton on 6 December that year. At least now his family knew where he was and that he could be contacted.

This was the beginning of the next stage of Sid's life – behind barbed wire as POW No. 24321 at Stalag VIII B in Silesia.

*

Meanwhile the war had moved on.

By September 1, seventy days had passed since the German invasion of the Soviet Union and Leningrad was surrounded. The siege of the city started in October 1941 and was to continue for over two years.

In Germany, September 1 marked the day on which all the remaining Jews of Germany, including 76,000 in Berlin, were ordered to wear a yellow Star of David on their clothing.

Two days later there was yet another experiment to find the most effective method of mass murder without the visible horrors of the pit executions. Six hundred Soviet POWs and three hundred Jews were brought to Auschwitz and gassed with prussic acid. This experiment was judged a success.[xxviii]

On September 9, the cryptologists at Bletchley decrypted the German orders for Operation Typhoon, the planned attack on Moscow.[xxix]

Also in September, Tito's partisans in Yugoslavia, 76,000 men in all, captured the town of Uzice with it's rifle factory. Once armed, the resistance in Yugoslavia like that on Crete, began to harrass and tie down considerable numbers of German troops.[xxx]

By the end of September, the first of many British convoys carrying war supplies to Russia, left Iceland for Archangel. Over the coming months the Russians were to receive British

Hurricanes and Spitfires, American fighters and bombers, submarine detection equipment, anti-aircraft guns and destroyers for the Soviet Navy and tanks and armoured cars for the Red Army. On top of this were industrial and medical supplies plus army boots and cloth for uniforms. Anything that could be provided to resist the renewed German attack, would be provided. Also in September the Russians were moving essential war machinery eastwards as far out of reach of the German armies as possible, while at the same time moving two and a half million soldiers in the other direction, westwards towards the front line.[xxxi]

By the time Sid arrived at Stalag VIIIB towards the end of October, the German army was within sixty-five miles of Moscow and Hitler thought it was within his grasp. In private conversations, he was talking about the Jews and *'exterminating this pest'* while at the same time being concerned about the architectural beautification of Berlin.[xxxii]

*

i Beevor, Anthony. Crete: the battle and the resistance. Penguin, 1991. p.218

ii Ibid. p.225

iii Stout, T. Duncan. Medical Services in New Zealand and the Pacific. Chapter 2: Crete, May-September, 1941. I: Galatos Camp. Part of: The Official History of New Zealand in the Second World War, 1939-1945. Historical Publications Branch, Wellington, 1958. www.nzetc.victoria.ac.nz/tm/scholarly/tei-WH2PMed-pt2-c2.html Accessed 15 January 2019

iv Waterfall, Sidney. Transcript of an interview undertaken by Fran and Duncan Elson. 2002

v Op cit endnote iii

vi Op cit endnote iii

vii Op cit endnote iii

viii Waterfall, Sidney. A wartime log. [Unpublished] Crete, 1941.

ix Https://en.wikipedia.org/wiki/Third_Geneva_Convention . Accessed 20 January 2019.

x Waterfall, Sidney. Personal papers. [unpublished].

xi Beevor, Anthony. Op cit endnote i. p236

xii Ibid endnote i. p247

xiii Op cit endnote iii

xiv Op cit endnote iv

xv Op cit endnote iii

xvi Stout, T. Duncan. Medical Services in New Zealand and the Pacific. Chapter 3: Salonika Transit Camp, 1941. Part of: The Official History of New Zealand in the Second World War, 1939-1945. Historical Publications Branch, Wellington, 1958. www.nzetc.victoria.ac.nz/tm/scholarly/tei-WH2PMed-pt2-c3.html . Accessed 20 January 2019.

xvii Charteris, D. L. Medical experiences as a prisoner of war in Germany. Reprinted from The Liverpool Medico-Chirurgical Journal. Vol.1, 1946

xviii Waterfall Sidney. Op cit endnote iv

xix Stout, T. Duncan. Op cit endnote xvi

xx Ibid endnote xvi

xxi Waite, Charles. Survivor of the Long March. Spellmount, 2012.

xxii Op cit endnote iv

xxiii Waite, Charles, Op cit endnote xxi

xxiv Stout, T. Duncan. Op cit endnote xvi

xxv Moreton, George. Doctor in chains. Corgi Books, 1980.

xxvi Jones, Ian. Relating his father's comments on Stalag VIIIB Facebook Group page. Accessed 30 August 2020.

xxvii Wickiewicz, Anna. Captivity in British uniforms: Stalag VIIIB (344) Lamsdorf. Opole, Cemtralne Muzeum Jencow Wojennych w Lambinowicach-Opolu, 2017

xxviii Gilbert, Martin. The Second World War: a complete history. Phoenix, 1989. p230

xxixIbid. endnote xxviii. p232
xxxIbid endnote xxviii p236
xxxiIbid endnote xxviii pp239-241
xxxiiIbid endnote xxviii p247.

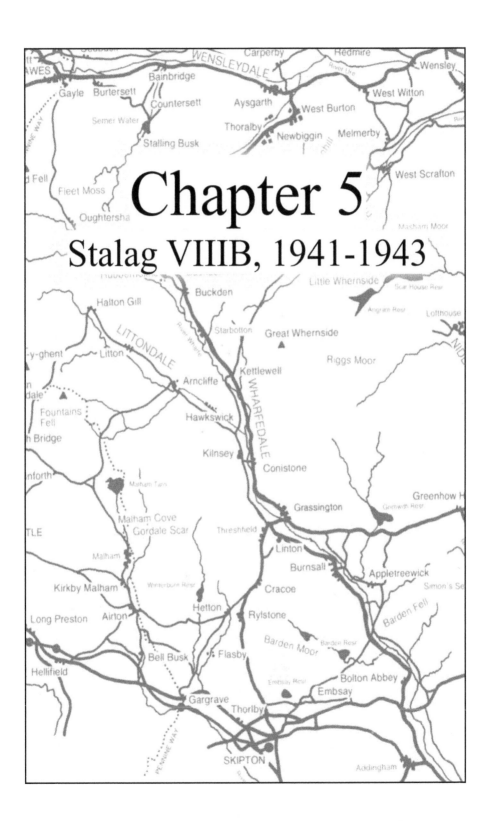

Chapter 5
Stalag VIIIB, 1941-1943

Chapter 5

2002

There was a pause in Sid's story and the three of them agreed to another break. As it was a lovely Spring day, they wandered outside into the garden to the seat below the back wall. Behind the seat was a lilac tree planted by Sid in memory of Frankie after she died in 1994.

The leaves were just beginning to sprout on the trees beyond the wall but Sid could still see through the branches to the view of the moors and Embsay Crag beyond.

He thought about his time as a prisoner of war and of how important memories of the hills of the Dales were to him at that time. They reminded him that there was a reason to survive and that better times would surely come.

He looked around the garden that he and Frankie had planned and planted and was grateful that she'd had time to enjoy it.

They wandered back inside and sat down again in the living room. Duncan switched on the voice recorder again and Sid continued.

He talked about his arrival at Stalag VIIIB and the conditions there. He talked about letters written and received, how he slowly settled into the new routine and the work he did there as a medic.

*

Stalag VIIIB (344) Lamsdorf

1941-43

By the time Sidney arrived at Stalag VIIIB there were already about 18,000 prisoners accommodated there – the numbers having doubled after the fall of Greece and Crete.

The highest number was recorded in October 1943 when an ICRC (International Commission of the Red Cross) report noted that there were 31,000 soldiers detained there. This was after several transportations from camps in Italy were made to various camps in Germany. The higher density of prisoners rapidly worsened the living conditions and made it necessary to reorganise the structure of camps in the area.

This was when Stalag VIII B Lamsdorf was formally renamed Stalag 344 Lamsdorf and a new Stalag VIII B camp was created at Teschen. 10,000 prisoners were transported to the new camp and from then on numbers at Stalag 344 Lamsdorf became more reasonable. There were 22,000 men imprisoned there when it was evacuated in 1945.

Altogether there were 48,000 POWs detained at the camp at one time or another during the four years it was in use. A third of all soldiers taken captive by the Germans, found themselves at Lamsdorf for longer or shorter periods. It was the largest camp accommodating British POWs during World War II. [i]

*

When Sidney first arrived, the camp was undergoing large alterations to extend it. Most of the plans of the camp still in existence today, show the camp in its final stage after the extensions were completed in 1942.

137

The camp was surrounded with a high fence of barbed wire with thirty-five foot watch towers equipped with searchlights at regular intervals, so the guards could keep a tight hold on what was going on both during daylight hours and at night. [ii]

It was divided into two parts – the German administrative sector and the POWs sector, each separated from the other by a high, barbed wire fence.

In the administrative sector were the buildings used by the German guards, a post office, food stores, a delousing station and the camp prison.

In the other sector there were five barracks for the POWs, equipped with sanitary facilities, baths and a laundry. Each barrack was divided into two, each part accommodating about 200 men. Along one side were two rows of three-storey bunks the lowest being six inches above the ground and the highest about seven feet from the ground. Each bunk had a mattress filled with straw and sawdust. Along the other side were ten tables and twenty benches at which the men would sit to eat.

Between the two divisions was a room containing a washing trough and a copper to boil water for tea. [iii] When Sid first arrived these washing troughs were the only bathing facilities available and in the bitterly cold winter of 1941-42 there was frequently a thick coating of ice on the bathroom floor. In March 1942 a bathhouse was built with twenty showers. This meant that 600-800 men could be showered each day and each man then had a shower every ten days. [iv]

Latrines were in concrete buildings built over deep pits which were emptied by pumping into horse-drawn tanks. Each latrine had forty seats and each seat had a lid until they were stolen by the men for firewood. [v]

Different nations were in separate compounds and these were often subdivided by different army sectors, regiments or ranks. The men were allowed to move between the different sectors but

138

Kriegsgefangenenlager **STALAG VIII B** — Datum _25-10-41._
Prisoner of War Camp — Date

Name — **WATERFALL** — Vorname **SIDNEY**
Surname — Christian Name

Dienstgrad u. Truppenteil **PRIVATE — R.A.M.C. — 7380174.**
Rank and Unit

Geburtsdatum **25 - 6 - 17** — Geburtsort **ENGLAND.**
Date of birth — Native-place

Letzter Wohnort **SKIPTON, YORKSHIRE, ENGLAND.**
Last dwelling

Adresse meiner Angehörigen **"LYNDHURST", SKIPTON ROAD,**
Home Address

EMBSAY, Nᵣ SKIPTON, YORKSHIRE,

Unverwundet — in deutsche Kriegsgefangenschaft geraten
Unwounded — prisoner of war in Germany —

befinde mich wohl.   COM. FAM.   **10 NOV 1941**
I am well.

(Nichtzutreffendes ist zu streichen)   _S. Waterfall -24321._
(Passages non apposite to the point to be cancelled)   Signature

Above and Below: Both sides of Sid's Prisoner of War card from Stalag VIIIB, completed on his arrival there, October 1941 and mailed to the ICRC (International Committee of the Red Cross)

Kriegsgefangenenpost
For Prisoner of War

Postkarte   Stalag VIII B
Postcard   Geprüft:
                       Nᵣ 60

An

das Internationale Komitee vom Roten Kreuz

9 NOV. 1941

Genf

Palais du Conseil général

Schweiz

Gebührenfrei!
Free postage

139

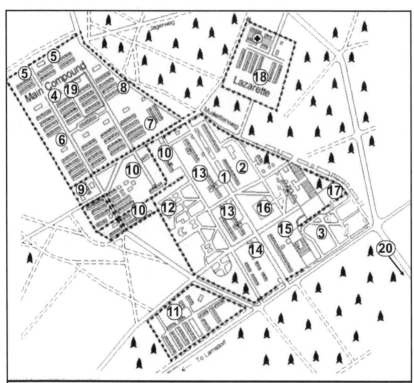

Stalag VIIIB/344-Lamsdorf, 1943-45

1. Chestnut Alley; 2. Stables, later Polish POWs; 3. Cemetery. 4. British POWs; 5. "Coolers"; 6. French POWs and other nationalities; 7. Ukranian and later British POWs; 8. Polish POWs; 9. De-lousing/bath huts; 10. Wehrmacht Camp HQ; 11. Wehrmacht guards accommodation; 12. Wehrmacht officers quarters; 13. POW huts; 14. Ante-camp (possibly new arrivals lodged here pending allocation to main camp); 15. Warehouse; 16. Football pitch; 17. Parking site; 18. Hospital; 19. RAF compound; 20. Road to Annahof Station.

Stalag VIIIB in winter

140

had to return to their own each evening in time for roll-call.[vi]

In each of the sectors there was a medical inspection room with a British medical officer in charge and there was a camp hospital (called a Revier) of 200 beds also with British staff.

Near the camp, but in its own barbed-wire-surrounded area, was a prisoner-of-war hospital, Lazarett Lamsdorf.[vii] Hospital facilities here were among the best at any of the Stalags. The hospital was made up of eleven concrete buildings, six of then self-contained wards each with space for up to one hundred patients. The others served as treatment blocks with operating theatres, X-Ray and laboratory facilities as well as kitchens, a morgue and accommodation for the medical staff.

The Lazarett was headed by a German officer with the title Oberst Arzt (Colonel Doctor) but the staff was made up entirely of prisoners. They included general physicians, surgeons, a neuro-surgeon, psychiatrist, anaesthiologist and radiologist.[viii]

Captured medical personnel were given duties in the camp medical inspection rooms, the camp hospitals, the Lazarett and with working parties.

The inspection rooms provided the first step for the sick to be seen by a doctor. The camp hospitals provided for medical, skin, venereal and minor surgical cases. It also looked after the chronic sick or injured who had passed the Repatriation Commission and were waiting for the first repatriation which eventually took place in October 1943. The Lazarett provided for the more serious surgical and medical cases.

Staff were therefore needed for the wards, the barracks, the laboratories, dispensary and theatre as well as staffing a large out-patients clinic which dealt with sick referred from the medical inspection rooms. Other medics found work as sanitation orderlies, attending to the cleanliness of latrines, staffing the camp delouser or organising the bath houses. Others worked on a daily fatigue party of cleaners and gardeners, working 8am to 5pm to keep both inside and outside areas of the camp in a clean and healthy condition. Sid mentioned working in the outside party in a later letter and he enjoyed the physical work outdoors.

In an interview he did for the local paper when he arrived home in May 1945, Sid said

It was a British camp and the Germans did not concern themselves with its internal running. This was left to the prisoners under the leadership of three British warrant officers who acted as trustees.[ix]

*

Sidney's first communication from the camp was a pre-printed Christmas card in December 1941 to which he just signed his name. The next letter that has survived was a card sent eleven months later in November 1942 where he mentions a football match that his team won 5-1 and a book he read – 'Garden of Delight' by W. Riley which was set in Burnsall and which he'd enjoyed very much. The next card was written two weeks later and mentions football again and asks how the business and the Christmas showroom is doing this year. [x]

*

No reason was given for this gap in the letters and it is always possible that they were simply lost. It's also possible that early 1942 was the worst period of Sid's captivity and he wanted to shield the people at home from what was happening to him – there was nothing good to report so he didn't write.

1941-42 was a terrible winter, starting with heavy falls of snow at the end of October around the time Sid arrived at Stalag VIIIB. From then on harsh frosts and fog continued through November accompanied by sporadic falls of snow until Christmas. From then on snow continued falling through January, February and much of March with very little

142

improvement until the beginning of April. Temperatures that winter would have been -20 to -25 degrees Celsius for much of the time.

1942 was also the year that there was a breakdown in the delivery of Red Cross parcels between January and May due to a bottleneck in the system at Lisbon. So for that period everyone was back on starvation rations, as well as not receiving the winter clothing rations usually provided to the POWs [xi]

It was also the year that the camp was being extended so until the extensions were completed, overcrowding would have been the norm.

Then there was the 'chain' crisis from autumn 1942 onwards. In revenge for the killing of German prisoners by British commandos during raids on Nazaire, Dieppe and the Isle of Sark, the Germans issued an order that in future all commandos would be treated as terrorist and sabotage groups and killed in action or given 'special treatment' in captivity. At Stalag VIIIB this included 1,544 soldiers and 800 RAF who were handcuffed between 8am and 9pm with an hour's break at noon. This lasted for 12 months until the ICRC negotiated a truce between the German and British governments.[xii] Sid would probably not have been involved but he would have known about it and it could have affected his morale.

*

The writing of letters played an important part in the lives of the POWs as it was their only means of keeping in touch with their families. The receiving of letters and news from outside the camp and from the 'ordinary' world was important psychologically and allayed the feelings of isolation, loneliness and home-sickness that was part of life in the camp with its 20,000 inhabitants.

According to camp regulations, the POWs had the right to send four letters and two postcards each month. They were written on special forms delivered regularly by camp authorities which made the work of the camp censors easier and resulted in all information leaving the camp being controlled. Only correspondence stamped *Gepruft* (censored) could be sent and all Sidneys letters had this stamp on them. Because of the censorship, the families had very little idea of what camp life was like as the writers were not able to mention any of the miseries or hardships they were enduring. However, it wasn't what was in the letters that was important – mainly the fact that they'd been written and that the writer was still alive. Both prisoners and families wrote a 'watered-down' version of reality, not wanting to worry their nearest and dearest about things that they couldn't do anything about. [xiii]

One of the privileges later granted to medical personnel was a double ration of letter cards per month which Sid undoubtedly made good use of.[xiv]

*

From November 1942 onwards Sidney wrote home regularly, mainly to his parents, his sister Barbara and his fiancee Amy. His letters have survived but not the ones he received as they probably had to be left in the camp as non-essential luggage when the prisoners were evacuated in January 1945. Of course the letters were censored. A lot of what he wrote repeats itself letter after letter and concerns news about letters and parcels received, the weather, books he's read, football and other activities. But every now and then a real nugget reveals itself and we get a hint of what real life was like for him.

A letter written in December 1942 says the weather has been good for the time of year and he hopes it continues that way as they have a good programme of sports planned for over the Christmas period. He mentions a visit to another barrack where they played them at Chess, Bridge, Table Tennis, Darts and Quoits and beat them at everything except Table Tennis. He also mentions a Whist Drive where he just missed a prize by one trick and the fact that school starts again soon and he is going to continue with his Shorthand. [xv]

He then talks about his allotment;

I don't know whether I mentioned that I had increased my allotment again. I increased it as from June – from 2/- to 2/3 per day and I have now sent in an application to increase it to 2/9 per day as from November – I hope you will have no difficulty with it – did you get notification of the last increase in June? I will make it up to 3/- per day next May.

All servicemen could allot a part of their pay to someone else – usually a wife or parents. It was taken automatically from their pay each month and the receiver (in Sidney's case, his parents) had a pension book that they could take to the post office to withdraw the money. There was a minimum sum that could be allotted but most men increased it from the minimum allowed. It was a means of giving the families access to money if the men were posted away.[xvi]

*

Sid's Christmas card for 1942 was another pre-printed card, this time with a sad little message on it:

I'd hoped I might be with you,
This year on Xmas Day,
But since my thoughts must still suffice,
I'll greet you in this way

In his next letter to his parents he tells them about his Christmas:

Well, another Xmas has been and gone and we managed to entertain ourselves fairly well under the circumstances, the weather helping as it was nice and sunny and we got two or three good football matches in – both soccer and rugby. In the evenings we had concerts etc. On Christmas Eve we had a very good variety show in our barrack room and since then the Camp

Panto 'Aladdin' has been on – this was not as good as usual, mainly because they only had three weeks for rehearsals.On Boxing Day I went across to the Church to hear the Camp Choir give a Carol Concert which was exceedingly good. [xvii]

Between the 4th and 10th January the weather turned very wintery with snow and wind and the snow lay deep on the ground and had blown into drifts against the barrack walls. Winter was a terrible time in the camp – the barracks were constructed of wood and were uninsulated and draughty – the small amount of heat from fires providing little warmth. However, the body heat from 130 men did make a difference. With all the windows and doors closed, broken panes of glass boarded up and cracks stuffed with paper, the temperature was kept above freezing during the day. During the coldest of weather all the men wore their greatcoat, hat and mitts continuously, went to bed fully clothed and spread their greatcoat over the blankets for extrawarmth. [xviii]

By the 16 January, the weather had changed again and *Everywhere, S*idney says, *Is ankle deep in mud.* This would have made the conditions in the barracks even worse as it was inevitable that the mud from outside would have been tramped inside.

Thank goodness, writes Sidney, *I am inside most of the time. I have been working hard this past week or two – six days a week and the odd hours on Sundays too. I haven't had time to do anything else.*[xix]

Maybe new transports of wounded had arrived from more recent battle areas, or maybe it was simply outbreaks of winter sickness brought on by the cold and hunger at this time of year. The hunger was ongoing and one prisoner wrote *"We went to bed hungry, we got up hungry, we rose from each mockery of a meal hungry and we sat, stood, lay or walked in a state of constant gnawing hunger"* [xx]- the cold during winter only made it worse.

*

Stalag VIIIB group photo. Sid standing far left.

Right: Distribution of Red Cross parcels, Stalag VIIIB

Left: Sid's Christmas card from Stalag VIIIB, 1941

Left: View of Stalag VIIIB

Right: Stalag VIIIB group photo. Sid standing, back row, fourth from right

Hospital building, Stalag VIII B

148

It was after this that the bottom fell out of Sidney's world with a letter from his fiancee, Amy, telling him she was going to marry someone else.

This was by no means an unusual occurrence and could have serious consequences as it brought to an end that hope of Home and a normal life that got the men through each day. It was at times like this that the strongly forged friendships between the men came to the fore as they supported each other. Most prisoners had their buddies - two or three, rarely more – and they looked after each other, sharing food, space and confidences. These close friendships acted as the substitute for the family at home that you could no longer turn to.

These friendships had an intensity that only occurred where men were thrown together in such a way that they cannot avoid each other, cannot choose when they will meet or separate. They existed in an absorbing, demanding and taut vacuum. Friends allowed each other to sulk, lose their temper and give way to almost every emotion quite unashamedly. Most had friends in other barracks who they saw on almost a daily basis, but it was essential to have someone who shared with you the periods of sadness and depression, who nursed you in illness and who accepted, without complaint, the anger that consumed a lot of the prisoners because of their circumstances. [xxi]

*

Sidney immediately wrote back to Amy:

Believe me I am truly sorry the present state of affairs has come to pass, but I only hope that everything is for the best. I must admit that since I read your letter I have felt very disappointed and have felt as if the bottom has dropped right out of everything and as for trying to visualise life at Skipton without you being with me – well I'm afraid it just can't be done at present. Anyway, there is an old saying "Don't worry it might never happen" and so to make life here a little brighter at present I am still living in hope, until I hear of anything further. You may think I am a fool but you see I am still as big an optimist as ever and I just can't bring myself to believe that things were meant to end like this. As you say, if I had been at Home this would never have happened and under the circumstances, please believe me when I say I do not blame you. I do realise what an unenviable task you have had as two or three years seems such a damned long time when one is young...........To end with, I want to whisper a little warning and say that if there have been no further developments before I get back I intend to lay siege again and do everything in my power to remedy this breach. [xxii]

Unfortunately, by the time Sidney got back to Skipton in 1945, there had been *further developments* and Amy was married with a daughter and soon after her husband was posted overseas and she went to live in married quarters in Germany for several years.

Nevertheless, for the time being Sidney continued to live in hope and asked his sister Barbara to be his intermediary *in my catastrophe.*

He then wrote to his parents. After apologising for not writing sooner but he said he felt he had to reply to Amy first. He then continued:

I am terribly sorry that this had to be and just at present I feel it pretty badly but I suppose that will pass. I don't blame Amy unduly and I want you to promise me that you won't either, as she has had a much harder job than mine has been and we youngsters are very prone to grasp at present certainties rather than future probabilities and she has done well to manage to wait so long as all my circle of pals here have been members of our so called 'Lost Legion' for a good six months or more. [xxiii]

The Lost Legion were probably those men who had been out of communication for long periods of time when their folks at home had not known whether they had survived or not.

Sidney also mentioned that he had written to Amy's parents and tried to explain the situation as Amy had told him that her parents were very much against her decision and that she was more or less in disgrace at home.

In a letter from Amy, written in 2004 soon after Sidney's death, she tries to explain what had happened from her point of view:

All that I can say was that I was young and had not seen Sidney for a long time. At first of course I just stayed at home at nights and then I was introduced to Frank by a mutual friend. He was a good looking, very smart soldier and when he asked me to go out with him that was the start of it. I know I should not have gone but I did and I thought I had grown to love him. We married in 1943 and Judith was born eighteen months later. Sidney came home in 1945 and as soon as we met again I realised that I had made a mistake and that he was the one I really was in love with.

However, it was too late for them and though they always kept in touch, they didn't see each other for several years. She says that *Frank was a loving husband but I have lived all my sixty years from that time being sorry for what I did.* [xxiv]

Sidney's first communication in February 1943 mentions that he is in good health which *makes a difference in these conditions.* He is also attending two or three classes at school which, he writes, *seems to make the time pass more quickly.*

In a letter to his parents he tells them he has had *a lovely letter from Amy's mother. She is awfully unhappy about the present state of affairs. Her letter bucked me up tremendously, it is nice to realise one has loyal friends at times like these.*

He has had some good news from Mr Harrison who would like him to take over Mr Whittingham's job in the Town Hall when he gets back. Sidney comments that he hopes he can cope with it as there would be good prospects there if he can. He tells his parents that he is taking a course in Criminal Law which should help a bit. [xxv]

Educational opportunities abounded and were seen as not only as training for a life after the war but also of psychological importance and a means for the men to use their brains and focus on other things beside their homesickness and the miserable conditions they were living in.

Lessons started in 1940 with an attempt to improve communication between captors and prisoners by teaching the men German. This was stopped in 1943 when the Germans realised that learning German enhanced the prisoners' chances of escape. But by this time the number of subjects taught had extended to English, French, History, Geography, Arithmetic, Electrical Engineering, Agriculture and crafts such as cobbling, tailoring, basket making, upholstering and lots more.

The school system targeted all the different levels of education including university level and in 1942 it was reported that there were 2,400 men coming to the school daily.

To support the educational opportunities, a collection of books was needed and already by 1941 the library at Stalag VIIB was one of the largest of its kind. In May 1943 the collection was comprised of thirteen thousand volumes and was expected to grow by another twenty-five thousand volumes by November that year. [xxvi]

*

In his next card home, amongst details of the weather and his good health Sid mentions that *we are all plodding on in the same old way here and praying for an early finish to our exile.*[xxvii] A hint at the boredom and homesickness that plagued a POW's life.

152

In a letter written in March he says that *on Tuesday I sat for the Royal Society of Arts first Shorthand Speed Exam and I think I have passed.* This was enabled by the visit of YMCA representatives who would have organised and overseen the exams. Success in such exams would have provided the men with the means of applying for jobs or even stepping up into further education once they got home. [xxviii]

His next letter mentions a visit to the dentist *which revealed three fillings needed, so I had them attended to straight away. I was surprised the way my teeth have stood up to it as for about twelve months I had no toothpaste at all and only an old, soft brush.* The Army Dental Corps was originally part of RAMC but split off to become a separate branch prior to World War II. After the war it was awarded the 'Royal' status to become the RADC in recognition of its service during the Second World War[xxix].

He ends the letter by asking his parents to remember him to Mr and Mrs Rushworth [neighbours] and all his other friends at Home.

In a letter to Barbara he talks about their cousin Kath:
I am very sorry to hear about Jim [her husband who had died]– *it will have been rather a blow to Kath. I wonder what she will be doing. It will be a blow to__us__ if she leaves Thorpe. But I expect she will.* [xxx]
However, Kath remained in Thorpe tucked away as it is in the Yorkshire Dales, and Sidney and his family continued to visit her in her little cottage, with it's huge and efficient black coal range, until the end of her life in the 1960s.

In the same letter he says he is feeling very fit because the football season has started again and he's getting in a bit of exercise. He also says that *the Woodheads have lent me their Old Scholars Report* [from Ackworth School] *….and I had an hour or so of very interesting reading. Nearly all of my pals except Fatty Auckland seem to have got 'hitched up'.*

*

In the next few cards and letters to various people, Sidney mentions the number of parcels he's received lately – nine since the beginning of February. These include clothing parcels, tobacco parcels, book parcels and one from the Embsay-with Eastby Institute. Some were from individuals (he thanks 'Auntie and Uncle' for one as well as his parents) others were Red Cross parcels.

Red Cross parcels, beginning in 1941 and arriving regularly by early 1943, allowed the POWs to survive in a relatively good physical condition. They were primarily food parcels that provided a supplement to the basic fare supplied by the Germans and consisted of items such as cans of meat, dried sausage and fish, vegetables, sugar, coffee, tea, condensed milk, cheeses, butter, dried fruit and porridge oats. Most British prisoners owed their life and their health to the continuing efforts of the British Red Cross. Heating the food was a problem to begin with until 1943 when the Klim (milk) tin blowers were invented as portable stoves. They were equipped with hand-propelled blowers which allowed the content of a POWs canteen or bowl to be heated very quickly, using very little fuel. They changed the POWs lives and it was reported that "the impact of this invention could be likened to the introduction of the microwave oven in modern times".

In separate parcels were sent cigarettes which were in particular demand as they were used as the informal camp currency and there was a rapid rise in bartering. Initially, swap shops were set up and if items changed hands, the price was a cigarette. Eventually this widened and German guards became part of the barter system although English and American cigarettes were more popular than the German ones. Something like a sharp knife, very useful for cutting bread, was worth a hundred cigarettes, while two Gold Flake cigarettes could buy a photo taken in the camp. [xxxi]

*

While Red Cross parcels were continuing to be increasingly important in Sid's world, the early months of 1943 brought more changes in the direction the war was heading.

January brought the tenth anniversary of Nazi rule and both Goering and Goebbels made radio broadcasts to mark the event. Goebells declared :

A thousand years hence, every German will speak in awe of Stalingrad and remember that it was here that Germany put the seal on her victory.

The Allies meanwhile bombed Berlin and Hamburg on the same night, these attacks being timed to coincide with these broadcasts. A day later the German forces in Stalingrad surrendered. Goebbel's boasting and Hitler's confidence were therefore held up to mockery. The news of the surrender brought renewed hope to the armies struggling against Germany as well as the captive peoples suffering throughout German-occupied Europe. For the first time the Nazis appeared vulnerable[xxxii]

A week later in Berlin, Himmler received a detailed report on the massive quantity of old clothing collected from Auschwitz and other death camps. The list included 22,000 pairs of children's shoes and 3000 kgs of women's hair. The women's hair filled a large railway wagon. Three weeks earlier, after a visit to Warsaw, Himmler had also raised the question of what to do with the hundreds of thousands of spectacles and eye-glasses lying in warehouses in that city.

The Jewish clothing sent to the centre of the Reich filled 825 railway wagons. Clothes, spectacles and hair – these were among the spoils of the Nazi's war against the Jews. Children and their parents were robbed of the very last of their possessions at the entrance to the gas chambers.

Also in February, as the deportation trains were continuing to travel from West to East, the Red Army was steadily advancing from East to West and Hitler, reflecting on Stalingrad to his confidantes announced:

What you are witnessing is a catastrophe of unheard-of magnitude.[xxxiii]

*

The struggle on the Eastern Front was aided by further successes in breaking the various Enigma keys. The 'Ermine' key used by one of the main Luftwaffe combat units in the East, was broken as was the 'Orchid' key of the German Air Force administrative units in the Ukraine. In North Africa, the ability to eavesdrop on Rommel's most secret messages resulted in the decryption of his plan to attack the British Eighth Army after he had failed to break through against the Americans in Tunisia. Montgomery was able to rush extra troops 200 miles along the single surfaced road to match and exceed the forces being gathered against him.

The Allies were also helping to finance partisans fighting behind the lines in occupied countries and in March 1943 the United States Treasury agreed to make five million dollars available to the Polish Resistance. The money, in small denomination notes was flown from Britain in a small plane which landed at night on Polish soil, left the money with members of the resistance, and flew back safely.[xxxiv]

The war against the Nazis was being fought on many fronts and in many different ways.

*

i   Wickiewicz, Anna. Captivity in British uniforms: Stalag VIII B (344) Lamsdorf. Opole, 2017 pp24-27

ii   Ibid endnote i, p31

iii Stout, T.Duncan.M. Medical services in New Zealand and the Pacific. Part of The official History of New Zealand in the Second world War 1939-1945. Wellington, Historical Publications Branch, 1958. www.nzetc.victoria.ac.nz/tm/scholarly/tei-WH2PMed-pt2-c5-1.html Accessed 29 August 2020.

iv Ibid endnote iii p127

v   Ibid endnote iii p128

vi Wickiewicz, Anna. Op cit endnote i p30

vii Https://stalagviiib.weebly.com/stalag-viii-b-pow-camp-344.html Accessed 20 January 2019

viii www.lamsdorf.com/history.html . Accessed 23 October 2020.

ix Waterfall, Sidney. Newspaper article. Skipton, Craven Herald. c. May 1945.

x   Postcard from Sidney Waterfall to Joseph John and Edith Waterfall, dated 1 November 1942

xi Stout, T.Duncan M.Op cit endnote iii

xii Wickiewicz, Anna. Op cit endnote i pp72-75.

xiii Ibid endnote i p34

xiv Stout, T.Duncan M. Op cit endnote iii

xv Letter from Sidney Waterfall to Joseph John and Edith Waterfall, dated 20 December 1942

xvi Stalag VIIIB Facebook Group

xvii Letter from Sidney Waterfall to Joseph John and Edith Waterfall, dated 4 January 1943

xviii Wickiewicz, Anna. Op cit endnote i p32

xix Letter from Sidney Waterfall to Joseph John and Edith Waterfall, dated 16 January, 1943

xx Nichol, John and Rennell, Tony. The last escape: the untold story of allied prisoners of war in Germany 1944-45. London, Penguin Books, 2003. p5

xxi Ibid endnote xx, p6

xxii Letter from Sidney Waterfall to Amy Wilkinson, dated 18 January 1943

xxiii Letter from Sidney Waterfall to Joseph John and Edith Waterfall, dated 24 January 1943

xxiv Letter from Amy Wilkinson to Sonia Waterfall, dated 12 July 2004

xxv Letter from Sidney Waterfall to Joseph John and Edith Waterfall, dated 7 February 1943

xxvi Wickiewicz, Anna. Op cit endnote i pp96-98

xxvii Postcard from Sidney Waterfall to Joseph John and Edith Waterfall, dated 14 February 1943

xxviii Letter from Sidney Waterfall to Joseph John and Edith Waterfall, dated 7 March 1943

xxix Www.en.wikipedia.org/wiki/Royal_Army_Dental_Corps. Acessed 29 August 2020.

xxxLetter from Sidney Waterfall to Barbara Waterfall, dated 21 March 1943

xxxiWickiewicz, Anna. Op cit endnote i pp38-39

xxxii Gilbert, Martin. The second world war: a complete history. Phoenix, 2009. p398-9.

xxxiiiIbid endnote xxxii p400

xxxiv Ibid endnote xxxii p407-412

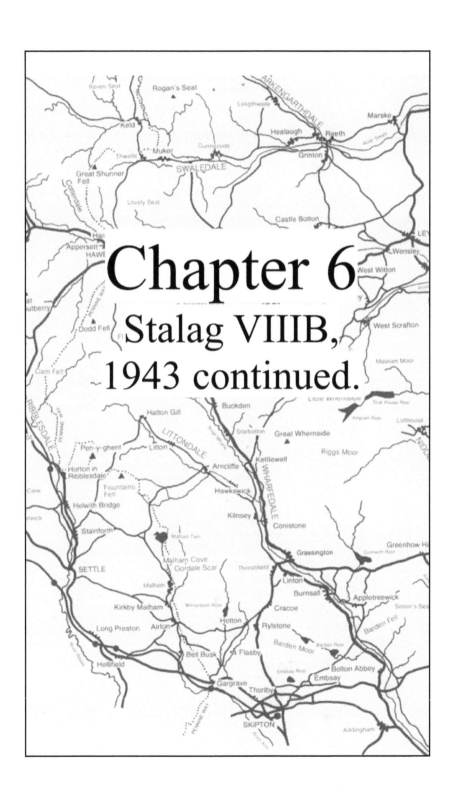

Chapter 6
Stalag VIIIB,
1943 continued.

Chapter 6

2002

Sid looked round the living room where the three of them were seated.

On the wall above the fireplace was a large oil painting of roses which had belonged to his mother at 'Lyndhurst' and which he'd refused to part with when they moved to the Park Home even though he knew Frankie wasn't keen on it.

She'd had her way with the two small watercolours of Austrian street scenes from before the war as well as the pre-war blue-and-white Dutch tiles showing the shop frontages of her Dutch in-laws before Rotterdam was bombed in 1940.

They both loved the wood carving of 'Lyndhurst' which had been a gift from the children on their 40th Wedding Anniversary

Their past history was reflected in what was displayed on the walls of their home.

On they went with the recording and Sid told Fran and Duncan more about life in a POW camp and his work as a medic.

He talked about playing football with one of the Stalag teams, the opportunities for further education that were offered and how hopes for repatriation were raised and then dashed during 1943. He talked about the importance of writing and receiving letters as a means of re-connecting with the world outside the camp.

*

1943 continued

By April 1943 Enigma messages being encrypted in Germany were being decrypted in Britain within a few hours of being received by those in the German Army who were to act on them. On 15 April it was Operation Citadel, the attack on the Kursk salient in Russia that was revealed.

It was also this month that the most prolonged Jewish revolt of all took place in the Warsaw ghetto when the Germans tried to continue deportations to Treblinka. Jewish fighters battled in the streets, apartments, cellars and sewers of the ghetto, armed only with seventeen rifles and hand-made grenades. Heavily out-numbered and out-armed, they still managed to kill three hundred soldiers before the revolt was crushed three weeks later. Thousands of Jews were killed and thousands more deported to Treblinka.

Resistance activity continued throughout Europe – in France, in Holland, in Norway and in Yugoslavia all aimed at breaking German morale and diverting troops from the front line.[i]

*

Sid's letters from Stalag VIIIB to family in Britain continued.

In a card to Barbara in early April 1943 he mentions a football match which his team drew 1-1. He says: *We should have won easily but just could NOT score. I am feeling very fit at present,* he says, - *more like 'civvy street'.* From a later letter we discover that this is 8 a-side football – the 11 a-side did not come until they had built a new and larger pitch two months later.[ii]

In his next letters to his parents, the subject of football continues and he tells them that his team had won their first League match 12-1 but lost the second one 4-2. He tells them about a book parcel he received which contained Wilsden's and Firth

Crossley's "Rest and Change" - *the photos of which,* he writes, *nearly made me weep with a desire to get back to our Dales.* He mentions again that he is feeling very fit and says that *even though being here is nearly enough to make anyone go mad, there is a lot we have to be thankful for.* In his next card home the subject of football continues and he tells his parents that the pitch is a quagmire but the team managed to win their League match 5-0 this week. He ends by saying *I wish mother had been here to wash my clothes after the match.* He has heard that Barbara [aged nineteen] has started working as a nurse in Bradford and is happy to hear that she is settling down well there. [iii]

In the next card to Barbara, he tells her that everyone is looking forward to the Easter weekend as there will be an Arts and Crafts Exhibition and a Sports Meeting. [iv]

The football news continued:

We won our football this week 2-1 against one of our chief opponents., Sidney writes to his parents. *We have now Won 4 and Drawn 1 out of 6 games and are 2nd in the League, 1 point behind the leaders who were the only team to beat us so far.* [v]

*

Sports had been a part of the POWs life since the first prisoners arrived in 1940 and the ICRC and YMCA had been involved from the beginning with the provision of equipment. By the time Sidney got involved it had become an inseparable part of everyday life in the camp and sports such as rugby, basketball, hockey, volleyball and cricket all had their followers.

However, no other sport provoked so many emotions as did the football matches. The popularity of this sport made it dominate the other disciplines as regards the amount of time devoted to it by the players or the number of dedicated supporters. The atmosphere at football matches in the camp would have matched that at today's stadiums. By October 1942 sports grounds had been marked out and benches built surrounding them, thus making miniature stadiums and several almost professional sports teams and competitions were organised on three levels.

Thanks to the aid provided by the ICRC and YMCA, sport continued to motivate the POWs and improve their morale and confidence as well as their physical condition. The involvement of these two international organisations proved to the POWs that they had not been forgotten by the outside world. [vi]

*

That Easter Sidney reported that a 7-A-Side Rugby International had been played with the Maori team beating the New Zealand team, 6-3 in the final. England lost to New Zealand in the Semis after beating Scotland 6-0. Then he moves on to the football when he says that his team has

a very good chance of heading the League as they only have one more hard game to play.

In a later letter he tells his parents that they have ended up equal top of their division after drawing a game they should have won. By the end of May they are top of their League by 2 points. [vii]

In a letter in May he mentions *a shortage of balls just at present* and a match between Stalag VIIIB and Stalag VIIA which *we just managed to win 4-2.*

He also writes about a very good Choral Concert in the church given by the Camp Choir and appears to go to any performance that is put on as he has previously mentioned 'Aladdin' the Panto at Christmas and the play 'The Schoolmaster' by Ian Gray. He also went to an Arts and Craft Exhibition over Easter and wrote in a later letter that *there were some very good paintings and sketches on view.* [viii]

*

Stalag VIIIB group photo. Sid standing, middle row, second left

Left: Original programme for a play performed at Stalag VIIIB to entertain the men

Below: View of Stalag VIIIB

168

One of the few times he mentions his friends was in a letter at the end of April when he says:

One of our little gang has been taken to Hospital with Pneumonia and Pleurisy and he has taken a turn for the worse.

A month later he writes about him again:

That pal of mine who I mentioned was in Hospital died on May 25th and I went to the funeral on the 27th. They get a very nice funeral, military of course, and it is the first I have been to here.[ix]

The POWs who died in the Stalag were buried in separate graves in the north-eastern part of the old POW cemetery behind the graves dating back to WWI. It is there that full burial ceremonies took place. The ceremony always started in a small chapel near a monument commemorating the British POWs who died at Lamsdorf during WWI. The funeral procession consisted of the dead POW's mates, a German guard of honour, the priest leading the ceremony and occasionally the camp band.[x]

*

In the same letter he mentions someone called Rod Gray who lives near Home.

I had a good talk to him, he says, *and funnily enough his pal, who is also from Leeds, was in the same unit as Ted Hole and Bert Howcroft so we had quite a lot to say to each other.*

This could have been the 'Bert' that Barabara had mentioned as having been captured – in a later letter in June it seems she mentions that she has started hearing from Bert again. [xi]

*

In May, he writes to his parents that

169

We have just finished building a new football pitch big enough for 11 a-side and they've just watched the opening match on the new pitch. *There was some lovely football,* he says, *considering the lads have been playing 8 a-side for so many years.* A week later and he has just played his first 11 a-side game for over three years, and says *it did seem strange.* [xii]

With the new season comes gardening and he tells his parents:
I have got some tomato plants in a little strip of garden we have got, but we have to grow them outside over here. I have also got radishes, lettuce, onions and peas and things are coming on nicely so far. In a later letter he says his garden is doing well due to some rain during the week and he has had a few radishes and lettuce from it. The gardening would have been part of the work he and his outside team would have been responsible for – as mentioned in a later letter in July.

He also tells them that he's been sitting out in the sun reading as well:
I am reading one of the best books I have read since I've been here...it is called "I Bought a Mountain" by Thomas Firbank, ;published by Harrap. ....it is all about sheep farming in North Wales between Snowden and the Glyders. Sidney would have known the area well because he had first climbed Snowden with his father and Arnold when he was only six years old and had visited the area several times since then.
Another book he mentions is "How Green was my Valley" by Llewellyn – also read out in the sun on a *glorious day.* [xiii]

One weekend in June seems to have been very busy – with *Camp Sports, a Boxing Tourney, Football and, for entertainment, a Naval Musical Revue called "Decko" and the Camp Choir giving "Merrie England"* which he said took him back to *Coronation Day and the Castle Grounds* [at Skipton]. Around the same time he also sent home the programme for a play called "Square Crooks" by James P. Judge which he says was *very good and funny.*

In the middle of June he took a week off from football as he
170

thought he needed a rest because he'd been a bit off form the last week or so. - *can't do a thing right,* he says – thinks he has been playing too much and has gone a bit stale. He has been to watch a couple of cricket matches and says *it comes as a change from football.* [xiv]

*

In July there is different news:

A week or two since I found a couple of skylarks' nests each with five eggs in and I am glad to say they have both fully hatched out this week. I found them in the course of my bit of work, a party of six of us are on the Camp gardening staff and we get all around the Camp every day, trimming road edges and keeping ditches clean etc. I have had this job about a year now, it is easy and you get about a good bit.

This was the first time he was specific about the work he did apart from the garden he mentioned earlier.

A week later he mentions the two nests again – he says they are still OK but he thinks they will be empty in another day or two as a couple of the youngsters have already flown from one nest. He has been reading *a very good book this week* - "The Crowthers of Bankdam" by Thomas Armstrong and says that *it was just like life in one of our West Riding towns and there was plenty of 'broad' talking in it.*

He writes about a Sports Day he went to at the New Camp Hospital and says it was *a good day out.* He later mentions that he played in a 'friendly' against a team from the New Hospital and his team won 8-1. Sidney was playing at centre-half and kicked five goals but says that *the opposing defence was weak..* [xv]

*

In his next letter home Sidney is worried about his father who it seems has had an operation. He says

I am very sorry to hear about Dad but I hope that everything has turned out successfully and that he is on the way to being quite well again.

He tells them both to take care of themselves and not to do too much work. At the end of July he writes *I hope Dad is getting well by now* and by the end of August he says that he's glad to hear that his Dad has got over his operation alright and expects that *he will have arrived home by now* and that it couldn't have come too soon for him. [xvi]

*

In July, while Sid was worrying about his father's health and what was happening in England, the tide of the war had turned yet again with the fall of Mussolini in Italy and the launch of the Allies' move into southern Europe when they landed troops at Palermo on the north coast of Sicily. Mussolini, the ruler of Italy since 1922, was suddenly shorn of his powers and had been informed by King Victor Emmanuel that Parliament had asked him [the king] to assume command of Italy's armed forces.

For Hitler, this meant calling a halt to any further advances on the eastern front and planning for military operations in Italy[xvii]

*

In a letter to Barbara on the 1 August he talks about her nineteenth birthday and says he hopes to be home for her 21st – [and he was].

He tells her that this weekend is a holiday with an Arts and Crafts Exhibition, a Boxing Tourney and a Grand Sports Day when the British Isles are competing against The British Empire and Allies.

Also that weekend, he says:

Football team, Stalag VIIIB. Sid standing second left.

Right: Morning roll call Stalag VIIIB

Left: German guard, Stalag VIIIB

this afternoon a small party of us went for a walk of about four miles to a lake and had a grand bathe, it was my first this year and only my second since I've been here. [xviii]

Being allowed out for a walk once a week was one of the privileges medical staff were allowed later in the war[xix] and it's no surprise that Sid took full advantage of it.

*

By the end of August a new season of the Football League has started and in the first two games, his team has drawn one match 2-2 and won one 3-2. The cricket season is underway with two Tests already played – England beat New Zealand by an innings and 15 runs and Australia beat New Zealand by 187 runs. England is still to play Australia at this stage but in a later letter he reports on *great gloom in England's Camp tonight – Australia won the Ashes by 83 runs – they were definitely the better team apart from the Keeper.*

In another August letter he mentions a Band and Choir Open Air Concert one evening:
In the band there were about 85 players and about 75 singers in the choir – it was very good and greatly appreciated. [xx]

*

In his first September letter he hopes that there have been no repercussions in his Dad's health and that he is well on the way to complete recovery. He tells his parents to look after themselves this coming winter and says that *I hope to be back to look after you myself for the next one.* In a later letter that month he says that he was pleased to hear that *Dad was getting on as well as possible and also getting about a little.* He talks about an exchange of photos and says he has had one taken and is expecting some from Arnold.

Back to sport and Ireland beat Scotland 5-2 in football and the

Army beat the RAF at cricket by 10 runs after being behind after the first innings. His team won their latest match 5-1 and at the half-way stage of the competition are in their usual place – second. They have not lost a match but have drawn one whereas the leaders have won all theirs.

He mentions his garden again – it is just about finished now but he's very happy with it as *I have had four or five dozen tomatoes and if there is a little bit more sun should get a few more.* [xxi]

*

Then he says in the same letter *Things have been very bright here this week especially as there has been movements with regard to repatting of medical men and wounded so who knows I MAY be lucky if it comes off.* [xxii]

Although the Geneva Convention makes provision for the repatriation of all POWs, it was only possible for the British and Germans to reach agreement over the seriously ill and disabled. Negotiations through the Red Cross had begun in late 1940 but did not progress very far at that time because there were far fewer German prisoners in this category than British. It was only after substantial numbers of Germans were taken prisoner in the desert campaign of 1942 that the talks resumed. The first actual exchange of prisoners took place in October 1943 and this is what Sidney had heard rumours about and what he hoped he might be a part of. [xxiii]

No more is heard about repatting until a letter at the end of October when it appears Sidney has missed out. He apologises for not writing and says:

We were all at sixes and sevens last week. After the lucky ones had left the camp, the Authorities decided they wanted the remainder of the Medics all together and we were removing from one Barrack to another.

Talking about the repatriated men, he continues: *I suppose they will have landed either yesterday or today, I saw a report in the paper that they had landed safely at Gothenburg on the 19th the lucky beggars. Still, I hope for better luck next time (if any).* xxiv

The repatriation exercise was a huge logistical undertaking. Trains bearing prisoners from Germany for repatriation to Britain began arriving in Gothenburg in the early hours of 19 October and the transfer to the Swedish steamship *Drottningholm,* was made during darkness. Before dawn more than 1,200 men were on board.

About noon on the same day, the German steamships *Ruegen* and *Meteor* brought a further 650 to the quays at Gothenburg just as *Drottningholm* was pulling out in preparation for sailing to England.

The British steamers *Empress of Russia* and *Atlantis* reached Gothenburg in the afternoon with 835 German repatriates. Meanwhile further trains with Allied prisoners from Germany, France and Holland were arriving, bringing besides servicemen, about fifty civilians.

The actual exchange of repatriated men depended on a signal that similar exchanges had reached the same stage in Oran in Algeria and Port Said in Egypt. The final movement of both German and British transports happened on the 22 October enabling the British ships to reach England during the weekend. xxv

*

Football continues to dominate Sid's letters and his team won their next match 6-1 with him shooting one of their goals. England beat Scotland 3-2 in the deciding match of the International League. Sidney comments: *One of my pals who was captain of the Jocks, missed a penalty and we did rag him.*

The repatriation has had repercussions on the football – matches had to be cancelled because things had been so unsettled and the

League had been abandoned as so many teams lost a lot of their players. However, he goes on to say say that he went to see a performance of 'Twelfth Night' at the Theatre and it was excellent – by far the best show he has seen. [xxvi]

*

In his first letter in November he says:
We are gradually settling down after the big movement and are getting quite used to the idea of having to stay.

Football is improving again and he says:
We have been having some good football lately. Some fresh talent having arrived including one or two League players, among them being the Stephens brothers who were on the books of Leeds United. Bill Stephens had a few games with the first team while I was at Home.

He has played in two games, both in knock-outs and both of them were wins, 3-2 and 2-1. The next letter tells his parents that his team has reached the semi-finals but he doesn't think they'll get any further as they are up against two of the best teams of the whole Camp. [xxvii]

*

In a letter at the end of October Sidney mentions briefly a *new job* which is going well and a week later in November he comments:

I am still working all day on my new job and it keeps fairly interesting as a great variety of cases come up for the clinics each week. I am at it 5 days a week and Saturday mornings if busy. My hours are the usual, 9 to 4.30 with a mid-day break.
[xxviii]

From these few comments it seems he could now be working in one of the medical inspection rooms or the camp hospitals.

He also mentions that they've had their first snow of the winter, that the frost has killed off all the greens and the trees are

177

looking very bare.

By mid November Sid has started sending Christmas greetings to all his correspondents and by the end of November in a letter to his parents he says:

Well Christmas will be over when you get this and I hope you have had no ill-effects from the rush and that business is as good as previous years.

He mentions that he has had three cigarette parcels of 500 each *which came in very useful as I was just about out.* They weren't really his but were for Wilfred Gibbs – one of his friends who had been repatted and had signed his parcels over to Sid,

No football at the moment because all the competitions have finished, however he watched a good match – the Army beat a combined RAF and Navy team 3-1. They have also had a delivery of a large amount of sports gear – enough to last a year and including over 100 footballs and many other things.[xxix]

*

By mid December he has heard that one of the repatted *boys* had called in to see his parents. He hasn't heard which one it was but expects it would be *Chappie from Bradford.*

Anyway, he says, *you will know now straight from the horse's mouth that I am not doing too badly and am in good health etc.*

He also tells them that he has received a big parcel – the first 4-Square parcel posted in August. He thanks them for it but also says *don't bother sending anything special in my parcels, you never know what is going to come off and I am pretty well off for things now.* Maybe he is still hoping to be a part of the next repatriation exchange.

In his last letter for 1943 he says that the men have started receiving letters from the repatts *and they all seem to have had a grand welcome.* Once again he says *Hope I have good luck next time (if any)*

He mentions that *everyone is helping to get their Barrack Rooms ready for Christmas and some of them are looking very nice. I have just been on a walking tour of inspection,* he says. He also mentions that he went to see the latest Camp show, *one of the more modern plays 'The Philadelphia Story' which was very good and very well acted and produced.*[xxx]

*

As 1943 came to an end, Germany and its allies could only look forward to more relentless attacks in the future, both from the unconquered nations fighting against them and from the ever-increasing partisan and resistance activity. Both Germany and Japan were determined to fight on, still believing they could break the power of the forces ranged against them who had vowed to continue until the Axis powers were forced into unconditional surrender.[xxxi]

i   Gilbert, Martin. The Second World War: a complete history. Phoenix, 1989. pp420-423

ii   Postcard from Sidney Waterfall to Barbara Waterfall, dated 4 April 1943

iii   Letter from Sidney Waterfall to Joseph John and edith Waterfall, dated 4 April 1943

iv   Postcard from Sidney Waterfall to Barbara Waterfall, dated 18 April 1943

v   Postcard from Sidney Waterfall to Joseph John and Edith Waterfall, dated 18 April 1943

vi   Wickiewicz, Anna. Captivity in British Uniforms: Stalag VIII B (344) Lamsdorf. Opole, 2017 pp108-112

vii   Letter ftom Sidney Waterfall to Joseph John and Edith Waterfall, dated 25 April 1943

viii   Letter from Sidney Waterfall to Joseph John and Edith Waterfall, dated2 May 1943

ix   Letters fom Sidney Waterfall to Joseph John and Edith Waterfall, dated 25 April and 6 June, 1943

x   Wickiewicz, Anna. Op cit endnote vi. p45

xi   Letter from Sidney Waterfall to Joseph John and Edith Waterfall, dated 6 June 1943

xii   Letters from Sidney Waterfall to Joseph John and Edith Waterfall, dated 16 May and 23 May 1943

xiii   Letter from Sidney Waterfall to Joseph John and Edith Waterfall, dated 20 June 1943

xiv   Letter from Sidney Waterfall to Joseph John and Edith Waterfall, dated 20 June 1943

xv   Letters from Sidney Waterfall to Joseph John and Edith Waterfall, dated 4 July and 12 July, 1943

xvi   Letters from Sidney Waterfall to Joseph John and Edith Waterfall, dated 12 July, 1 August and 22 August 1943

xvii   Gilbert, Martin. Op cit endnote i. pp446-7.

xviii   Letter from Sidney Waterfall to Barbara Waterfall, dated 1 August 1943

xix   Stout, T. Duncan M. Medical services in New Zealand and the Pacific. Part of: The Official History of New Zealand in the Second World War 1939-1945. Wellington, Historical Publications Branch, 1958. **nzetc.victoria.ac.nz/tm/scholarly/tei-WH2PMed-pt2-c5-2.html** . Accessed 9 September 2020.

xx   Letters from Sidney Waterfall to Joseph John and Edith Waterfall, dated 22 and 29 August 1943

xxi   Letters ftom Sidney Waterfall to Joseph John and Edith Waterfall, dated 6 September and 18 September 1943

xxii   Letter from Sidney Waterfall to Joseph John and Edith Waterfall, dated 12 September 1943

xxiii   The Times newspaper, 20 October 1943

xxiv   Letter from Sidney Waterfall to Joseph John and Edith Waterfall, dated 24 October 1943

xxv   The Times newspaper, 20 October 1943

xxviWaterfall, Sidney. Op cit endnote xxi

xxviiLetter from Sidney Waterfall to joseph John and Edith Waterfall, dated 1 November 1943

xxviiiLetter from Sidney Waterfall to Joseph John and Edith Waterfall, dated 7 November 1943

xxix Letter from Sidney Waterfall to Joseph John and Edith Waterfall, dated 28 November 1943

xxxLetters from Sidney Waterfall tyo Joseph John and Edith Waterfall, dated 12 and 21 December 1943

xxxiGilbert, Martin. Op cit endnote i. p484.

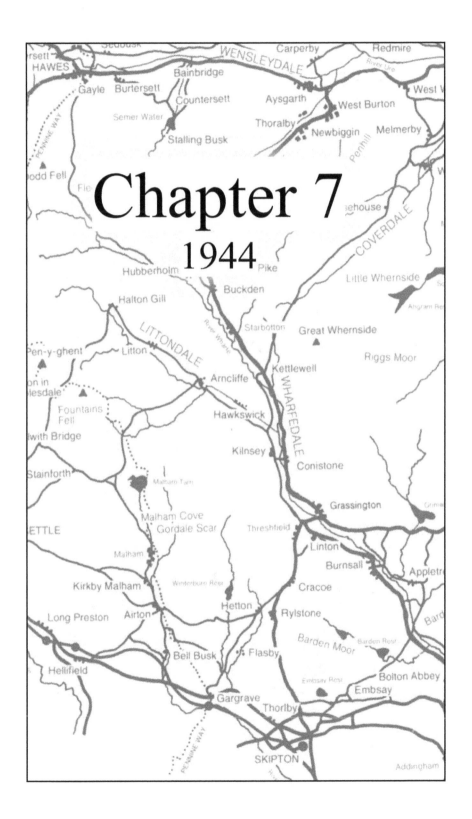

Chapter 7
1944

Chapter 7

2002

As Sid looked round the Park Home, he realised how much of Frankie's crafts and interests surrounded him.

Her lace work was everywhere and there were a few examples of her decoupage which was her major occupation right up until her death. Her fabric collage of a couple in national costume hung in one of the bedrooms and her cross-stitch tapestry wall-hanging was hung between the two windows in the living room.

Her thimble collection was displayed on the open shelves along the end wall of the living room. He knew that in the drawers of the display cabinet were the silverware and linen belonging to her mother, Hulda, and grandmother, Gisela, most of which Frankie had smuggled out of Austria when she'd escaped in 1938.

The Park Home reflected her family and history as much as it did his.

He looked up at Fran as she encouraged him to talk more about life as a POW. This time he talked about the next hospital at Tost that he was transferred to in 1944. Conditions were a lot better here and medics were allowed out of the camp on a regular basis. By this time the men knew that the war was coming to an end and their hopes were high.

*

1944

In the wider world of the European war, the New Year of 1944 opened with the establishment of yet another German concentration camp on Polish soil, at Plaszow, a suburb of Cracow. It had been a forced-labour camp since March 1943, run by a notorious sadist, Amnon Goeth, and now it joined the ranks of those places where thousands of people were worked and tortured to death. Amnon Goeth would later gain worldwide notoriety when he was portrayed by Ralph Fiennes in the film 'Schindler's List'.

The New Year was also characterised by increased resistance behind enemy lines. On the Eastern Front, as the Red Army continued its advance, more than sixty thousand partisans were active in five distinct areas, a constant threat to German troops and supplies moving up to the front.[i]

*

For Sid, 1944 began with more of the same. In his first letter home in the that year, he mentions a large number of parcels and letters having arrived during January - from Miriam, Aunty Kate, Aunty Bell, Aunty Angie, Dorothy Harrison, Geoff, Dot Holmes, Irene Keegan, Barbara and Little Kathleen as well as his parents. He says:

We had a very nice Xmas and New Year under the circs; I went to 3 shows and we did our fair share of eating and drinking (home made wine).

Once again there is no football as the place is ankle deep in mud but he is being kept busy at work which is good as it helps to pass the time. [ii]

The theme of no football, lots of mud and busy at work continues through the next few letters and life seems to be very routine apart from a Saturday evening's relaxation at the theatre to see Shaw's "Pygmalian".

I*t* wa*s*, he says, *quite the best show I have seen here and each show nowadays seems to be better and better* [iii]

In the next letter he reports that

On Friday evening a blizzard started and has been blowing ever since and we are getting quite a depth of snow now. I hope it won't freeze to solid as it will take weeks to go again. Needless to say it has put a stop to all sports. [iv]

An interesting postcard to Barbara at the end of February gives us the only detail we have about Sid's work in the hospital. He says:

I am pleased to hear you have moved to the Surgical side. I think you will like it as it is far better than Medical and much more interesting. All my work is Surgical. [v]

A letter to his parents on the same day tells us that Winter is slowly moving towards Spring and conditions are improving:

We have had 3 weeks of snow covered ground and it is still with us. It has also been very cold but for the past few days the sun has been managing to get through during the day and it is gradually melting the snow. It is fairly easy to tell that it is now really March as the sun has now got a good bit of warmth in it. Yesterday I had my first game of football in 3 months and don't I know it. All this time I've kept on telling you I was fit but after yesterday I found out I had been 'fibbing'. We played a full 1½ hours in 6" of snow and I was 'winded' after it?? I'm going to get another game or two in shortly to work off my excess avoirdupois and I'll then be as right as rain. [vi]

This is the first letter that Sid mentions 'Phyl' and the 'new addition' - his nephew, Roger, was born on 15 February, 1944. The first of the next generation in the immediate family.

In March his first letter home mentions that he's glad to hear that Uncle Harry is home and he hopes that *it won't be long before he and Dad are water-cressing together.*[vii]

The next letter records two pieces of news that he'd received in letters at the end of February and the beginning of March. His reply is addressed to *My Dearest Mother* and mentions the fact that she has become a grandmother and then goes on to say

The second lot of news was a very great shock, although perhaps not quite as big as if I hadn't received Arnold's letter of the previous week which more or less prepared me. I am very glad he saw Roger before he passed away and I'm feeling very much as though I let Dad down by being the only absent one.

His father, Joseph John had died on 27 February 1944, aged 70 and only twelve days after the birth of his first grandson. His thoughts are with his mother and he tells her

Please Mother, try not to fret and worry too much and it is a great blessing that his passing was, by all accounts, a peaceful one [viii]

Towards the end of the letter he hints again at the possibility of repatriation when he says

Shortly I hope you may get a pleasant surprise, but no better than mine will be.

*

In his next letter to his mother he apologises for the lack of letters because he missed writing the last two weeks. He says

We have had official notification of a further repatriation and as I am 'on the list' this time and with any small amount of luck I should be with you all sometime next month. He continues *I do hope the above* [repatriation] *comes off as then I would be able to do my share of trying to fill the empty place left by Dad's passing* ix

His next letter begins again with apologies for not writing and goes on to explain

The reason I am now writing again is because there appears to be some hitch in the subject of the news I gave you and it is now doubtful, in our minds although nothing official has been said, whether the projected move of medical personnel will take place, so please try your best not to worry if I do not come strolling in on you in the near future. I feel very badly about not having written to anyone for so long and I hope you will understand why I have been lax in this respect, as no doubt you will be able to imagine how excited we all were at the prospect of returning home.

He goes on to tell his mother that the weather has been glorious that day and he has had his first bout of sun-bathing for the year. [x]

A week later and there is still no news about the proposed repatriation:

Still another week gone by and no definite news about our move being cancelled, but now we are all firmly resigned to the fact that in all probability we are here for the duration.

Later he mentions the good weather again and says he's getting in a good deal of sun-bathing and feeling a lot better for it. He ends with the hope that the *'little'un'* (his nephew, Roger) is getting on well and growing into a lusty young lad. [xi]

At the end of May he mentions the coming weekend which will be very full:

Sports, Art & Craft Exhibition, A Procession of Tableaux on Carts, Fun Fair and the Civvie Internees are here giving 'The Ghost Train' which is an excellent show.

For the first time he mentions that he might be changing his address the following week

as, all being well, I am going on the staff of a new POW Hospital which is being opened. [xii]

*

190

Tost Hospital staff, 1944. Sid second row from the top, seventh from the left.

Left: Tost Reserve Hospital, 1944

Below: New Year's greetings from Barbara to Sid, December 1944

The next letter from Sid is very interesting and deserves to be quoted in full:

… as I intimated last week I have changed my home. The new address is my old one, I know that sounds Irish, but I mean that it is once again Stalag VIII B. [earlier that year in a reorganisation of prison camps in the area, Stalag VIII B had changed it's name to 344 Lamsdorf and Teschen had become Stalag VIII B Teschen. His new address at Tost comes under Stalag VIIIB Teschen] *We moved on Wednesday and had a three hour train journey which was quite an experience after over two years of not travelling in one. The new hospital is a very nice place and is situated in a small town the size of Settle* [in Yorkshire]. *We are living in small rooms about 20 feet by 10 feet (4 to a room) in 2 double tier beds and we also have a wardrobe and table and chairs. It seems very quiet and private after a Stalag Barrack Room, but is very pleasant. We have a good view from our window and see quite a lot of the civilian world. If anything it makes one feel more homesick seeing all the kiddies and girls strolling about.* [xiii]

*

Sid had been moved to a new hospital which was in the process of being prepared for patients. It was called Tost Reserve Lazarett and was in the small township of Tost which had a population of about 3,500 and was around 78 kilometres south-east of Stalag VIIIB (now 344 Lamsdorf).[xiv] When ready it would be a 600-bed hospital with a staff of 140 including the doctors. It would be a General Hospital for all the POWs in both Teschen VIIIB and the work camps in that area. In an interview for the local paper that he did when he returned home in May 1945 Sid said:

While at the camp [Tost] *the treatment by the German authorities was in strict accordance with the provisions laid down by the Geneva Convention and therefore we had a comfortable stay.*

He also mentioned

The German medical personnel encountered in the hospital did all they could for the sick and wounded[xv]

192

*

There had been a Civilian Internment Camp situated at Tost [now Toszek] (Ilag VIII) and many of those held there had originally been transferred from Kamp Schoorl in the Netherlands in 1940.

Ilag was an abbreviation of Internierungslager and the Ilags were used to house civilians typically those living in an occupied country but who were citizens of countries with whom Germany was at war. At Tost, P.G Wodehouse was one of those internees, having been 'captured' by the Germans when his French residence was over-run.

Ilag VIII was housed in former barracks which had previously been used as a mental hospital. In 1943, the camp was cleared, the internees moved elsewhere, and it was this building that became Tost Reserve Lazarett.

*

While Sid was settling in to his new duties and accommodation, D-Day had happened in France. At dawn on 6 June 1944, eighteen thousand Allied parachutists were on the ground in Normandy, capturing essential bridges and disrupting German lines of communication. At 6.30am American troops came ashore at 'Utah' Beach, at 7.25am British soldiers came ashore at 'Gold' and 'Sword' beaches, followed by Canadians at 'Juno' beach.

Rommel was ordered by Hitler to drive the invaders 'back into the sea' by midnight but by then 155,000 Allied troops were already ashore – only at 'Omaha' beach had the Germans managed to halt the American assault.[xvi]*

*

The next communication from Sid is a typed postcard and he says

I am still liking my new place, and think I can stick it here until they are going to send me home. [xvii]

*

The day after Sid wrote this postcard, on 13 June 1944, the first of Hitler's secret super weapons, the V1, landed in Britain. Also known as the *Buzz Bomb* or *Doodlebug,* this jet powered flying bomb had been specifically designed for terror bombing of London. It would go on to cause more than 22,000 casualties, mainly civilian. It was like an early version of the cruise missile and was launched from sites along the French coast. Attacks continued until September by which time all launch sites had been overrun by the advancing Allies.[xviii]

*

After a couple of brief postcards to his mother and an aunt and uncle, he writes again to his brother Arnold and sister-in-law, Phyllis.

I hope that both of you and the youngster are keeping well, and I am glad to say I am feeling as fit and well as ever. The change to my new address, which is now Stalag VIII B again, has done me a lot of good, as the old place was getting on my nerves a bit, after being there so long without a move. Our living accommodation here is much more comfortable and as we are in rooms of 4 one can get a bit of privacy. There are 140 of us, including Doctors, and we are setting up a Hospital for POWs for all this area. We have not as much space for games etc as at the Stalag but as we get out for walks 3 times a week, it does not seem so bad, and we will soon be working full time so that our time will be pretty well filled. We are situated in a small country town and it is a great change to have green fields, trees and civilian houses just outside one's bedroom window again.[xix]

*

The new billets obviously needed a bit of upgrading as in his next letter to his mother, Sid describes their spring cleaning. He writes on his twenty-seventh birthday, the fourth he has spent in captivity but he is quite philosophical about it.

Well once again the 25th has come round and I am still another year older. All I have got to do now is to start hoping that I will

194

be back again before the next one rolls round, and as things seem to be brighter now there may be a chance.

He goes on to say

Talk about your spring cleaning [his mother must have written to him about her spring cleaning] *the four of us in our room started this morning and did our room out. We scrubbed everything from ceiling to floor, including all the furniture, and then did the interior decoration – distempered the walls and white-washed the top. We started at 9-0 this morning and just finished at 8-0 tonight so you can see I have had a busy day. It was a terrible job but I must say it looks and smells a lot fresher, and it is twice as light.* [xx]

*

His next letter starts off all about parcels and money

In the last few days I have received 5 cigarette parcels, 2 from you, 1 from Frank and Lucy [Whincup], *1 from RAMC Comforts and 1 off Wilf Gibbs, the chappie who left me his parcels when he was repatted. I should be alright for a while now eh!*

The Comforts Guild was established in 1940 to provide woollens, games and books to men of the RAMC and the Army Dental Corps (ADC). Subscriptions and donations were requested and the money received was spent on wool for their knitters and on books and games. Wives of men overseas helped both in the production of woollens and in the packing of parcels[xxi]

By the way I have made out a remittance of 750 marks (£50) out of my German Credits this last week, so please let me know when and as soon as you hear anything. I hope you are still getting my allotment alright.

He goes on to describe the walks he has been on

I have had a walk nearly every day this past week and have enjoyed them immensely. It is good to get out walking in the country again. It is quite like England round here, although of course all features of the country are on a larger scale. There are lots of flowers out and cherry trees line every road. The cherries are just coming ripe and the trees are a mass of orange and red.[xxii]

*

In his next letter he mentions a parcel from the Embsay Ladies and asks Edith to thank whoever was responsible for sending it.

I know you told me in a letter but after the supposed repat move was mooted I burnt all my letters [presumably because he knew he wouldn't be able to carry them with him] *and consequently have not now got the above address.*

In one parcel he has received a book called *"Yorkshire Tour"* and writes *I am enjoying it immensely and reading all about the old places is making me want to get back and visit them all again.* [xxiii]

He says, in his next letter, that the weather hasn't been too good lately

I have however managed to get two showery walks in and on yesterday's walk I managed to find about 8 mushrooms so had a real treat for breakfast this morning. The first time I have had them for 4 years.

I am still liking my new place, and am hoping I won't have to change again, as I am quite content to stop here for the duration. [xxiv]

His next letter is to his sister Barbara

Well the BIG news is that I have managed to get 3 swims in this last 10 days and if the weather holds up I should get at least 2 every week in the future. Oh Boy! Was it great to get in the "briny" again. I am still wearing my old "Jantzen" - not doing bad is it. This is the 10th season it has seen, although it is getting a little the worse for wear of course.

He goes on to mention his health

Well I am glad to say I am still keeping well, and also a lot fitter than when I first came here, as I am now doing a bit of training and also I get a bit more exercise than I did the last 2 or 3 months in Stalag.

Then he mentions the fact that he is now typing his letters

I hope you people at Home don't mind me typing my letters. It is really so much easier and one can get more on. [xxv]

*

It was while he was at Tost that he met a young German girl who was working in the German office of the hospital. Elisabeth Wieland was having trouble with her typewriter and phoned her counterpoint in the British office. Sid picked up the phone, fixed her typewriter and so began a friendship that would last until they were both evacuated at the beginning of 1945. [xxvi]

What the nature of the relationship was is unsure, the only hint of something deeper than friendship is a brief mention of the exchange of 'Liebenspaketen' [love packages] at Christmas 1944 when it had to be done secretly through a go-between.

*

The next letter to Edith reports that the weather has improved:

This week we have had quite a bit of lovely hot sunshine. We went for a swim this afternoon, and it has been one of the best afternoons since I left Crete. We lounged about in the water and on the grass for a good 2 hours.

It really did one good to see a crowd of people having a few hours off and enjoying themselves as we all used to before the present trying times. Everyone from the smallest toddlers to the elder [sic] people seemed to have dropped their cares for a short time.

I am glad to say I am feeling as well as I ever did and am more than glad that I left the Stalag as that place was getting me down

197

a bit. [probably another example of understatement from Sidney]
xxvii

*

For the first time, in a September letter, Sid mentions that everyone is *"in a state of readiness"*. He says

It is getting very difficult to write to people again, we are all in a state of readiness and when you are like that you find it very unsettling and difficult to write, especially as at the best of times a POW life is monotonous, there being very little of interest to tell the people at Home about. xxviii

For the most part, time stood still in the camp. Life had its own rhythms, its ups based on mail, parcels, friendships and, for Sid, keeping fit, and its downs based on homesickness, hunger, fear for the future, lack of privacy and anger at the world in general. By and large, if a man kept his head down and his nose clean, didn't get involved in the antics of the escapers – the 'tally-ho boys' - and concentrated his mind on getting enough to eat and survival, it was a safe life, defined by military rituals and routines. Life behind the wire had a sense of security but when the outside world threatened to take over life in camp, that sense of security was threatened and fear dominated.xxix

It was probably this fear of an uncertain future that left the men at Tost feeling unsettled.

*

The men in the camp would, by this time, have been aware that the war was slowly coming to a close. Most POW camps had an underground radio system (often home made) that kept them in touch with what was happening in the outside world. By September 1944 they would have known about the Allied advance through France from the west, through Italy from the south and through Russia and the Baltic States from the east.

By then, Paris, Antwerp and Ghent had been liberated and Eisenhower had agreed to the start of 'Operation Market Garden', the attack on Arnhem led by Mongomery.

The men probably realised that it would be the Russians who would get to them first as, by this time, they were only about 300 miles east of the camp and had reached the border of Bulgaria and were advancing through Poland.

It was probably a sense of uncertainty about what would happen to them over the next few months that was unsettling the men, both patients and medical personnel, at the hospital.

They may have also heard that the first POW camp, near the Baltic Sea in East Prussia close to the border with Lithuania had already been evacuated in July 1944 together with the German civilian population of the area.[xxx]

The chaos that accompanies the end of a war had already begun – people in the east moving west trying to keep ahead of the Russian advance and people in the west moving east trying to keep away from the battle zones of the Allied advance.

*

Back in Tost Reserve Lazarett, what was worrying Sid most was the lack of mail and parcels. By October the weather was cooling down and the swimming had stopped. He notes that

Autumn seems to be coming slightly early this year. There are a lot of leaves on the ground already, but the colours of the trees are a sight for sore eyes, all the different shades of yellow and brown mixed in with the greens of the evergreens. [xxxi]

Later letters in the same month mention that

I had a trip out to the nearest city this week to get fitted for some new spectacles and it was a grand break.

They will be about a month in arriving. It will be a good thing when they come as this prescription is very old and not quite strong enough. [xxxii]

At the end of October he mentions again the remittance and his allotment that he had first mentioned in a letter written in July.

I am not worrying about the non arrival of the remittance as I fully expect it will take a good six months to arrive. Glad to hear you are getting my allotment OK and that it appears to be mounting up, as it should by now. If being taken a prisoner has done nothing else for me it has enabled me to save a little more than I would otherwise have done.

He also mentions a walk he did

I managed to get a good walk in on Thursday afternoon, only about 8 miles but you see we are only allowed 2½ hours. The trees were marvellous, every different shade imaginable. We were in woods for about 4 miles and the smell of the decaying leaves and the feel of pine needles under ones feet was grand. It is great to be able to get about a bit again. [xxxiii]

By mid November it seems winter has arrived bringing with it a few slight falls of snow that didn't lay very long – just turned the ground wet and muddy.

One thing about this place is you have got somewhere to go and have a decent wash and warm up.

His mother must have mentioned in a letter that the "Black-out" had come to an end and he comments

I am glad to hear that you have abolished the "Black-out" it makes things so much easier. I know when I was in Durban it seemed so pleasant to walk down fully lit streets after England's "black-out". [xxxiv]

In a letter at the end of November (which has a hand-written note at the top of the page saying it was received on 1 Feb 1945) Sid apologises to his mother for not having written the weekend previously

I was still busy getting off my Xmas mail. Can you believe it I sat down and wrote over 24 letters during the two weekends.

He mentions the weather – no more snowstorms like the week before – just cold and damp.

Christmas, it seems, started early

The staff here gave a concert to the patients last night and it was excellent considering the limitations one has to put up with, it was an ordinary variety show but everyone seemed to enjoy it. [xxxv]

The last letter of 1944 is mainly concerned with a death in the extended family at Pateley Bridge in Yorkshire and the fact that there's been a heavy fall of snow in Tost leaving three inches on the ground. Sid hopes it will stay for Xmas so that they have a white Christmas.[xxxvi]

By the end of 1944, the Russian advance was getting ever closer to the camps in Silesia and the sound of their artillery could be heard in the distance.

*

Outside the camps that December, the Germans launched their last counter-offensive against the Allied forces in the Ardennes in an attempt to push the Allied line back to Antwerp and the River Scheldt. The fighting was vicious and several times the Allied forces were offered the opportunity to surrender which they refused. On December 22 General Eisenhower issued an order to all Allied troops:

Let everyone hold before him a single thought – to destroy the enemy on the ground, in the air, everywhere to destroy him.

On 23 December, American forces launched their first counter-attack against the southern edge of the Ardennes 'bulge' and by Christmas Eve the German offensive towards Antwerp had been halted.

In Europe, by the end of 1944, almost every square mile of territory conquered by Germany between 1939 and 1942 had been recovered.[xxxvii]

i   Gilbert, Martin. The Second World War: a complete history. Phoenix, 1989. p485

ii   Letter from Sidney Waterfall to Joseph John and Edith Waterfall, dated 2 January 1944

iii Letter from Sidney Waterfall to Joseph John and Edith Waterfall, dated 6 February 1944

iv Letter from Sidney Waterfall to Joseph John and Edith Waterfall, dated 14 February 1944

v   Letter from Sidney Waterfall to Barbara Waterfall, dated 28 February 1944

vi Letter from Sidney Waterfall to Joseph John and Edith Waterfall, dated 28 February 1944

vii Letter from Sidney Waterfall to Joseph john and Edith Waterfall, dated 6 March 1944

viii Letter from Sidney Waterfall to Edith Waterfall, dated 26 March 1944

ix Letter from Sidney Waterfall to Edith Waterfall, dated 12 April 1944

x   Letter from Sidney Waterfall to Edith Waterfall, dated 14 May 1944

xi Letter from Sidney Waterfall to Edith Waterfall, dated 2 May 1944

xii Letter from Sidney Waterfall to Edith Waterfall, dated 28 May 1944

xiii Letter from Sidney Waterfall to Edith Waterfall, dated 4 June 1944

xiv Waterfall, Sidney. Newspaper article. Skipton, Craven Herald, c.May 1945

xv Ibid endnote xiv.

xvi Gilbert, Martin. Op cit endnote i. p534.

xvii Postcard from Sidney Waterfall to Edith Waterfall, dated 12 June 1944

xviii Nichol, John and Rennell, Tony. The last escape; the untold story of Allied prisoners of war in Germany 1944-45. London, Penguin Books, 2003

xix Letter from Sidney Waterfall to Arnold and Phyllis Waterfall, dated 18 June 1944

xx Letter from sidney Waterfall to Edith Waterfall, dated 25 June 1944

xxi Journal of the Royal Army Medical Corps, Novemver 1940. http://jramc.bmj.com/. Accessed on 13 November 2019

xxii Letter from Sidney Waterfall to Edith Waterfall, dated 2 July 1944

xxiii Letter from Sidney Waterfall to Edith Waterfall, dated 16 July 1944

xxiv Letter from Sidney Waterfall to Edith Waterfall, dated 23 July 1944

xxv Letter from Sidney waterfall to Barbara Waterfall, dated 6 August 1944

xxvi Letter from Elisabeth Wieland to Sidney Waterfall, dated 26 November 1946

xxvii Letter from Sidney Waterfall to Edith Waterfall, dated 15 August 1944

xxviii Letter from Sidney Waterfall to Edith Waterfall, dated 18 September 1944

xxix Nichol, John and Rennell, Tony. Op cit endnote xiv pp6-7

xxx Ibid, endnote xxiv, pp 2, 30

xxxi Letter from Sidney Waterfall to Edith Waterfall, dated 2 Ocober 1944

xxxii Letters from Sidney waterfall to Edith Waterfall, dated 16 and 22

October 1944

xxxiiiLetter from Sidney Waterfall to Edith Waterfall, dated 28 October 1944

xxxivLetter from Sidney Waterfall to Edith Waterfal;, dated 12 November 1944

xxxvLetter fromSidney Waterfall to Edith Waterfall, dated 28 November 1944

xxxviLetter from Sidney Waterfall to Edith Waterfall, dated 18 December 1944

xxxvii Gilbert, Martin. Op cit endnote i. pp618-624

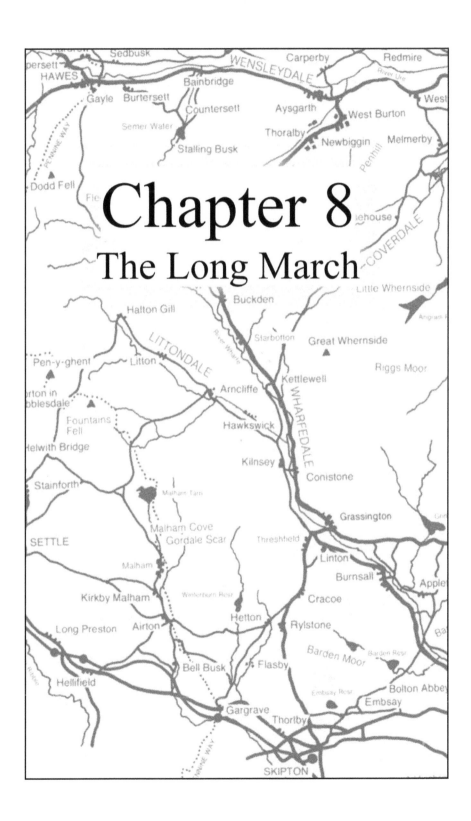

Chapter 8
The Long March

Chapter 8

2002

Books had played an important role in Sid's life and he looked round at the books that surrounded him in the Park Home.

The tall glass fronted shelving opposite the front door had originally come from 10 Sheep Street where he had been born and the other, more elegant, cabinet with double glass doors had belonged to his parents when they moved to 'Lyndhurst' in 1939. Both were crammed full of books.

There was a collection of historic books on Yorkshire that had originated at J.J. Waterfall's, a complete set of Wainright guides, some of them first editions, and a collection of more recent publications that covered his and Frankie's interests and their travels. The different periods of his life were reflected in his book collection.

Fran posed him another question and he took his mind back to the period right at the end of his captivity.

He talked about the Russian advance, the Germans evacuating the POW camps and the forced march across Europe. He talked about the freezing cold at the beginning of the march and the miserable damp towards the end. He talked about the hunger, the disease and the deaths.

*

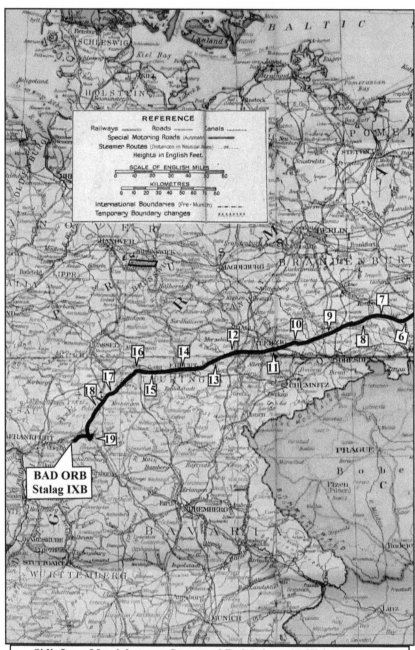

Sid's Long March between Sagan and Bad Orb (6) Weisswasser (7)
Spremberg (8) Senftenberg (9) Grossenhain (10) Grimma (11) Bohlen (12) Bad
Sulza (13) Apolda (14) Erfurt (15) Gotha (16) Mechterstadt (17)
Heimboldhausen (18) Fulda (19) Steinau an der Strasse

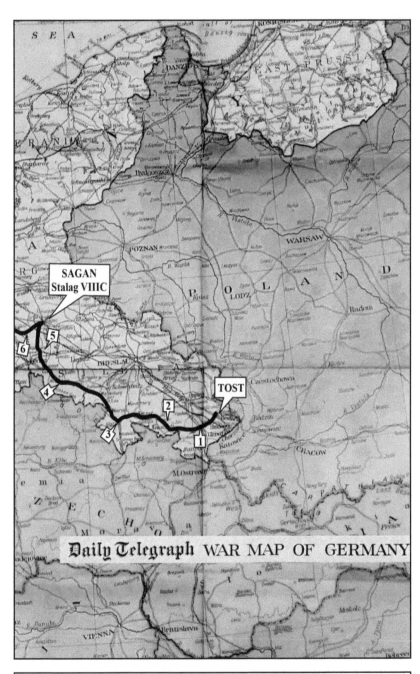

The train journey between Tost and Sagan

(1) Cosel (2) Neustadt (3) Glatz (4) Hirschberg (5) Kohlfurt

The Long March

1945

The Long March is well documented and the detail in the following chapter is taken from various sources. There were, in fact, several different routes that were undertaken by thousands of men moving west from POW camps in the east. There is general agreement that there were three main routes: the northern one that stayed close to the Baltic coast and north of Berlin; the central route that included the 20,000 men from Stalag 344 Lamsdorf and travelled north of the Czech border and south of Berlin; the southern route that travelled across Czecholsovakia towards Nuremberg.[i]

Sid's Long March fits mostly into the central route simply because he and the patients he was accompanying were taken by train to Sagan and that's where they started walking.

*

Rumours of the Russian advance coming closer and the possible end of the war, had been rife for weeks, if not months, in the POW camps spread across the Reich. For most prisoners, the end of the war had been a dream for years but now it was approaching, they met the idea with mixed feelings. Of course they wanted to go home but what would happen to them between now and then was unknown and therefore worrying. For many, life in the the camp, however unpleasant, had become a source of security and what was happening outside the camp was a long way away and didn't concern them. Now, it was coming closer and it was an unsettling experience.

*

As long ago as July 1944, Hitler had been preparing for the

defence of the Reich and the time when the war would be fought on German soil. Amongst many other instructions including the evacuation of the civilian population, he had also called for *'preparations for moving prisoners of war to the rear*[ii]

The reasons for this decision are unclear, some thought the Germans were attempting to abide by the rules of the Geneva Convention and keep the POWs away from the war zones. Others thought they were keeping them as hostages and would use them to barter a better peace deal once the war was ended. The prisoners themselves feared that they might be marched out into the countryside and shot as a way of solving the problem of what to do with them.

*

All the POWs knew was that on a certain day they were informed that they would be leaving the camp at a certain time, some were given twenty-four hours notice, others a lot less.

*

In an interview that Sid did for the local newspaper when he returned home in May 1945 he said

All hospital patients who were fit to move were certified by the British Government and the Germans accepted their ruling without question. Those remaining in the hospital were later liberated by the Russians and repatriated via Odessa.[iii]

Sid mentioned that they were transferred by train from Tost to Sagan where it was planned that they were to change trains. Sid's group left Tost on the 21 January 1945 only one day ahead of the Russians who arrived on the 22nd. The train journey went via Cosel and arrived at Sagan on 4 February 1945. [iv]

We know that the train journey from Tost went via Cosel because a later letter from Elisabeth Wieland to Sid mentioned that it was here that they went in separate directions. They didn't

212

have time to say goodbye as the evacuation of the German workers happened with no warning and before she knew it she was in a truck heading away from the Russian advance.[v] She joined the thousands of civilians trying to keep one step ahead of the battle zones while Sid continued with the thousands of POWs whose German minders were trying to do the same.

(Elisabeth's experiences over the following two years can be found in Appendix 1).

*

The train journey to Sagan took 14 days according to the aforementioned article in the *Craven Herald* (the local Skipton paper). From a map Sid drew in 1946, we know of the route the train took. The highlighted numbers in brackets in the text relate to the numbers on the map at the beginning of this chapter.

Instead of taking a direct route it wound its way along a minor railway line that followed the Czechoslovakian border, first heading south-west from Tost to Cosel **(1)** then west through Neustadt **(2)** and Neisse to Glatz **(3)**. From there it was north-west as far as Hirschberg **(4)**, before turning more directly north until Kohlfurt **(5)** and finally north-east to Sagan. There would have been numerous stopping places during the 14-day journey but the only one there is any record of was the one at Cosel. In any case they would not have been the only convoy using that line and it would have been a stop-start affair even when they were on the move.

At Sagan there were two stalags, Stalag Luft III (of Great Escape fame) and Stalag VIII C. Stalag Luft III was evacuated on 27 January, the same day that the Russians marched into Lamsdorf 344 further south.[vi] Stalag VIII C, built in 1939 and occupying 120 acres, was evacuated on 8 February 1944[vii]

Most of what we know about Sid's Long March comes from a hand-written record produced by Arthur Pattinson who had

213

arrived at Tost as a patient in August 1944. He was a sailor who had survived the sinking of his ship in 1941, had been imprisoned at a number of work camps, including one at Auschwitz, before ending up at Tost.

He kept a detailed record of the places they walked through on their Long March, daily kilometres walked and the rations they were given en route. The map that Sid produced confirms Arthur's route and puts his details into a wider context.

Arthur's record begins on 8 February, the same date that Stalag VIIIC was evacuated so it is highly likely that it was here that the Tost arrivals spent four days waiting for a train that never arrived, before it was decided they would have to walk with the rest of the evacuees from the camp

*

During the eighteen days between leaving Tost and then leaving Sagan momentous events were taking place in the world some of which the POWs would have been aware of but others they would have had no idea about.

The German forces continued to fall back on the Eastern Front and increasing numbers of concentration camps and slave-labour camps were evacuated. Columns of prisoners of war, concentration camp prisoners and civilian refugees crowded the same roads during the day and fought for the same shelter at night. All trying to cross the River Oder before the bridges were blown.

On January 26 the SS blew up the last of Auschwitz's five gas chambers and crematoria and then left the camp. Behind them they left the sick and dying. One of those who remained, an Italian Jew, Primo Levi, later a Nobel Laureate, recalled:

We lay in a world of death and phantoms. The last trace of civilisation had vanished around and inside us. The work of bestial degradation, begun by the victorious Germans, had been
214

carried to its conclusion by the Germans in defeat.[viii]

On the Western Front, three American divisions launched an attack on the Siegfried Line on January 30 and on January 31, on the Eastern Front, Soviet tanks crossed the River Oder.

By this time, Hitler had returned to the Reich Chancellery in Berlin, one of his staff commenting

Berlin will be most practical as our headquarters: we'll soon be able to take the streetcar from the Eastern to the Western Front.[ix]

On 1 February 1945, with the Red Army less than fifty miles away, Berlin was declared a Fortress City. Young and old were now set to work to build fortifications – trenches, earthworks and tank traps. A new slogan appeared on the walls of buildings: *'Victory or Siberia'*

On 4 February, in the Crimean resort town of Yalta, Stalin, Roosevelt and Churchill met to discuss the political problems of post-war Europe. It was also at Yalta that the decision was made to use bombers to attack the German lines of communication in the Berlin-Dresden-Leipzig region. This decision resulted in fire storms in Berlin and the destruction of Dresden.

(Elisabeth Wieland's description of life amidst the fire storms in Berlin, can be found in Appendix 1)

On 8 February, the German army pulled back across the Upper Rhine for the first time in five years.[x]

*

Around two thousand men gathered at Sagan on the morning of 8 February including the patients and medics from Tost. Leaving the camp only six days ahead of the Russians, they split up into smaller groups, each of which took a slightly different route mainly walking along back roads and farm tracks.

There were probably between two and three hundred men in Sid's group from Tost, the medics marching alongside the patients. The highlighted numbers in brackets in the following description, relate to the numbers on the map accompanying this chapter,

The men walked two, three or four abreast depending on the width of the road. The column of the march was, in some places, over a mile long and German guards accompanied the marchers at regular intervals, armed with rifles and hand grenades and some of them leading dogs on a leash.

Because of the large number of men in each group, it made sense to split up into small groups of between three to five men, medics and patients both, who would look after each other, scavenge for food together, eat together and sleep together, sharing belongings, blankets and body warmth to make sure that all of them survived each night and were able to continue each morning when they were forced to march again. [xi]

They were walking in the depths of winter and the snow was deep on the ground. January and February that year were among the coldest winter months of the twentieth century, with blizzards and temperatures as low as -25 degrees Centigrade.[xii]

One marcher described the effect of the cold:

It was exhausting – every icy breath drawn in hurt your lungs and made your teeth and head ache. Every movement was painful, every step was potentially dangerous. It was so slippery that you had to watch every step to make sure you didn't fall. The continuous, gnawing cold made your eyes water and your head ache. Your feet were so cold that you couldn't feel them and you felt you had to keep checking that they were still there on the end of your legs. Even with gloves on and your hands stuffed into your pockets, they still felt as if they were burning With cold.[xiii]

Daily record of march from
Stalag VIII C Sagan to Bad Orb. Stalag IX B

Feb.	8		WIESAU.	22 Kl
	9		BIRKTAMEE	23
	10		SLEISNAU.	15
	11		SPREMBERG	18
	12		LEISRE.	20
	13	VIA SEMENBERG.	RUHLANA.	25
	14	(BIRTHDAY)	DLOCKURTZ.	19
	15	VIA GROSSENHIAN.	VEISSIS	21
	16	REISA.	OSCHATZ	25
	17		GOTTWITZ	17
	18		GRIMMA	18
	19	CHANGED OUT	DALZ SRAU	15
	20	NR. LEIPZIG.	WIEDERODA.	24
	21	VIA BOHLEN.	BUNTHAL	8
	22		GROSSJENIA	28
	23	STALAG IX C	BAD SULSA	16
	24	WERMAR (HOLOA)	KAPOLLENDORF.	13
	25		LINDERDACH.	28
	26	VIA ERFURT.	SIEPELDEM.	25
	27		MACHTERSTADT.	16.
	28	EISENACH.	STADFALD.	20
MARCH	1st	VIA GESSUNGEN.	OBERSUHL.	25
	2	RESTED FOR ONE DAY.	HEIMBOLDHAUSEN	13
	3			
	4	VIA VACHA	GROSSENBACH.	32
	5		RÜCKERS	7
	6	REST DAY		
	7		NEUHOF.	27
	8	LANCASTERN	STEINAU	25

The original daily record written by Arthur Pattinson of the Long March from Sagan to Bad Orb undertaken by the patients and medics (including Sid) from Tost

Right: Long March photo,

217

If you were at the head of the column you had to force your way through the drifted snow and it was slow going, cold and wet, as it was impossible to prevent the snow from getting into your boots and freezing your feet. At the rear of the column life was a bit easier as you had other people's footsteps to step into. However, as the march went on, dysentery became rife and the further back you were, the more mud mixed with faeces you found yourself walking through.

One report said:

You just followed in the footsteps of the guy in front of you. You bowed your head because snow was falling and somebody said that if you bowed your head as you walked or shuffled, you'd be less affected by the wind coming at you.

You didn't talk because that was an effort. You concentrated on walking. You concentrated on putting your foot into the foot-mark of the person in front of you. You didn't think.

It was called the Long March but it was more of a long shuffle to be honest because the snow was about a foot deep.[xiv]

*

The Tost group walked twenty-two kilometres that first day through deep snow which had fallen overnight. Their day ended at a place called Wiesau. Most overnight stops were undercover in barns, churches, factories, empty POW camps anywhere that the Germans could commandeer to get themselves and the prisoners out of the freezing winter weather. Occasionally they had to sleep outside and there are reports of groups sleeping in woodlands and on playing fields.[xv]

Another account of that first day says that the day was dull and overcast with the clouds seeming to hang very low[xvi] Next day was similar to the previous one, cold and dull. No more snow had fallen but the twenty-three kilometres to Birktmare seemed to go on forever especially as the meagre rations distributed by the Germans that morning, hadn't lasted past mid-day.

The following day, the weather deteriorated into rain to begin with but with sun coming through the trees after a stop at mid-day. After only fifteen kilometres they stopped at Gleisnau for the night. Here it snowed again overnight which made walking next day more difficult.

On 11 Fenruary after another eighteen kilometres and a total of four days of walking they reached the rail hub of Spremberg bypassing en route the town of Weisswasser **(6)**. Little did Sid know at this point that this was where his future wife Ilse Frankenbusch had spent her early years.

At Spremberg **(7)** the Tost group were expecting to find a train for the rest of their journey but once again they were disappointed – the Russian advance had cut the rail tracks and they would have to continue moving west under their own steam.[xvii] The Russians were not far behind them and they had to keep going.

That night, one of the groups stopping in Spremberg was herded into a sports stadium where they had to sleep on the playing fields. The snow was three feet deep and the men felt like Eskimos. One of the marcher's reported:

Between the six of us we had a couple of groundsheets and six gas capes [a large oilskin sheet intended to cover a soldier and his equipment in case of gas attack] *Everyone was trying their best to flatten down the snow. When we were more or less successful, we laid 2 groundsheets down and then three of the gas capes which left three capes to put over us.*[xviii]

*

It was on the 11 February 1945 that a secret document was sent from the War Office to SHAEF (The Supreme Headquarters of the Allied Expeditionary Force) for the attention General Eisenhower who was the Commander of Allied forces in NW Europe.

It outlines the information received concerning *'the German intention to transfer PW* [sic] *to the centre of Germany'.*

It details, amongst other items:
Stalag 344 moving southwest across Bohemia
Stalag VIII B to move to Stalag 344 and subsequently on foot across N Bohemia
Stalag Luft III to move to Spremberg. PW to be dispersed to various camps
Stalag 8C to be evacuated destination unknown

It continues:
'Evacuation generally on foot owing lack of transport. Departure from 344 witnessed by inspector of protecting power. Guards accompanying PW had rifles and some hand grenades, 2 had police dogs. 1 Home Guard Coy detailed to 4 groups PW each containing 1,000. Move to be on foot by daily stages 20/30km. Route along side roads. Arrangements made to accommodate PW at night. Before departure each issued with Red Cross parcel and loaf of bread'.

So the British government and the High Command in Europe both knew in some detail exactly what was happening to the POWs.[xix]

*

On 12 February 1944 the Tost group had no choice but to move on, this time twenty kilometres to Leiske, again following the back roads. From Spremberg they headed south-west, crossed the railway line then followed it as it turned north-west. For the last eight kilometres they left the route of the railway and headed directly west to Leiske situated on the banks of the Sedlitzer See.

The following day they headed north-west for a few kilometres then turned south-west following the route of a road and railway line. They came to Senftenberg **(8)** on the Senftenberger See, the centre of an area of lakes, forest and flat land. Their over night that day was at Ruhland after a total of 25 kilometres. The last two nights had also been spent out in the snow in similar conditions to the one in Spremberg.

*

14 February 1944, as well as being Valentine's Day was also Arthur Pattinson's birthday and he spent it walking in sleet for another nineteen kilometres, mostly through a Nature Reserve to Blochwitz where they found shelter in a pottery. They were under cover and their evening ration of soup and a slice of bread arrived. Whatever was in the soup, it was hot and they were dry, unlike the weather outside.[xx]

It was dismal weather when they set off on the 15th after their slice of bread and coffee which had to last them all day. By this time, after a week on the road, the sound of gunfire had been left behind. They never seemed to take a direct route and bypassed a lot of built up areas. This day they seemed to be walking in circles, through Grossenhain **(9)**, then back to Weissig. After 21 kilometres they arrived at a large farmstead where they found shelter in a barn which was warm and had plenty of straw

The next day was a long one of twenty-six kilometres mainly through open country. They headed directly west through Riesa, where they crossed the River Elbe, and on to the outskirts of Oschatz for the night.

Three shorter days followed - firstly just seventeen kilometres, travelling south-west to Gottwitz, near Horstsee, a large dam complex with forest to the north and open country to the south. Then eighteen kilometres in the same direction to Grimma, **(10)** situated on a floodplain on the river Mulde, and finally fifteen kilometres to Oelzschau, south-east of Leipzig.. This last day, 19

February was the day that Arthur Pattinson noted a change of guard in his diary, the first he'd noted since leaving Sagan. Other reports noted more frequent guard changes.

*

By this time many men were beginning to fall ill. Dysentery was rife and easily spread from one group to another when they followed the same route and rested in the same places. Sufferers had the indignity of soiling themselves whilst still having to continue marching and being further weakened by the debilitating effects of the illness. Some told how they owed their survival to their mates who helped them carry on. There was always the danger that if they fell by the wayside, they would be left there to die or to be shot by the German guards. Such a shooting was witnessed by a POW marching the same route as Sid but in a different group.[xxi]

Many POWs suffered from frostbite which could lead to gangrene and these men too were in danger of slowing down because of the pain and ultimately giving up.

Typhus, spread by body lice, was always a risk for POWs but the risk was increased now by using overnight shelter previously occupied by other infected groups.[xxii]

Sid blamed some deaths on the POW's addiction to cigarettes:

The Germans knew where they were marching us but they didn't know where the next food depots would be and they used to give us two or three days of rations and a lot of the soldiers, as soon as they got their rations, would go to the Germans and swap all their rations for cigarettes ... and then of course, they'd no food to eat[xxiii]

He also mentioned that

Many men suffered because of a shortage of medical equipment.

He estimated the death rate at one man per day.[xxiv]

Sid, having kept himself fit in camp and having been an outdoorsman from an early age, would have survived the march better than most despite the hunger and cold. He had a good pair of boots – he had thanked his mother for them in a letter from Tost – and he would have relished the freedom of being able to walk through interesting countryside. A comment he made about his childhood was

I was never more thankful [about the way he was brought up] *than when I was a POW – especially towards the end of the war when we were marched right across Germany from Silesia*[xxv]

*

The next day of marching was a long one, twenty-four kilometres to Wiederoda, and from there on through Bohlen, **(11)** south of Leipzig to Bunthal, a day of eighteen kilometres. All the time heading directly west across a heavily built-up area of the country while still trying to keep to the backroads.

On 22 February the Tost group reached Grossjenia on the River Unstrut and surrounded by nature reserves. This marked a turning point in their march as from then onwards they stopped marching west and started moving in a more southwesterly direction.

The next night's halt was only sixteen kilometres away at Stalag IX C at Bad Sulza **(12)**, situated on the River Ilm, a tributary of the River Saale. The camp was already overcrowded by other marchers following various routes, however room was found for the Tost group and they bedded down for a night in the dry.

From Bad Sulza, the march continued on 24 February, first following the River Ilm as far as Apolda **(13)** and then veering almost directly south to Kapellendorf, a day of 18 kilometres. Here, according to an account from someone in another group but following the same route, they spent the night in a fortress complete with a moat. It was also here that the men got a shower after two weeks of living and sleeping in the same clothes, sleeping in the rough, not having had a decent wash or a shave and being sick with dysentery or stomach upsets. They were ordered to strip off in groups of twenty, leave their clothes on the floor and go into a shower room where there were ten showers.

One report describes this:

We thought lovely, except for the fact that it was two to a shower and the tiniest square of soap between two. After only two minutes the water was turned off. ... We were then ushered into another room which was very hot. Our clothes ... had been put into a big oven-like appliance. That's where the heat was coming from. After a few minutes they were taken out with large wooden forks and we had to sort out our belongings as best we could. They still felt a little damp but smelt cleaner ... we had been de-loused. It was warm enough in the castle and by morning we were dry and so were our clothes. Some slept on straw and others on the wooden floor.[xxvi]

*

The weather next day had improved although by mid afternoon it became cloudy and by four o'clock it had become quite dark. This time it was a barn at Lindenbach on the outskirts of Erfurt **(14)** after twenty-eight kilometres on the road. That night the rains came down and what with the howling wind and the banging of unfastened windows, not many slept despite being thankful that they were undercover and dry.

The next day, 26 February, the rain had ceased though it still felt damp as the men marched on through wooded areas to the south of the city of Erfurt. The direct route to the next night's stop would have been west but in order to avoid Erfurt, they were taken south then west then north-west to Siebleben, just outside

Gotha **(15).**

If Sid had marched through the centre of Erfurt he would no doubt have been interested to find a mainly medieval city and learn about the city's most famous inhabitant, Martin Luther, the father of the Protestant Reformation, who lived there for ten years. He studied at the university between 1501 and 1505 and lived at St Augustine's Monastery as a friar between 1505 and 1511.[xxvii] before moving on to Wittenburg.

*

Part of the column almost came under 'friendly fire' at Gotha. One report says:

About mid-afternoon we heard the wailing of air raid sirens. We were approaching a small town called Gotha and from the hillside where we stood we could see the town below. The RAF bombers came roaring in flying very low, then released their bombs and veered away. We could see the palls of smoke rising from various parts of the town below.[xxviii]

Sid also mentioned 'friendly fire' in his account though whether this was at Gotha or elsewhere is unclear as he couldn't remember the name of the town.
He said:

We were even bombed by our own people at one stage ... the town we were going through ... well, we had to get out of town and up onto a hillside ... there we crouched down in the heather ... while the British planes came over and strafed the town[xxix]

After the bombing of Gotha one of the columns of POWs was marched through the town and a participant described the experience:

The guards were almost doubled with SS thrown in and as we marched down the hillside towards the town the guards became really aggressive – shouting and knocking us into line. All through the town the people were really hostile, shouting, jeering and calling us English Pigs. It was a frightening experience as anything could have happened. We thought afterwards, maybe that's why the guards had been increased.[xxx]

This group carried on that day until they were clear of Gotha, whereas the Tost group spent the night in a barn at Siebleben to the east of the town.

*

The next day was a trek of just sixteen kilometres heading directly west to Mechterstadt **(16)**, a village on the edge of a forested, mountainous area called Thuringer Wald where the highest peaks were around one thousand metres. This was another night in a barn and once they'd eaten their soup and bread and talked a while, they settled down. By this stage in the march most of the talk was about food, as hunger was a fact of life for them and the continuous physical effort required to keep going on very little sustenance was getting them down. No-one wanted to leave the barn once they were inside because, at that time of year, the farmyards were a quagmire. Only a call of nature could make them leave their warm and dry safe haven and in that case they had to be accompanied by a guard. As it got dark, one report noted;

the chatter would gradually die down, a few goodnights and the snoring would start. Complete bliss![xxxi]

*

The next day was the last day of February and they'd been on the road for three weeks. Their march continued along the Nesse River valley below the Thuringer Wald ridge and despite his hunger, Sid would have appreciated the scenery if he'd raised his eyes from the feet of the man in front of him. However the weather was wet and miserable, the men were dripping wet and any rest stops were spent on their feet as there was nowhere dry to sit. Their route that day was again almost directly west, around the town of Eisenach with Wartburg Castle overlooking the town. Wartburg Castle is where Martin Luther lived while he translated the New Testament into German in 1521[xxxii]. The Tost men would have been more interested in where they were going to stop that night - it was in another barn, this time at Stedtfeld a village on the north bank of a tributary of the River Werra, after a march of twenty kilometres.

From Stedtfeld the route took the men first south-west then south. On the first day of March 1945 they followed the River Werra through Gerstungen and Untersuhl with its round church, to Obersuhl a total of twenty-five kilometres. It was mainly along the valley bottom, the weather was dry and cold that day so the walking wasn't too bad. There was also a rumour doing the rounds that the end was in sight so hopes were higher than usual.

From here it was only another thirteen kilometres to the small market town of Heimboldhausen **(17)** on the south east bank of the River Werra. Here they stayed for two nights and had a day of rest which gave the men the opportunity to wash themselves and their clothes and prepare themselves for what they hoped was the final push.

*

4 March 1945 was a long day of thirty-two kilometres, firstly heading south-east to Vacha on the south bank of the river Werra and then finally leaving the River Werra, climbing away from the river and walking through forested hills in a south-west direction to Grusselbach. After another night in yet another barn, they continued on for a further twelve kilometres to Ruckers, a small village near Fulda **(18)**, where they stayed for another two nights with another rest day in between. The men began to think that the Germans didn't know where they were going and the rest days gave them time to communicate with their bosses and

work out their onwards route.

Two days later they left Ruckers and travelled the twelve kilometres into the city of Fulda followed by another fifteen kilometres to the small town of Neuhof with its potash mining dump rising above the town and dwarfing it.

After a night here they moved on fifteen kilometres to Schluctern on the River Kinzig which they followed in a south-west direction for another ten kilometres to Steinau an der Strasse **(19)**. Here they spent the next six nights in a barn before, on 14 March 1945, being moved the last sixteen kilometres to Stalag IX B near Bad Orb and the end of their Long March.

*

According to Arthur Pattinson's estimation of the distances walked, the Tost group walked 580 kilometres on twenty-nine days, including seven rest days towards the end of the march.

He lists the rations supplied over the twenty-nine days for each man by the Germans as the following:

Bread	7 ½ loaves
Meat	6 lbs
Knackerbrot	3 x 125 grm packets
Margarine	125 grms
Soup	6 pints
Cheese	5 issues totalling 280 grms
Fat	1 issue totalling 10 grms

*

While the men had been marching across Germany entirely focused on surviving one day then the next, the major centres of the country were being bombed by the Allies in an attempt to delay as long as possible German troop reinforcements being transferred from Norway, Italy and Holland to the eastern battle zone around Breslau.

On 14 February British Bombers struck at Dresden in an attempt to destroy the city's railway marshalling yards, this being followed up by an American raid the next day. By this time Dresden was on fire and some of the fires were to burn for seven days and nights. The death toll at Dresden was never able to be calculated precisely. Nearly 40,000 were officially identified dead but at least another 20,000 were buried beneath the ruins or incinerated beyond recognition.

British and American prisoners of war were brought into the city to dig out the bodies. One of these was Kurt Vonnegut who later wrote

Every day we walked into the city and dug into basements and shelters to get corpses out ... just a typical shelter, an ordinary basement looked like a streetcar full of people who had simultaneously had a heart attack. Just people sitting there in their chairs, all dead.

On the Western Front, American forces reached the Rhine opposite Dusseldorf on 2 March but found that all the bridges had been destroyed. The same day, German forces still held the Russians at bay in Breslau. So far, no Allied soldiers had crossed the Rhine and on the Eastern Front, the Oder, though bridged in several places was still serving as an effective barrier to the Red Army.

On 3 March Finland declared war on Germany. Turkey had already done so ten days earlier. Both countries therefore earning their right to be part of the post-war negotiations. The same day, Churchill was visiting the Western Front at Julich, the first time a British Prime minister had been on German soil since Neville Chamberlain had gone to Munich in 1939 to concede the Sudetanland region of Czechoslovakia to Germany.

On 7 March, American troops crossed the Rhine at Remagen.

No enemy or invader had crossed the Rhine into Germany since Napoleon had done so in 1805.

On 11 March, Hitler drove from Berlin to the western bamk of the River Oder to see for himself the preparations for defense being made between the Oder and the capital. This was the last time he was ever to leave Berlin.

On 14 March, the same day that Sid and the Tost contingent reached Bad Orb and the end of their Long March, the Allies ended their bombing attacks aiming at cutting all communication links leading up to the River Rhine.

On 27 March, Churchill crossed the Rhine to the eastern side. It was a moment of deep satisfaction for him. He wrote

A beaten army not long ago the Master of Europe, retreats before its pursuers. The goal is not long to be denied to those who have come so far and fought so well under proud and faithful leadership. Forward all on wings of flame to final Victory.[xxxiii]

The end of the war was in sight.

*

i   Nichol, John and Rennell, Tony. The last escape: the untold story of Allied prisoners of war in Germany 1944-45. London, Penguin Books, 2003. p.152-3

ii   Ibid endnote i. p.15

iii Waterfall, Sidney. Newspaper article. Skipton, Craven Herald. c. May 1945

iv Ibid endnote iii.

v   Letter from Elisabeth Wieland to Sidney Waterfall, dated 2 October 1945

vi Nichol, John and Rennell, Tony. Op cit endnote i p. 67

vii Sorsby, John. The beginning of the end – Part One. Www.bbc.co.uk/history/ww2peopleswar/stories/94/a6953394.shtml Accessed 22/11/2019

viii Gilbert, Martin. The second world war: a complete history. Phoenix, 2009. p.634.

ix Ibid endnote viii p.629.

x   Ibid endnote viii p. 639

xi Waite, Charles. Survivor of the Long March. Spellmount, an imprint of History Press, 2012.

xii Www.lamsdorf.com/the-long-march.html Accessed on varioius dates, 2019

xiii Waite, Charles. Op.cit. endnote xi

xiv Wiseman,Andy. Www.dailymail.co.uk/news/article-1246442/British-veterans-forced-gruelling-Long-March-Poland-enact-journey-65-years-later.html

xv Sorsby, John. Op cit endnote vii p.2

xvi Ibid endnote vii p.3

xvii Waterfall, Sidney. Op.cit. endnote iii

xviii Sorsby, John. Op.cit.endnote vii p.3

xix Www.lamsdorf.com/the-long-march.html . Accessed November 2019.

xx Sorsby, John. Op.cit. endnote vii p.4

xxi Sorsby, John. The beginning of the end – Part Three. Www.bbc.co.uk/history/ww2peopleswar/stories/81/a6979981.shtml. Accessed 23/11/2019

xxii https://en.wikipedia.org/wiki/The_March_(1945)#Main_evacuation_routes_to_the_west

xxiii Waterfall, Sidney. Op cit endnote iii

xxiv Ibid endnote iii

xxv Ibid endnote iii

xxvi Sorsby, John. Op.cit.endnote xxi

xxvii Https://en.wikipedia.org/wiki/Erfurt Accessed 23/11/2019

xxviii Sorsby, John. Op cit endnote xxi p.3

xxix Waterfall, Sidney. Op.cit. endnote iii

xxx Sorsby, John. Op.cit. endnote xxi p.3

xxxi Ibid endnote xxi p.3

xxxii Https://en.wikipedia.org/wiki/Eisenach. Accessed 24/11/2019

xxxiii Gibert, Martin. Op cit endnote viii. pp640-652

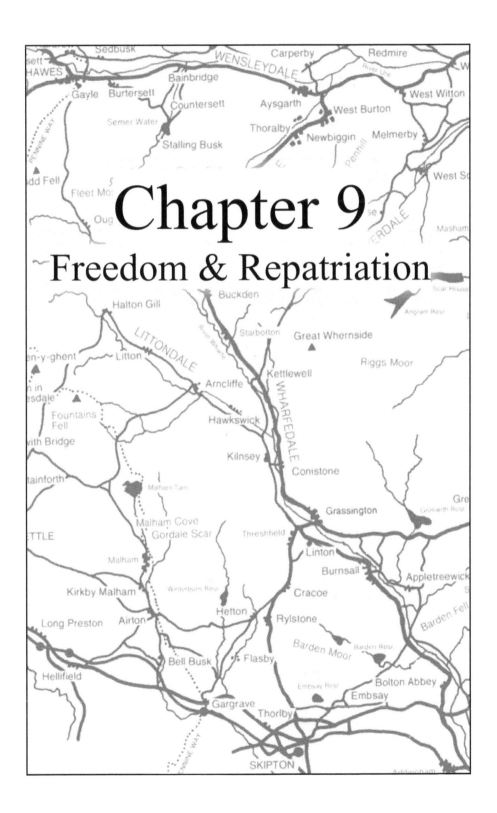

Chapter 9
Freedom & Repatriation

Chapter 9

2002

They decided on another break and while Fran made the necessary cups of tea, Sid walked through to his bedroom to get a handkerchief.

Looking through the back window he noticed that the Lavateria against the fence was just coming into bud and remembered the trip he, Frankie and Sonia had made to Leighton Moss RSPB (Royal Society for the Protection of Birds) reserve near Carnforth when they had first noticed the plant in flower and had determined to buy one for their garden.

He also noticed the activity on the bird table next to the shed in the back garden. This had given him many hours of pleasure in the later years of his life as he sat in bed reading with a cup of tea first thing in the morning. He had always been a keen bird watcher and the bird table enabled him to continue his interest as he got older and slower.

He went back through to the living room, picked up his cup of tea, took a sip and then continued talking.

He talked about the liberation of the camp by the Americans and the flight back to England and his beloved Yorkshire Dales. He talked about the reunion with his family and about meeting Amy once again. He talked about his work in an army camp at Crookham, how he met Frankie, the death of his mother and finally his and Frankie's marriage, their honeymoon and their move into 'Lyndhurst' in Embsay.

*

Freedom and Repatriation

1945-6

Sid and the rest of the Tost group arrived at Bad Orb (Stalag IX B) on 14 March 1945 at the end of their 'Long March' which had started at Sagan (Stalag VIII C) thirty-four days and 580 kilometres earlier. They were to spend another nineteen days there before liberation and a further six before repatriation.

Also known as Bad Orb-Wegscheide, Stalag IX B was located south east of the town of Bad Orb in Hesse. During WWII, more than 25,000 POWs from at least eight countries were housed here at any one time. Overcrowding was the norm and conditions were appalling, especially after the Battle of the Bulge in early 1945 when nearly 5,000 US infantrymen were moved here as POWs.[i] The addition of another 2,000 Long Marchers from Sagan in March would have stretched facilities to breaking point. However, for them, anything would have been an improvement on continuous marching and sleeping in barns.

*

Another member of the Sagan contingent who had arrived at Bad Orb four days earlier than Sid and the Tost group, described happenings over the next couple of weeks.

The worst job we had to do in those last few weeks was to bury our own dead. We had to dig a big hole and then push the ... cart up the hill with just a blanket covering the body. The Padre took off the identity tags and finalised the burial. ... Not a very pleasant job.[ii]

He said that the days passed slowly, mainly talking and thinking about food and what recipes could be concocted from the next Red Cross parcel. The Klim box was in evidence again, as it had been throughout the time in Stalag VIII B and on the Long

March. Another way of heating food was to fix up a wire from a light socket and hold the insulated ends into the soup or stew. He also describes how a radio was hidden in an Army water bottle which was in two halves and held together by the canvas cover. It had to be assembled each time it was used, and as soon as the news was over it was dismantled and put back in the bottle. No-one knew who owned it and the Germans searched for it at regular intervals but never found it.[iii]

*

Easter that year fell right at the end of March with Good Friday on the 30 March and Easter Monday on 2 April 1945. On Good Friday nearly all the 2,000 men who had taken part in the long march across Germany from Sagan, joined together on the hill above the camp singing the traditional Easter hymns and listening to the Padre conducting the service. He talked about the happenings of that Easter long ago and prayed for peace in the world that was the present.

The next day rumours were rife and gunfire could be heard in the distance. There were very few guards left and those that were still in evidence were acting a little edgy. Everyone who could manage it was up the hill trying to catch a glimpse of what was happening. Saturday night was tense with excitement with most men outside after dark, talking long into the night. Heavy gun fire could be heard and occasional flashes seen.

Easter Sunday dawned and everyone was outside in the compound waiting to see what would happen. During the day, the Camp Commandant organised for the letters POW to be laid out on the ground to attract the attention of friendly aircraft. The Padre called everyone to a service at five o'clock and it was well under way – the hymn 'Christ the Lord is risen today' had been sung and a second one ' The strife is o'er, the battle done' had been started when pandemonium had broken out. Two Hurricanes came down towards the assembly, read the POW letters and both pilots waved to the men. They zoomed upwards a couple of thousand feet, looped the loop and came screaming

238

down towards the camp doing the Victory Roll all the way down. There wasn't a dry eye in the whole compound. Everyone to a man closed their eyes in prayer and the Padre said a prayer of thanksgiving. After a short silence, the noise started, everyone chattering away. It took a long time to settle down that night and not many men got a lot of sleep – all of them lying there thinking about a future life of freedom at Home.

On Easter Monday, 2 April 1945, Bad Orb, Stalag IX B, was liberated. The remaining guards had disappeared, there was very little heavy gun fire, some small arms fire and the sound of rumbling getting closer. Then, an amazing sight, American tanks coming up the hill, tank crews waving. The gates were knocked down, followed by the flattening of the perimeter wire. Bars of chocolate and sweets were thrown in all directions and eagerly snapped up. As many men as possible clambering all over the tanks.[iv] Men were cheering, crying, embracing each other, praying. It was mass hysteria – freedom at last.

The task force were made up of the 2nd Battalion, 114th Regiment, US 44th Infantry Division, reinforced with light tanks and armoured cars from the 106th Cavalry Group and 76th Tank Destroyer Battalion. They had broken through the German lines and driven north over sixty kilometres through enemy held territory to liberate the camp.[v]

Sid's description of liberation comes from a newspaper article he was interviewed for when he arrived home in May:

The tanks were quickly followed by ration lorries. The following day an American canteen wagon arrived and prisoners were issued with doughnuts, coffee, cigarettes, matches and gum by American WACs.[vi]

Things calmed down after a while and when the transport arrived the American Engineers decided it was better to keep the POWs behind the wire for the time being to prevent them roaming all over the countryside. Not a popular decision with the POWs but probably a reasonable reaction to the hysteria.

239

The American medics decided they had to ration the food intake as already some of the men had made themselves ill. The lack of food during the previous few months had caused stomachs to contract. By the time Tuesday 3 April dawned, all the men were back behind barbed wire although under much better conditions than before.[vii]

*

Next morning, medical orderlies started sorting through the worst cases and lists were prepared as to who should be repatriated first and in what order. The Tost patients and their medics would probably have come somewhere near the top of the list. Arthur Pattinson, the patient from Tost who kept a record of his long march, also kept a record of the steps of his repatriation. On 4 April he was moved to a Field Hospital and from there he was flown to Paris on 6 April, put on a train to St. Val on 7 April and finally flown to England by the RAF on 10 April 1945.[viii]

Meanwhile Engineers were preparing a landing strip for the DC47s to land and take off from.

After three days everything was ready for the evacuation which took place over the next six days. Arthur must have been on one of the first planes out on 6 April. Sid left Bad Orb on 8 April 1945 and arrived at No. 92 Reception Camp at Pipers Wood, Amersham, Bucks on 9 April after stops at Paris and Le Havre.[ix] The last flight out of Bad Orb, Stalag IX B, was on 11 April. Before it left the bulldozers flattened all the buildings and the remains were set alight[x]

*

Over the previous few days German forces had evacuated Sarajevo on 7 April and begun their withdrawal from the Dalmatian Coast. On the same day in Czechoslovakia, Bratislava fell to the Red Army and in Austria, the battle for Vienna continued. In Silesia, the Germans holding out in Breslau were being slowly overcome.

By the time Sid arrived back on British soil, the Red Army had signed a treaty of friendship and post-war collaboration with Tito's Yugoslavia. The Red Army was now the master of Hungary and eastern Czechoslovakia and had reached the city centre of liberated Vienna. Also, by the 11 April, American forces had reached the Elbe south of Wittenberg, only eighty-five miles from the centre of Berlin..

On the same day, the inmates of Buchenwald were liberated when American troops entered the camp where emaciated corpses and starving survivors awaited them. One of those they liberated, Elie Wiesel, later wrote

You were our liberators, but we, the diseased, emaciated, barely human survivors were your teachers. We taught you to understand the Kingdom of Night.[xi]

*

At the Reception Camp, returning POWs were provided with arrival postcards (or telegrams, depending on when their onward travel home was planned) alerting their next-of-kin that they had arrived safely and would be with them soon. All the men had to do was address them and they were posted free of charge immediately.

Each man went through a medical examination and if deemed medically fit they were granted leave. They were given a new uniform, provided with paperwork such as identity cards, a leave pass, ration cards, a pay advance, a rail warrant and clothing coupons. It was at this stage that POW Liberation Questionnaires were completed.[xii]

Sid's Army record had a handwritten note at the top of the page saying '*not to be sent overseas before 8th October 45'*. He was posted to no.7 List 'D' and was given six weeks home leave until 24 May 1945.[xiii]

On Sid's 'Notification of Impending Release' form completed on 8 May 1945, his military conduct was noted as *Exemplary* and his Testimonial said

Pte Waterfall is a well educated soldier of good address and manners, courteous and thoroughly good living. He can confidently be recommended to work efficiently without supervision. I have pleasure in saying that he has served the Corps well and he takes my best wishes with him on his return to civil life where he will do well in any post to which his talents are best suited.

With this under his belt, Sid headed for home to contemplate his future.

*

There was a lot to catch up with in Yorkshire. Sid's mother Edith was a lot frailer than he remembered and obviously, the death of Joseph John in February 1944 had added to her worries and the deterioration of her health.

Arnold had set his stamp on the family business and now shouldered the major responsibility for its growth into the future. Arnold and Phyllis had a son, Roger, the first of the next generation, born ten days before his grandfather's death, also in February 1944. They had moved out of 10 Sheep Street and were now living at Airton as the wardens of the Friends Meeting house there.

Sid would probably have felt a bit like a fish out of water to begin with but had to concentrate on improving his health, putting on weight and adjusting mentally to the idea of being a free man by re-acquainting himself with his beloved fells and dales. It was memories of the freedom he knew when walking the dales that had brought him solace during the worst times behind barbed wire and now those same open spaces comforted him again as he attempted to settle back in to life in post-war England.

A runway in France showing planes taking part in Operation Exodus, the repatriation of Prisoners of War from camps in Germany to the UK, 1945

Army Form W4098

ARMY

FOR ....AVE TRAVEL ONLY

PASS (to be surrendered on rejoining unit)

Regiment ....R.A.M.C.

No. 7380174 Rank Pte

Name Waterfall S

has permission to be absent from his*/her* unit from

8 APR 1945 to 24 MAY 1945

Any number or letter identifying the unit, etc., must be obliterated

*No. 91 RECEPTION CAMP Commanding.

DOCUMENTATION BRANCH STAMP

No. 91 RECEPTION CAMP

1. From London District	4. Reporting Centre	7. Ration Card Issued
✓		Yes.
2. To London	5.—	8. For use of C.M.P.
✓	6. Nearest Hospital	
3. Through London	Yorks.	9. Authorized to travel over 50 miles at concession fares

*Items not applicable to be deleted and initialled by Issuing Officer.

Important.—See back.   [P.T.O.

Sid's Travel Pass for his six weeks of repatriation leave, 8th April to 24th May, on arriving back in the UK, April 1945.

He would probably have spent time with the extended family further up the Dales, his cousin Kath at Thorpe and the family at Pateley Bridge about whom he'd told his mother he'd felt a bit guilty because he hadn't written to them while he was a POW. He'd also have gone to visit his best friends including Geoff and Dorothy who were having problems of their own: Dorothy had an affair with someone else while Geoff was at war and when Sid got home the two of them were at loggerheads and it was he who persuaded them to stay together – he understood the difficulties they were having because of what had happened between him and Amy.[xiv]

He would also probably have investigated possible employment opportunities – would he return to Knowles & Harrison, the solicitor's office, where he had worked for five years prior to the war or was it possible for him to join Arnold in the family business – did it have the potential to support two families instead of one? He still had commitments to the Army for the foreseeable future but he might need to start thinking about a plan for the longer term.

It would have been an unsettling and worrying period as well as a reassuring one. For the last five years he hadn't had to make any life-changing decisions, he'd just had to do as he was told, live within the parameters of military routines and be satisfied that at least he was alive and there was a sliver of hope for the future. Over the next few months, all that was about to change.

*

In a letter to Amy after Sid had received her 'Dear John' letter in 1943, he had told her that the first thing he would do when he got home was to come and see her and this he did.

A number of letters from Amy written during this period tell us that the couple had met again, Amy had realised that she still loved Sid and was contemplating a divorce from Frank so that she and Sid could be together again. The letters cover a period from around May 1945 until Easter 1946 long after Sid had met the woman he was to marry and had married her. Only one of them was dated but some provide a hint of when they were written from events mentioned in the text. Unfortunately none of Sid's replies have survived.

It is uncertain what exactly their relationship was. There are a couple of hints that it could have been sexual in nature when she writes in one letter

I would love to see you and spend a very enjoyable night with you

and in a second she says she is writing to him from her bedroom and continues

wouldn't you like to be here with me.

Most of the letters however are just declarations of her love for Sid and how much she is longing for him and wants to be with him. She mentions a lot of the memories they shared together, such as their special seat in the Regal Cinema in *the second row of the second circle*, walks they took up *our beloved Crookrise*, the moors, *our moors*, the day out they had at Bridlington and the photo she has of them there. She remembers

the last morning at Bridlington when we sat on the sea wall on the Princess Parade and listened to Lionel John's orchestra, they were playing a certain tune and every time I hear it I think of you. It is six years ago this week, pet.[probably summer 1939]

Another day out at Waterford Ghyll and the photo of them together there. She keeps both of the photos, together with the birthday card she received from Sid in May, under her pillow and each night, she writes, *I say goodnight to your photographs and go to sleep thinking of you.*

*

245

She writes about her choice of Frank and the 'Dear John' letter she wrote to Sid in December 1942. She says

I always wrote and told you if I was going out with someone else and I never did anything I was ashamed of for you were always No. 1 to me until Frank swept me off my feet.

She continues,

I realise I made a grave mistake in thinking infatuation was love. To make a success of life together I realise that there must be more than sexual attraction and I am afraid that Frank and I haven't a great deal in common. ... I did realise this long ago before there was any chance of you getting home ... but I didn't want to admit I'd made a mistake when everyone warned me against it. I thought I could go through with it but God knows how I will.

The first hint of the possibility of divorce comes in this same letter when she says

What have I to say to Frank for I don't want to do anything without your permission, but just think if he did agree, within a year we could be married.

In another letter she says that if she told Frank that she still loved Sid then

I probably should have to get out from home as Elsie said I wouldn't have their friendship if I went away with you.

She also tells him of a couple she met, a friend of hers who had lived with a married man for fourteen years before his divorce became absolute and says

They seem to be quite well respected around here and I thought if they could do it, you and I could.

246

*

It seems that her family is stepping in by keeping her at home and trying to stop her from seeing Sid when he is home on leave and writes

For my sake I shall be glad when tomorrow comes and you have gone back for knowing you are here I would do almost anything to see you, but for your sake dearest I mustn't wish your days at home away, but God alone knows how I shall endure your next seven days.

There is mention of a five year pact between them but no details – maybe they agreed that if they still felt the same after five years they would do something about it. She writes

I hold you to that five years Sidney for although they stop us seeing each other they can't stop our hopes or the plans we cherish in our hearts.[xv]

Four days later she writes again to tell Sid that she will be away or have visitors during July and then Frank arrives back from Germany for two week's leave in August, so, she says

at present my chances of seeing you look to be as low as they possibly can be.

In the same letter she talks about an empty flat she has heard of and has looked at a furniture catalogue and estimated how much it would cost to furnish it.

What wishful thinking, isn't it? It's still nice to have my castles though and it affords me some small measure of comfort.[xvi]

She mentions Grassmere in a couple of letters and it seems that at this time there was the possibility of the family buying a property in the Lake District and extending the business with the establishment of a new branch there. Amy writes

Do let me know as soon as you have some definite news of that proposition. If I could only hope that in the not too distant future, I should have a chance to live there with you. Darling I am sure we should both love it and make a great success of it.

In another letter she asks if Arnold has been up to Grassmere to have a look at the property.

*

Meanwhile, up in Glasgow, a young woman had decided to join the ATS (Auxilliary Territorial Service). Her name was Ilse Frankenbusch. She was from a Jewish family and had been a refugee from Hitler's Europe, coming to England in early 1939 and finding work near Aberdeen, then Birmingham and London before ending up back in Scotland working for a Seafarer's charity in Glasgow.[xvii]

She signed up on 4 April 1945, a few days before Sid arrived back in England. On 11 May she was assigned to Ambulance No.11, T&H Unit for a month before being transferred to No.1 MTTC (Military Transport Training Centre) at Amberley, Surrey on 13 June 1945. This was the same unit that Princess Elizabeth had trained at earlier in the year. Ilse was at Amberley until 29 August 1945 when she was transferred to No.1 E/Command HU at Fleet.[xviii]

It was probably during this period of her life that friends started calling her 'Frankie' instead of Ilse – presumably a shortened version of her last name and easier to remember than Ilse Frankenbusch. From now on she was more usually known as Frankie.

Meanwhile Sid had returned from leave on 24 May 1945 and his Army record says *'Arrived P Coy, Depot RAMC from 7 list (Repat P.O.W.) on 24.5.45. To 5 same date'.* The next entry on 17 August 1945, tells us that at Crookham, Hants, Sid had been *'Confirmed in pre-captured trade of Clerk Class III at a trade test at the Depot RAMC'*

91 RECEPTION CAMP.

DIET SUGGESTED WHEN RETURNING HOME.

(1)   Avoid large amounts of fat and fried foods at first.

(2)   Take plenty of milk and milk puddings,porridge,bread,
        jam etc.

(3)   Do not try to eat too much at each meal, but consume
        small meals frequently.

(4)   A Certificate for 1 pint of milk per day may be
        obtained from the local hospital or General
        Practitioner.   This is handed to your milkman.

Hodgemoor Wood,
Amersham, BUCKS.

Repatriation diet suggestions for returned POWs, 1945

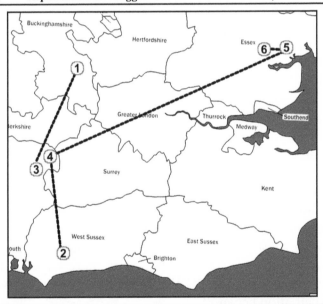

Sidney and Frankie's Army postings, April 1945 to May/June, 1946.
1. Hodgemoor Wood, Amersham (Sid) 9 April -; 2. Amberley, Surrey (Frankie)
13 June - ; 3. Depot RAMC, Crookham, Hants, (Sid) 17 Aug - ; 4. No 1 E
Command, Fleet (Frankie) 29 Aug - ;5. Royal Army Servuce Corps, Earlscone,
Nr Colchester (Frankie) 6 Sept -; 6. Braintree

Right: Marriage announcement from the Craven Herald (Skipton) newspaper,	**WATERFALL—FRANKENBUSCH.**—On Jan. 29, 1946, at the Registrar's Office, Sidney, younger son of the late Mr. and Mrs. J. J. Waterfall, to Ilse Felicitas Frankenbusch of Czechoslovakia.

On 18 August 1945 he *'Passed to No.18 Coy RAMC'* and on 19 August 1945 he *'Joined No.18 Coy from the Depot RAMC for duty at RAMC Records Office.*[xix]

With Frankie now at Fleet and Sid at Crookham, they were only a few miles apart and this was presumably when they first met. They met at a swimming pool when, so family oral history has it, Frankie saw Sid, fancied him and dived in on top of him. Sid, being a gentleman, apologised and things went on from there. Sid denied this version of the story and said he took the initiative and dived in on top of Frankie.[xx] Whichever version is to be believed the end result was the same and they were married at Skipton Register Office on 29 January 1946 as both their army records tell us.

*

By the middle of August the war was over. Victory in Europe (VE) Day had been celebrated on 8 May 1945 after the last document of surrender was signed in Berlin thirty minutes before midnight that day.

The war with Japan continued for three further months until, on 15 May, after the bombing of Hiroshima and Nagasaki with a combined death toll of almost 200,000, the Emperor made a radio announcement to his people acknowledging the need to surrender because of *a new and most cruel bomb, the power of which to do damage is indeed incalculable, taking the toll of many innocent lives*. It took a few more days for the news to reach the Japanese POW camps and a few more weeks before repatriation began.[xxi]

*

Frankie's last move was on 6 September 1945 to 578 Coy C(M)T RASC (Royal Army Service Corps) at Earlscone, Nr Colchester, Essex. The RASC was responsible for land, coastal and lake transport amongst other things, so Frankie, as a driver, suddenly found herself posted quite a distance from Sid. The officer she was driving lived at Braintree, west of Colchester, so Frankie lodged with Mrs Woods who had a boarding house there. When Sid visited her over the next few months, he also stayed at Mrs Woods' boarding house[xxii]

On 15 October 1945 Sid's mother Edith died of colon cancer and presumably Sid got compassionate leave to attend the Funeral.

Frankie was still at Earlscone, Colchester on her thirtieth birthday in November when she received two birthday telegrams addressed to her there.

A letter exists, written in November, from 'Cass' of Bury St. Edmonds, obviously a friend of Sid's, who writes to apologise for not having been able to meet up with him last weekend. He was going to stay at Mrs Woods with Sid and Frankie and asks Sid to convey his apologies. He goes on to say

Did you have a good weekend again? I suppose that's a silly question really ...

Have you decided whether you will get married yet? Getting old you know - bald head – all that - won't have to wait too long – this fits my own case too! I suppose you will take the plunge when you get demobbed eh?[xxiii]

So it seems that marriage was on the agenda by mid-November.

*

Amy and Sid were still meeting occasionally and writing to each other but the affair seems to have been winding down

There were frequent mentions of her visiting Sid at Fleet but nothing seems to have come of these plans.

A letter that brings things between them to a head mentions 'Joe' who knows them both and who has passed on a message from

Sid that he doesn't want to see her again or have anything more to do with her. She asks

do I have to forget all our plans and hopes and also our five year bargain?

She doesn't know whether to believe what 'Joe' has said and thinks

at least we are entitled to see each other and finish our affair ourselves.

There are a couple of letters written in December 1945 when Amy says she won't be able to write for about three weeks because Frank will be home until after Christmas. Sid must have been home on leave in early December and they had met up again and she writes that she hopes he had a good journey back. She tells him about a trip with a friend to a dressmaker in Embsay and says

We had to walk to a house almost on the moors, right up the lane we used to go up to get to Crookrise. I looked very longingly at Lyndhurst as we passed in the bus.

She asks him not to write while Frank is at home and suggests that he saves Judith's Christmas gift until he comes back for Barbara and Jack's wedding on the 29th.

Three days later she writes again just before Frank arrives and says

I am afraid this is my last letter to you dearest for it is no good going on, there must be a proper break for in fact I dare not risk it any more. ... Frank and I had a good talk and I realise from it what I can expect if he ever gets to know about you and I. We were talking about Dorothy and Geoff and he says any woman who goes off the rails after she is married deserves it [sic] whether it comes now or years ahead. It is very unfair to Frankie and to Frank and as we can't alter things, we may as

252

well make the best of things and do what is right.

She says that very soon she is hoping to join Frank in Germany. She wishes him a *grand time at Christmas for it means a lot to be at home and especially to have Frankie with you.* She continues by saying that she presumes the engagement has taken place.

*

Barbara, Sid's younger sister, was living at 'Lyndhurst' at this time and presumably she and her future husband, Jack Dewhurst from Silsden, spent Christmas there with Sid and Frankie that year. Barbara and Jack were married four days later at the Friends Meeting House in Skipton on 29 December 1945 and after that they moved to a house at Steeton Top.

Once the estate was settled, Arnold inherited the business, Sid, the house, and Barbara, a sum of money.

Sid and Frankie's wedding at Skipton Registry Office took place on 29 January 1946 This brought this period of change in the family to a close with all three siblings married and starting their own lives.

*

A diary kept by Sid on their wedding day and during the honeymoon gives the reader the facts of this period – the places stayed at, the routes taken, the costs involved and some of the events. Every now and then a hint of Sid's dry sense of humour shows through the facts and practicalities. It deserves to be copied in full.

He describes the wedding day as follows:

29th *January 1946*

11am   *Zero hour: we take the plunge*

11-20 to 12-30 "Much ado about petrol"
12-45 to 1-30 Lunch: "We were 7"
1-30 to 2-30 Auntie Angies
2-30 to 5-15 Lyndhurst [Home]

Journey over Black Park to Barden midst heavy snow storm and finally to Red Lion, Burnsall for our "first night". Garaged "Baby" [the car] *in Mr Bailey's garage. Arrived about 6-00pm, had dinner at 7-00 and then settled down in the lounge until 9-30 writing letters. Drink or two in the bar, had an hour's billiards while Frankie watched, so to bed at 10-45pm.*

Red Lion Hotel: *One night's board residence £2-2-0 inc early tea (Room No 5)*

o

30th January 1946

Rose 8.30 after a splendid nights sleep??? and a cup of tea at 8-00. Breakfast 9-00. Walked up to and through the church and along the river path past Loup Scar (photo of Frankie 50th @ 5.6) to Suspension Bridge (photo of me 50th @5.6) and then back by Postman's Hill to Red Lion. Got "Baby" ready for the days drive. Had lunch at 1-00pm.
2-00pm left Burnsall – first stop 2.30 top of Kidstones (snowfight and photo of Frankie with "Baby" 50th @ 8).

3-30 passed through Hawes and took Sedburgh road at Moorcock Inn arriving Sedburgh 4-15 and put up at White Hart hotel. Much snow falling in upper Garsdale. Went to .... cinema to see W Beery in "This man's navy".

White Hart Hotel: *Room 17/-, Breakfast 6/-, Tea and Coffee 1/-, Afternoon tea 3/-, Dinner 9/-, Garage 1/6 (Room No 8)*

31st January 1946

Left Sedburgh 10-20 arrived Kendal 11-00. First called on Bill for half an hour – called County Hall re licence and did a little shopping. Lunch 1-00pm at Marvic Private Hotel and left Kendal 1-30. Settled down for "over Shap". Baby took it like a bird. Much snow high up but lorries had packed it down nicely. 2-25 top. Glissaded down the north side as if were on skis – very icy. Rain started as we dropped down and by the time we reached Lowther Castle and turned off onto the Ullswater road it was very heavy. In spite of the rain the lakes and hills looked lovely especially the latter with their snow caps. Reached Patterdale and tried Patterdale Hotel but alterations in progress. Recommended Brotherswater Hotel and glad they did as it has proved our best "bunk". Very unpretentious outside but real Lakeland pub cum farm and very cosy inside. Food excellent. Extremely wild night – gale winds and sheets of rain. Retired 10-00pm.

Brotherswater Hotel: Room £1-1-0, Breakfast 7/-, Tea 4/-, Dinner 10/- (Room No 4)

1st February 1946

When we woke practically all snow had been washed away by rain. Still very windy but fair. Hills look very dark and forbidding with usual storm rivulets cascading down their flanks. Breakfast IN BED. Rose 11-30.

We have more or less decided to go to Coniston or Langdale for tonight then return here for Sat and Sun nights as it is so comfortable. Photo bedroom window.

Left Brotherswater after lunch (1-30) proceeding over Kirkstone Pass to Windermere via Troutbeck. Stopped for a few minutes at Bowness (Photos Swans, Frankie and Baby, and lake and myself). Down Windermere to Newby Bridge (Photo of bridge) and across country to Lowick and thence up old road on East of Coniston Water to head of lake. Over past the Drunken Duck to Little Langdale, Elterwater, finally stopping at Langdale Hotel. (4-45). Weather fair although heavy rain at night after we had "bedded down". Lovely old roads. (Photo bedroom window).

255

Langdale Hotel: *Dinner Bed and Breakfast £1-3-0, Tea and Coffee 3/-, Motor Hire 1/-*

2nd *February 1946*

Left Langdale 10-30 and went by Chapel Stile and down Red Bank to Grasmere and up Dumail Rise round west of Thirlmere by old road (2 photos of lake) and so to Keswick. Stopped for half an hour, looked in Abrahams and bought photos at Judges Ltd. Left Keswick 11.45 down Borrowdale to Seatoller and over Honiston (Baby's hardest test so far) to Buttermere, Crummock and Loweswater. Over the tops by the old road to Ennerdale catching a glimpse of the lake and on to Gosforth. Between Ennerdale and Gosforth (lovely unfenced moorland road) we had good views of the coast. Gosforth 2-30 filled up with petrol, oil and water and set off on the last stage of the days journey up Wasdale to Wasdale Head and Wastwater Hotel. Lake looked very fine and the screes dark and forbidding with their tops hidden in cloud. Yewbarrow just clear but Scafell and Gable invisible. Fine until Kewswick when it started to rain. This gradually got worse to Buttermere and Crummock but sun came out at Loweswater and it remained fine until we got to Wasdale Head. Decided to stay the weekend and spend our last night (Monday) at Brotherswater.

3rd *February 1946*

Breakfast 9-00am, set off from hotel at 10-0 and looked in Wasdale Head church. Then set off to climb to the top of Sty Head. Ran into low clouds at the gateway and remained in them all the time until about the same place on the descent. Strong wind, however, kept them constantly on the move and occasionally got some brief but lovely views of Lingmell Crag and Great End with Piers Gill in between. Mist became denser and wetter as we climbed. Reached the top at 11-10 and sat on stretcher case for a smoke. Last minute decision to make a try for Great Gable. What a try. Mist getting even thicker and Frankie puffing like a model steam engine. Finally succeeded by

12-5 with visibility between 50 and 100 yds. Thank goodness for the cairns on the return route but got to Sty Head again by 12-25. Now it was a race against time as lunch was at 1-0pm. Just managed to make Burnthwaite by that time and the hotel by 1-5 in spite of Frankie insisting on a bathe fully clad in a little stream which crossed the path. After lunch it commenced raining so stayed in for the rest of the day. Browsed in the FRCC library. Both had a lovely hot bath before retiring.

Wastwater Hotel: Rooms £1-5-0, Teas 7/-, Dinners 8/-, Suppers 6/-, Luncheons 8/-, Garage 2/- (Room No 3)

4th February 1946

Left Wasdale 10-30 and on our way past the lake saw the Eskdale Hounds on the slopes of Middle Fell. Proceeded on the moorland road to Ennerdale where Baby had her first fit of "moodiness" of the week. Patched it up and we managed to get over Whinlatter without mishap. Called at Keswick to phone through to Brotherswater to let them know we were coming. Baby had a couple more "moods" before Patterdale but we just managed to persuade her to take us back to Brotherswater. (Photo (2) of Ullswater). Very fine day until we got to Patterdale when it started a slight shower. Turned out to be quite a wild wet night but quite snug in front of the fire. Reached our dozen eggs each. Cleaned up Baby.

Brotherswater Hotel: room £1-1-0, Tea 4/6, Dinner 10/-, Drinks 6/6 (Room No 4)

5th February 1946

The day we have to wend our way homewards after a really marvellous week.

Journey summary

Day	Date	Journey	Milea ge	Petrol

1	Tues 29	Embsay to Burnsall	8	1 1/2
2	Wed	Burnsall to Sedburgh	45	2
3	Thur	Sedburgh to Brotherswater	56	2
4	Frid	Brotherswater to Langdale	43	2
5	Sat	Langdale to Wasdale	67	2
6	Sun	Wasdale		
7	Mon	Wasdale to Brotherswater	59	
8	Tues	Brotherswater to Embsay	68	2
		Total	346	11 1/2

xxiv

*

After returning to Embsay and a few days there, both Sidney and Frankie returned to their Army duties, Sidney to the RAMC Records Office at Crookham and Frankie to 578 Coy RASC C(M)T near Colchester, still boarding with Mrs Woods and continuing to drive her officer.

*

Amy and Sid were still in communication two months later as Easter approached, when she writes to apologise for not having answered his last letter but asks him not to write again because it's too risky. Her father has sold 7 Brougham Street and he has moved in with 'Jack' at 38 Regent Crescent. Amy and Judith are going to move to Durham *until we can go to Frank.* She is expecting Frank home on leave next week for six weeks and she hopes it won't be long after that that before she can join him. She is hoping to spend an evening with Barbara before Sid and Frankie come home for Easter. She ends by saying

Don't think it isn't that I don't want to hear from you, you understand how it is. Take care of yourself Sidney and give a little thought to me now and again.

258

This was the last letter of the batch that has survived.

*

Frankie very soon realised that she was pregnant and a letter she wrote to Sidney in Spring (only dated Wednesday 27th but possibly April or May) says

I am sitting in the grass, baking in the sun and I must say, Junior and I enjoy it very much. ... We can hardly wait for Saturday to come along again. I think we'll come and fetch you from Chelmsford. As Junior doesn't take much space up, there will be plenty of room for you in the cab![xxv]

Their Army records complete this part of their story.

Frankie's says that *R/L Commences 18/4/46, R/L Expires 12/6/46, Relegated to D List 18/6/46, Discharged 1st Apr 54. Services no on Termination of Engagement Authority ATS Regs 1945 App VII Para 9.*[xxvi]

R/L was probably leave prior to discharge.

Sid's tell us that *on 7/5/46 he was medically examined prior to release on 8/5/46* and *posted to 'Y' List (7) on 9/5/46. On 23/8 46 he was released to Class 'Z' (T) Royal Army Reserve (Class 'A' Release) and finally on 30/6/59 he was discharged from Reserve.*[xxvii]

The 'Y' List was a means of accounting for personnel who were not where they were initially posted, usually to cover a change in status – secondments or transfers from one unit or place of employment to another.[xxviii]

Class 'Z' Reserve is for a previously enlisted soldier available for recall if under 45 years of age.[xxix]

The world had moved on from the war but new threats appeared. On 6 March 1946 Churchill warned

From Stettin in the Baltic to Trieste in the Adriatic, an iron curtain has descended across the Continent. Behind that line lie all the capitals of the ancient states of Central and Eastern Europe. Warsaw, Berlin, Prague, Vienna, Budapest, Belgrade, Bucharest and Sofia, all these famous cities and the populations around them lie in what I must call the Soviet sphere.

New alliances emerged with the Western bloc creating the North Atlantic Treaty Organisation (NATO) and the Eastern bloc reciprocating with the Warsaw Pact.

Punishment dominated the autumn and winter months of 1945 and on into 1946 and over the following years military trials and the sentencing of war criminals brought some peace to those who had lost much during the war although there was nothing that could ever bring back those who had been murdered against all the accepted rules and codes of war.[xxx]

Nothing could stop Frankie remembering that most of her extended family had lost their lives during the previous five Years. However, her life with Sid and the new life developing inside her reminded her that she had a future that could bring her many years of happiness.

By August 1946 they were both able to put the war and their Army careers behind them, make a final move to 'Lyndhurst', the home that was waiting for them in Embsay, near Skipton in Yorkshire and settle into married life.

*

i   https://en.wikipedia.org/wiki/Stalag_IX-B . Accessed 29 December 2019

ii Sorsby, John Lesley. The beginning of the end – Part Five. www.bbc.co.uk/history/ww2peopleswar/stories/12/a6980312.shtml . Accessed 29 December 2019.

iii Ibid endnote ii

iv Ibid endnote ii

v   https://en.wikipedia.org/wiki/stalag_IX-B . Accessed 30 December 2018

vi Waterfall, Sidney. Newspaper article. Skipton, Craven Herald, c.May 1945.

vii Sorsby, John Lesley. Op cit endnote ii

viii Pattinson, Arthur. Handwritten record. [unpublished] 1945.

ix Army record of Sidney Waterfall

x   Sorsby, John Lesley. Op cit endnote ii

xi Gilbert, Martin. The Second World War: a complete history. Phoenix, 1989.p 661

xii Stalag VIIIB/344 Lamsdorf Facebook page. Accessed 5 October 2019.

xiii Op cit endnote ix

xiv Transcript of an interview conducted by Fran and Duncan Elson with Sidney Waterfall. [unpublished] 2002.

xv Letter from Amy Wilkinson to Sidney Waterfall, dated 25 June 1945.

xvi Letter from Amy Wilkinson to Sidney Waterfall, dated 29 June 1945.

xvii Waterfall, Sonia. Escape to Auschwitz: Hulda's story. Feedaread, 2013.

xviii Army record of Ilse Frankenbusch

xix Op cit endnote ix

xx Op cit endnote xiv

xxi Gilbert, Martin. Op cit endnote x p692 and p717

xxii Op cit endnote xxiv

xxiii Letter from Cass to Sidney Waterfall, dated 12 November 1945.

xxiv Waterfall, Sidney. Honeymoon diary. [unpublished] 1946.

xxv Letter from Frankie Waterfall to Sidney Waterfall dated Wednesday 27th, Spring 1946

xxvi Op cit endnote xviii

xxvii Op cit endnote ix

xxviii www.ww2talk.com/index.php?threads/info-on-y-list-please.61446/ . Accessed 30 December 2019

xxix www.british-genealogy.com/forum/threads/83538-My-dad's-army-service . Accessed 30 December 2019.

xxx Gilbert, Martin. Op cit endnote xi pp724 -728

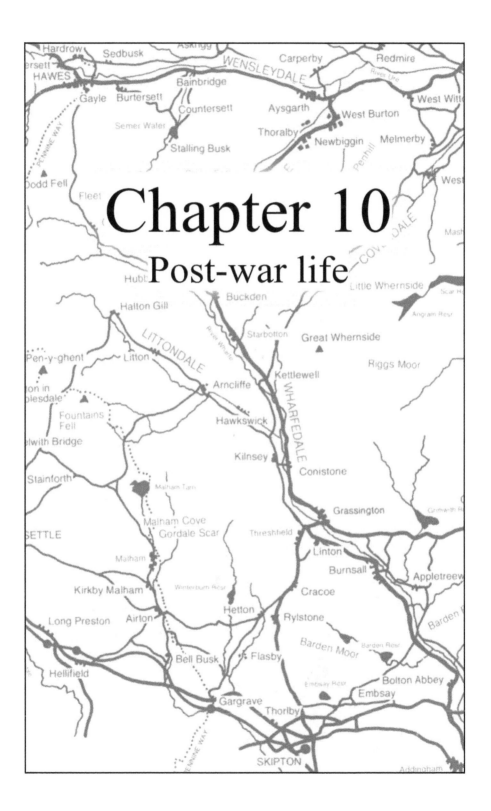

Chapter 10
Post-war life

Chapter 10

2002

The three of them decided to wind-up the interview at this point. Sid had reached the post-war period when he and Frankie had settled down into family life in Embsay. The three children had their own memories of this period and forwards into the later years of the twentieth century.

There was no more to tell of a past that they hadn't shared, a past that the next generations had no knowledge of before the interview began.

Duncan unplugged the voice recorder, Fran went into the kitchen to organise the evening meal for the three of them and they settled down for an evening in front of the TV.

In future, the interview would be saved to disc, transcribed and shared amongst the family.

*

Post war life

The next generation of Waterfalls began to be produced in earnest in 1946. Roger, the eldest, had been born to Arnold and Phyllis in February 1944, but 1946 was a bumper year with the birth of Barbara and Jack's son, Anthony, in September while they were living at Steeton Top and the birth of Sidney and Frankie's daughter, Sonia, in November at Embsay. Both were born a mere nine months after the weddings of the two couples! It seems they were keen to repopulate the family after the deaths of Joseph John and Edith in 1944 and 1945.

The last four of this generation were born over the next four years. John and Frances were born to Sidney and Frankie in January 1948 and June 1949 respectively. Brendalyn was born to Arnold and Phyllis in July 1947 and Jane was born to Barbara and Jack at Farnhill in June 1950. The Dewhurst family emigrated to Canada in November 1953.

The first few years after the war must have all been about family and work.

*

Once the Army had finally finished with Sid in August 1946, he started working with Arnold in the family business. Arnold had offered him a third of the business if he wanted to come in as he felt it would have been the wish of their parents. Sid had the option of continuing his old job as a solicitor's clerk but decided to accept Arnold's offer instead. He knew that the financial rewards would not be great but he would be able to have time off and would be more of his own man working with his brother.[i]

From then on, Sidney worked five days a week with Tuesday and Thursday afternoons off as well as Sunday when the shop was closed. Sidney and Arnold worked together for the next thirty-three years.

The first few years in Embsay must have been particularly lonely years for Frankie. For most of the time she would have been alone, either pregnant or with a small baby. Sidney was at work most of the time but he did make a point of coming home for lunch each day, catching a bus home, having his meal with Frankie then returning to work each afternoon.

The midday meal was their main one of the day and Frankie would cook things such as tripe (bought from the fish shop near the Odeon Cinema in Skipton), pork pies with aspic jelly (bought from.Stanforth's Pie shop) and jellied eels. He quite often had to work late at the shop, especially at busy times of the year when he was needed behind the counter during the day and had to find time once the shop closed to catch up on the paperwork.

Tuesday and Thursday afternoons he usually had three hours to himself until the children got home from school. Then he took over from Frankie and she could get a break while he had time with the kids and cooked their tea. On Tuesdays it was quite often 'bubble and squeak' to use up the leftovers from the weekend and Thursdays it was something on toast like baked beans or scrambled eggs.

*

Sid took over two departments in the shop. One was the Map Room which over time he developed into a state-of-the-art map department located in the Minstrel's Gallery to which customers came from all over Yorkshire. This built on the technical skills he had learned at Ackworth in the geography and surveying classes and the practical skills he had learnt as he roamed the Dales and further afield pot holing, rock climbing and walking with his father and brother in the 1930s.

In an article on shopping in Skipton from *'The Leeds Graphic'* magazine in 1963, the author says

In Sheep Street, at No.10, J.J.Waterfall...have the largest selection of maps and guides in the North of England ... you will find Blue, Red and Baedekers guides to every Continental country and, of course, every inch of the U.K. is covered[ii]

In an article in the *'Craven Pothole Club Record'*, describing 10 Sheep Street after the war, the shop is described as

A venue known to everyone who passed through Skipton in the cause of caving. They kept what always seemed to be a veritable treasure house of which the most entrancing part was a beautiful map room. Here you could buy a map of Equador just as easily as a six inch map of Grassington Moor.

The writer goes on to say

Many of the post-war explorations started out from 10 Sheep Street on a Saturday afternoon. [The Waterfall brothers] ... could always be relied on to know what was going on and where and were willing to spend time with the young novices[iii] who had wandered into the shop.

In his autobiography, Arnold notes

Our bookshop was often the venue for climbers passing through Skipton for the Lakes or Scotland. We naturally always tried to have a good selection of pot-holing and climbing books in stock. Whilst sitting round a camp fire on the Yeti Expedition, sponsored by the Daily Mail in 1982, the Waterfall Brothers were mentioned and five out of the seven expedition members knew of us.[iv]

For many years the headquarters of the Craven Pothole Club was above Waterfall's shop in Skipton which became a rendezvous for Club members where, post-war, both Arnold and Sidney provided a warm welcome. It was above the shop that the library was housed during the twenty years Sid was the librarian.

A snippet from the *'Craven Pothole Club Record'* of 1991 tells us of another side to this connection between the Craven Pothole Club and *J.J. Waterfall's*. This was that the shop had a curious under-the-counter sideline – explosives.

There was an explosives store in the cellar which was used to supply those club members who had explosives licences. They could go into the shop and buy gelignite and detonators over the counter.

*

Sidney's second responsibility was the Greeting Cards department that was first established in the room at the top of the first flight of stairs – formerly Edith's birthing room where Sid himself had been born. This was another busy department which, for three months every year also became the Christmas showroom. No sooner was Christmas over for one year than Sid had to begin ordering for the following Christmas as well as preparing for Valentine's Day in February, Mothers' Day in March and Easter, usually in April.[v]

*

As well as working in the family business, Sidney also worked as Deputy Superintendent Registrar in Skipton for which he was paid about £100 a year. It was this money that paid for the annual Bridlington holidays which the family started taking after the birth of Frances in 1949.[vi]

The first Bridlington holiday was in 1950 – the first of four that were taken there until 1953. Each year the family travelled by train and always went to the same guest house chosen because of a very accommodating landlady who was willing to babysit while Sidney and Frankie went out on the town in the evenings.

It was in Bridlington that Sidney mastered the art of sandcastle building as a means of keeping Sonia and John occupied, while

Left: 'Lyndhurst', Skipton Road, Embsay, 1950s

Left and Above: Bridlington 1950

Right: Bridlington, 1953. Sidney, Fran, John and Sonia

Frankie looked after Frances who was still a baby in 1950. The two elder children had the job of filling buckets with sand and each bucketful became part of the wall of the castle with double-bucket sized towers at each corner, turrets at intervals around the walls and battlements along the top of the walls.

The castles always had moats with trenches dug by the two children from the edge of the water to the moat so it filled with water as the tide came in. Building sand-castles was a daily job for Sid and the two children as high tide always demolished them so a new one needed to be built each day. Each one had to be bigger and better than the one before in order to keep Sonia and John interested and Sid's imagination was stretched on a daily basis.

Still, it was a relaxing time with walks on the beach, paddles in the sea, walks along the promenade, donkey rides and funfairs and finally the evenings to themselves for Sid and Frankie when they could forget they were parents for a time and just have fun.[vii]

*

Sid managed to continue rock climbing whenever he could get time off from working or parenting.

In the late 1940s he continued to pioneer routes on Simon's Seat and Crookrise and in 1965 he recorded a number of short routes on Eastby Crag at the end of his climbing career (see map on page 66)

It was in 1948 that he first met John Wilson who was to become a firm friend and play a large part in his life from then on. John told the story that he was fishing in Ellerbeck, a stream that runs through the centre of the village in Embsay when Sid walked past and stopped to talk to him. John was aged seventeen and Sid thirty-one at the time, but they immediately got on and found that they had rock-climbing in common.[viii]

272

John (together with Brian Hartley) went on to pioneer many new routes on the crags that Sid had known so well before the war.[ix] David Handley, a later friend of Sid's, called John *"Sid's student"*[x] and in *'Yorkshire Gritstone'* John and Brian are called *two notable apprentices* of the original pioneers.[xi]

John also introduced Sidney to the snooker tables at Embsay Village Institute and it was at John's house that Sid first enjoyed watching sport on TV – long before this new technology found its way into 'Lyndhurst' at 26 Skipton Road.[xii]

*

In 1949 an important piece of legislation was passed with all-party support as part of the reconstruction of the UK by the Labour Party after World War II. This was the National Parks and Access to the Countryside Act, 1949. As well as taking responsibility for national parks and nature reserves, it also conferred on the Nature Conservancy and local authorities the right to make further provision for the *recording, creation, maintenance and improvement of public paths,* for *securing access to open country* and for *amending the law relating to rights of way.*[xiii] All of these issues were dear to Sidney's heart and his beliefs and he became involved in the local survey of footpaths for the Embsay with Eastby Parish Council.

In 1950/51, together with T. M. Read of 17 East Lane, Embsay, he walked, described and reported on twenty-four local footpaths, from high-level moorland paths covering many miles to short walks around the villages, across agricultural land and over stiles that had been in place for generations.

All the reports produced were very detailed and revealed a lot of interesting data as well as, in places, personal opinion.

The footpath from Embsay Moor Gate over Crookrise to Waterford Ghyll is a *Clearly marked moorland footpath approximately 2 feet wide.* It is also *One of the finest panoramic paths in the Craven District, Crookrise Crag Top being a widely known viewpoint.*

On the other hand, the walk from Brackenley Lane to Skipton Road is a *Field footpath... well defined with gates, bridge and stile in good condition.* It *commences... at Swaley Grange Farm. Through the farmyard by means of 2 field gates, diagonally across the field to a squeezer stile to the right of a gateway at a small shippen, continuing straight down the field to a stone slab bridge over Embsay Beck and to an iron gate leading onto Skipton Road at the bottom of Cross Bank.*

There is sometimes the hint of conflict between the landowner and their needs and the public and their traditional rights of way. On one report it is noted that *the field before rejoining Brackenley Lane had been recently ploughed but the footpath across the corner of the field had been left intact.* On another there is the report that *the step stile leading from Rowten Lane ... is totally blocked by stones.* Another stile is also reported as *blocked by stones and a single strand of barbed wire.* Three other paths lead past notice boards saying *'No Right of Way'*

The past usage of each path is usually noted with the phrase *Uninterrupted usage by the public within living memory* thus indicating that, historically, these are traditional rights of way used by man and beast long before motorised transport came into being. One footpath is described as *Part of an ancient footpath from Eastby to Halton East* and another as *Part of an ancient footpath from Eastby to Flasby*

Some have had recent work done on them and two leading off from Brackenley Lane are listed as a *Metalled footpath 4 foot in width* and have been *Repaired at Public Expense in the latter part of 1947* and *29th July 1949* respectively. A few are described as *well defined cart roads with an average width of 10 feet.* Only one stile is described as being *in a dangerous condition.*

All paths are described only as far as the boundary with the next parish – two as far as Halton East Parish, another as far as Barden Parish, yet another as far as the Stirton with Thorlby

Parish and a fourth as far as the *boundary of the parish of Skipton UDC* [Urban District Council].[xiv]

This survey was the start of Sid's interest in the traditional rights of way in his part of the country. For the rest of his life he would ensure that they were all walked at least once a year and reported to the Parish Council in writing to prove that they were still in use and therefore needed to be kept open and in good condition.

*

Once living back in Skipton, Sid continued playing football, the sport that had kept him sane and healthy during his time in Stalag VIIIB. From 1946 onwards he played for the Mild & Bitters, a group of 'local lads' who played on the Skipton LMS Sports Club ground until a broken leg and two weeks spent immobile on the settee at home in the early 1950s brought his football career to an end.[xv]

*

Sidney also continued his pre-war involvement with the Craven Pothole Club on his return to the district in 1946. He was Librarian for the club until 1958 and a Trustee until 1968. The *Craven Pothole Club Journal* commenced publication in 1949 and as well as producing regular lists of new additions to the library, Sid also contributed by publishing for the first time the details of rock climbing routes he and Arnold had pioneered in the 1930s. These included *'Rock Climbing at Rylstone'* in 1950[xvi] and *'Rock Climbing on Simon's Seat'* in 1951[xvii], both of which included sketches drawn by Sidney and access details from the nearest main road. A third was *'Rock Climbing at Crookrise Crag',* but this time without a sketch. (For all these climbs see the map on page 66) There was, however, an interest--ing comment under the heading *'A Piton Problem':*

Whilst climbing at Rylstone a party of club members received something of a shock whilst doing "Dental Slab" - the discovery of an iron piton at the top of the diagonal traverse. It is to be hoped that the perpetrators of this crime are not going to make a habit of driving in pitons on our local gritstone slabs.

Another regular column in the Journal (*A year passes by*) mentions that S. Waterfall led the Borrowdale Meet in 1950 *in ideal weather* [when] *a great day was had by all. Fell walking, climbing and bathing were the chief attractions.*[xviii]

*

In the last half of the 1950s Sid also contributed an annual column *On and off the rocks* which, he says, are not written primarily as a record

but in an endeavour to bring back to those involved, pleasant memories of times spent in the hills and on the rocks, as well as to recapture those incidents, both humorous and otherwise which inevitably appear to be an essential part of any gathering of we "hill-folk".

In 1955, he starts with the meet held locally each December, the last one at Crookrise in 1954. He continues

In spite of snow and low cloud it was very gratifying to see a total of 17 members attending. Though not much climbing was done we had a most enjoyable day. In the afternoon we walked across Embsay Moor to the top of Black Park and down to the Mason's Arms at Eastby for the Climber's Annual Dinner. Much to the amusement of the remainder of the party, John Wilson and the writer managed to temporarily lose themselves on the Moor. Intending to strike across the Moor to Deer Gallows, I must admit we never even saw the place.

In May the following year, the first Lakeland weekend was held at the YRC [Yorkshire Rambler's Club] cottage in Little Langdale.

14 members and friends attended ...Climbing parties were out on Doe Crag, Tor, and Raven Crag, Langdale, whilst walking

276

parties covered Bow Fell, Scafell and the Pikes.

The final meet of the year was also held at Low Hall Garth, Little Langdale in September when 9 members attended. Sid writes that the highlight of the weekend for him

was not any particular climb or fell walk but the sing-song in the Three Shires on the Saturday night when 5 of us were entertained by the locals to renderings of most of the old Lakeland Hunting and Folk songs.

On the Saturday two parties went out, the one Sid was with doing Tilberthwaite Gill and then on to Hen Tor and Wetherlam. This party, Sid writes

could not entirely overcome their underground tendencies and simply had to try one or two of the copper mine shafts above Tilberthwaute Gill

The summer of 1955 had been a fine one and had seen

the re-birth of our weekly Wednesday evening meets and parties of members and friends numbering between 4 and 10 have been on the rocks practically every week since the beginning of May having visited Rylstone, Crookrise and Widdop three times each,and Eastby, Deer Gallows and Hawbank Quarry once each.[xix]

'This was the first recorded mention of the Wednesday night group which was to continue for over forty years. (See the maps on pages 50 and 66 for these walks and climbs)

*

It was in 1955 that Sid joined the Yorkshire Ramblers Club (YRC) for the first time. Albert Chapman who was to become a close friend of Sid's from the 1960s onwards, commented in his later years, that 1955 was a bumper year for the YRC because both he and Sid joined that year. Wilfred (Andy) Anderson had joined two years earlier in 1953 and he too was to become one of Sid's merry band of Wednesday Nighters. Andy also went on to conquer many Alpine climbs with John Wilson.

*

Low Hall Garth, Little Langdale, as mentioned in the article '*On and off the rocks*' for 1955 was to feature large in future weekend meets for the climbers and walkers of the CPC and the ramblers of YRC.

It was opened in October 1950 with the following list of amenities:

Running water in every room (given suitable weather conditions)
Sleeping accommodation for 10-15 people
Beds fitted with mattresses of an improved type ... these however would not be noticed unduly if good thick pyjamas were worn
A large airy bathroom (with directions to Little Langdale Tarn)
A lofty fitted garage well fitted with everything the mechanic might need – provided he brought it with him
Every room fitted with windows designed to open and shut and glazed with twentieth century transparent glass.[xx]

Its basic facilities and location in the Langdales of the Lake District provided a perfect home-from-home for the Yorkshire outdoorsmen on their weekends away.

*

Meanwhile, for Arnold, 1955 had brought a skiing trip to Scotland. He describes it in an article for the CPC Journal and says

I was privileged to attend one of the most strenuous holidays I've ever had, as a guest of the Gritstone Club – on a ski-ing holiday in the Cairngorms.

The party of nine over eight days of fine weather climbed over

278

15,000 ft and travelled 80 miles and Arnold's description is well worth reading. He described it as a holiday that would always linger in his memory.[xxi]

Sid's *On and off the rocks* for 1956 began with the December Meet and Dinner at Cracoe at the end of 1955. This time

some 16 members and friends passed the morning on Rolling Gate Crag in brilliant sunshine. After lunch we walked across the fell to Rylstone where all the more popular climbs were patronised before retiring to the Devonshire Arms where a splendid meal rounded off a memorable day.

At the beginning of 1956 members were lucky enough to get a couple of days of skiing up the Dales. Then came the first official meet of the year in May at Low Hall Garth in Langdale.

A really grand meet with a burning sun overhead. On the Saturday walking parties were out on the Pikes and Bowfell and climbing was done on Gimmer and Doe Crag whilst on Sunday the climbers spent the day in White Gill and on Scout Crag. Yet another party of six members spent the day doing a 'direct' of Greenburn Gill, in process of which two members had involuntary bathes – fully clothed – in the beck much to the amusement of the rest of the party.

For the September Meet at Low Garth, the weather was equally kind

and the outstanding memory for most will no doubt be the glorious Sunday spent by the majority of members on the sun-baked Napes Ridges. The main topic of conversation of the weekend was undoubtably the roster of duties which appeared on the notice board by direction of the leader whose name was conspicuous by its absence. In view of all the mumbling and grumbling however, his conscience must have been stricken as he supplied the early morning cup of tea on Sunday.

The Wednesday Meets were also mentioned as a great success

with an average attendance of 7.

Crookrise (5 times), Rylstone and Widdop (twice each) and Simon's Seat and Cowling were visited during the summer.

New climbs that had been pioneered that year at Rylstone andCrookrise were also listed.[xxii] (See the map on page 66)

Where family life was concerned, Sid learned to drive, taught by Frankie who had driven for the ATS during 1945/46. He passed his test and bought a hand-me-down Austin 8 (registration number CFV 550) from Arnold who was upgrading. This car was well remembered for its leaking roof so that when it rained umbrellas were needed.

With Sid driving, the family never knew where they would end up. He always believed he knew which way to go and loved his 'short cuts' – mystery trips into the middle of nowhere which often ended up in farmyards. The number of times he had to turn round and retrace his steps became a family joke and every time he mentioned a 'short cut' there were groans from the rest of the family but they always let him have his way because sometimes, amazingly, he was right.

*

Having a car and a second driver in the family meant that holidays could be taken further afield and the family started venturing down south.

In 1954 Sid and Frankie drove the family down to Perranporth in Cornwall, 1955 was Rhossilli on the Gower Peninsula and 1956 brought the first camping holiday – to Whitesands Bay near St. David's in South Wales. By this time the family had bought a small trailer to carry the camping gear and the marathon of packing up, travelling with three children in the back seat and then unpacking and setting up camp, became an annual event for the next six years.

It was after one of these last two holidays that Frankie decided to stop off in Merthyr Tydfil to visit her father and introduce the children to their grandfather. He only lived two more years after this visit, dying in 1957 and Frankie had to travel down to Wales to organise his funeral, leaving Sidney with the three children for a few days.

For five of those six camping years, the holiday was spent with another family, sometimes two families and once three. That meant that the adults could share the childcare and the chores and once the children were in bed, could have a social evening together on the beach while still being able to keep an eye on the tents.

1957 brought a holiday to Angle on the northern shore of the Pembrokeshire Peninsula and in 1958 it was Mwnt on Cardigan Bay in South Wales. This was also the year of the second car that was purchased – again a hand-me-down from Arnold. This time it was an Austin A40, a step up from the Austin 8 because the roof didn't leak - its registration was LKY 79. The last holiday of the 1950s was in 1959 to Llangeneth on the Gower Peninsula where the camp was set up in the dunes.[xxiii]

*

Back in Yorkshire, swimming in the River Wharfe and picnics on its bank at Appletreewick were the norm for fine Sundays in summer and bank holiday weekend camps at Barden as well as Appletreewick became a welcome break in the warmer months. Sidney would run the family out after school on Fridays, set up camp, spend the night there, go back to work for the day on Saturday then return for the rest of the weekend on Saturday evening.

Easter Sunday was special if it was fine. Sid used to meet the children from Sunday School and take them Easter egg rolling up on Eastby Brow. Frankie had spent the morning boiling and

281

dyeing hard-boiled eggs and it was these multi-coloured eggs that Sid and the children rolled down the hill until the shells had cracked and they could be eaten. After all this excitement the four of them walked down the green lane to Halton East where Frankie would be waiting for them in the car with a picnic, usually eaten at Bolton Abbey.

Often on Sundays, the children used to come out of Sunday School to find Sidney waiting for them to go for a walk on the moors. These outings were treats for all of them including Frankie who got a few hours of peace and quiet while they were away. However she wasn't impressed with the state of their clothes (usually their Sunday best) when they got back and, more often than not, Sidney got a ticking off.[xxiv]

*

Winter in the 1950s brought snow and ice on a regular basis. This meant ski-ing for Sid and Frankie on Manby Castle Hill while the children sledged and tried not to plough into the fence at the bottom. It also meant skating on the flooded land at Millholme, often joined by John Wilson and Alec Breare, another Embsay-ite and the joint owner (with his brother Eric) of the mens-wear shop at No 12 Sheep Street in Skipton. It was the Breare family (2 adults and two children) who accompanied the Waterfall family on one of the above-mentioned camping trips.

Winter was also the time for entertaining and Sidney and Frankie used to have parties when the three children (who were supposed to be in bed) would watch people arriving from behind the banister at the top of the stairs. As they got older, Sonia, John and Frances were often roped in as waiters handing the finger food round. As well as entertaining at home Sidney and Frankie used to enjoy going out to balls and dinners, Frankie looking glamorous in ball-gowns she had made herself and Sidney looking very handsome in his dinner jacket.[xxv]

*

Above: The 'Mild and Bitters' football team, Skipton LMS Sports Club, early 1950s. Sid standing, second left

Left: Sid and Andy in the Dales, mid 1950s

Right: A family camp in the dunes, Llangeneth, South Wales, 1959

Meanwhile, Sonia had moved on to Skipton Girls' High School in 1958, closely followed a year later by John starting at Ermysted's Grammar School and, in 1960, Frances attending Aireville Secondary Modern School, also in Skipton.

*

On the work front, the shop at 10 Sheep Street underwent extensions in 1958. Arnold and Sid's dream had, for a long time, been of a shop forty yards long from front to back. It finally came to fruition starting in 1957 with Arnold chatting to a fellow pot-holer who also happened to be an architect by profession.

Arnold happened to mention that the business could do with more room but it would mean pulling down the old living quarters and incorporating the back kitchen, the backyard, wash-house, old outdoor toilets and midden and then breaking through into the first three cottages of Craven Terrace.

The pot-holer/architect, Malcolm Riley, produced plans that would increase the sales area to around three thousand square foot plus warehouse and stockrooms to another two thousand square foot. The brothers decided to go for it.

It meant that the three tenants in the cottages had to be moved out but over the year between planning and the work starting, this happened quite amicably. They also had to deal with Council objections and the fact that there was a debit balance at the bank. However, all the problems were overcome, the Building Society were enthusiastic about the scheme and loaned them more on the cottages than they were worth and Arnold raised the balance from the sale of some stamps.

The work started in January 1958. The old kitchen and living room came down first, the backyard was excavated and the whole area roofed. The breakthrough into the cottages was made and they were gutted, leaving just one staircase to the upstairs rooms which were all joined into one, big enough to take the

Craven Pothole Club's full sized billiard table. The Council insisted on including extra heavy girders to support the upstairs floors but apart from this it all went smoothly.

Their accountant was not happy with the developments and reminded them that they would have to double their takings because of the capital investment involved. They did just that though it meant heavier buying of stock.

The brothers settled down to what would be another twenty years of business at No 10 Sheep Street. At the end of this period Arnold wrote

We've had a wonderful life at Number 10. We have worked hard, played hard and have always remembered the Thai motto "Why be angry for a minute, when you can have sixty seconds of happiness"[xxvi]

It was a good summary of Arnold's forty-eight years in business and the thirty-three years he and Sid spent working together.

*

i Waterfall, Arnold. Life at 10 Sheep Street. [unpublished] p10.

ii Fickes, Renee. Shopping in Skipton. The Leeds Grahic Vol. 8, No. 63. August 1963 p.71.

iii Anonymous obituary for Arnold Waterfall. Craven Pothole Club Record, August 1990 (19). pp1-3

iv Waterfall Arnold. Autobiography. [unpublished] c.1987 p198

v Op cit endnote i. p10.

vi Waterfall, Sidney. Transcription of an interview with Fran and Duncan Elson. [unpublished] c.2002.

vii Waterfall, Sonia. Choices and Opportunities: memories of a baby boomer. Feedaread, 2019.

viii Wilson, John. Interview with Sonia Waterfall and Fran Elson. [unpublished] 2017.

ix Yorkshire gritstone. Edited by Graham Desroy. Yorkshire Mountaineering Club, 1989

x Handley, David. Interview with Sonia Waterfall. [unpublished] 2017.

xi Op cit endnote ix p202.

xii Wilson, John. Op cit endnote vii

xiii https://en.wikipedia.org/wiki/National_Parks_and_Access_to_the_Countr yside_Act_1949 . Accessed 3 February 2020.

xiv Report sheets. National Parks and Access to the Countryside Act, 1949. Part IV. Public Rights of Way – Ascertainment of footpaths etc. Schedule to accompany Map No 17/EY/2.

xv Waterfall, John. Email to Sonia Waterfall dated11 February 2020.

xvi Waterfall, Sidney. Rock climbing at Rylstone. Journal of the Craven Pothole Club, 1950. 1(2) pp90-93.

xvii Waterfall, Sidney. Rock climbing on Simon's Seat. Journal of the Craven Pothole Club, 1951. 1(3) pp119-122.

xviii B.C. A year passes by:meets in 1950. Journal of the Craven Pothole Club, 1950. 1(2) p86.

xix Waterfall, Sidney. On and off the rocks. Journal of the Craven Pothole Club, 1955. 2(1) p53

xx Anonymous. Yorkshire Ramblers' Club Journal, 1950. vol 7 pp298-299

xxi Waterfall, Arnold. Journal of the Craven Pothole Club, 1955. 2(3) pp161-162.

xxii Waterfall, Sidney. On and off the rocks. Journal of the Craven Pothole Club, 1956. 2(2) pp115-116.

xxiii Waterfall, Sonia. Op cit endnote vii

xxiv Waterfall, Nicola. Sidney Waterfall, 1917-2004. [unpublished] p17.

xxv Op cit endnote vii. p17.

xxvi Waterfall, Arnold. Op cit endnote i. pp13-14.

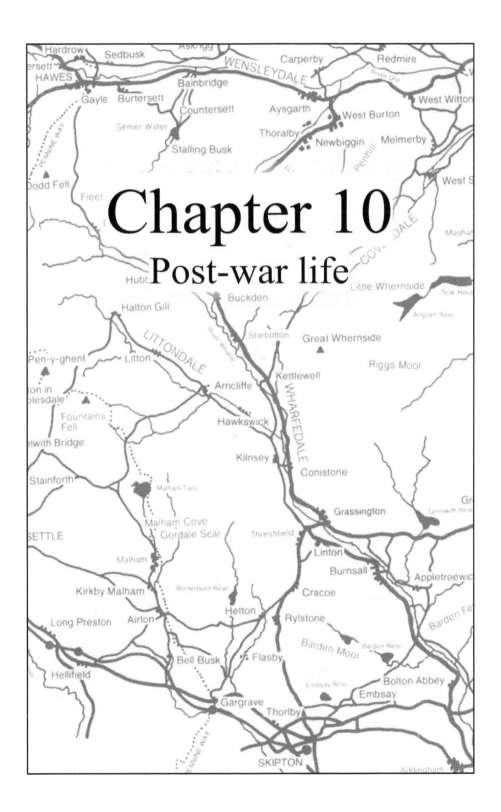

Chapter 10
Post-war life

Above: South Wales holiday, 1961. L-R: Sidney, Frankie, Cousin Hazel, Aunty Phyllis, Fran and John

Left: St David's camping holiday, 1961. L-R, standing: Irene, Dick, Jack and Sidney. L-R, middle row: Floss, Betty and Frankie. L-R front row: Shiela, Martin, Chris, Jenny and John

Family group, Sonia's graduation, 1969. L-R: Fran, John, Sonia, Frankie and Sidney

Chapter 11

The 1960s and 1970s

The 1960s saw the children move into their teenage years with all the usual issues of them wanting to become more independent as well as have more privacy. Once they were all in secondary school, homework and where to do it became an issue. To solve the problem, in 1960, the wall between the dining room and living room at 'Lyndhurst' was knocked through and a folding door installed. This way it could be one big space if needed for family gatherings but could also provide a private space to study in the downstairs warmth but away from the distraction of the newly acquired TV.

The family holidays continued for a few years more, 1960 to Brighouse Bay in Kirkudbrightshire in Scotland. That was the year of four families; eight adults and ten kids and after a panic when John was lost for four hours, counting of kids was the order of the day before the group set off anywhere. 1961 was back to Pembrokeshire, South Wales and 1962 was the last UK family holiday and was to Devon.

1963 was to Austria and was the last family camping holiday together. Frankie wanted to visit the country of her youth , introduce Sidney and the children to it and visit some old friends in Vienna. In Austria the camp was at Hallstat by the side of the lake and from here the whole family walked the hills, took day trips into the surrounding area and swam in the lake. The scenery was glorious – mountains, forests, lakes and idyllic small settlements – and it was a holiday that everyone enjoyed and remembered forever.[i]

*

It was also in the 60s that Frankie decided she needed a life outside the family and from then on always had a part-time job of one kind or another.

She became a courier for the travel firm Wallace Arnold and for a few years accompanied coach trips on holidays to Austria, Germany, Italy and France – she had a working knowledge of each of the latter two languages as well as being fluent in German and English.

After this she became a beauty consultant for Beauty Counselor, giving demonstrations and selling their products. She held similar positions for other organisations and continued selling beauty products well into her seventies.

She also taught German in one-on-one sessions, usually from 'Lyndhurst' but occasionally at her student's home and later on at Eshton Hall School near Gargrave.

She was an enterprising woman, a brilliant salesperson and the secret of her success, whatever she took on, was that she was always interested in people.

*

It was also in the 1960s that Sidney became a Parish Councillor on the Embsay with Eastby Parish Council. He was first elected in 1963 and continued his involvement until 1982. These dates mark a period of huge change in the world and this, to some extent, was reflected in the work of the Council. Sidney's vote on Council helped change his tiny corner of the world, sometimes for the better, sometime not, but in order to try and effect change people have to be involved and, by standing for | Council, he was.

Being interested in the environment Sidney would have supported the creation of a Nature Reserve in Embsay and a Tree Planting Committee that worked on small areas of plantations throughout the two parishes. A lot of their work involved negotiating with landholders and Bolton Abbey Estate to provide pieces of land on which to plant, deciding who was to be responsible for the upkeep of fences and walls, what trees would be planted and the costs involved. Usually, the Council covered the cost of fencing and trees and members of the committee, with the help of community groups, did the planting.[ii]

The 1970s were a period of development in villages everywhere and this was largely the time when Embsay changed from a small agricultural village to part of the commuter belt for Bradford and Leeds. In just over a decade, its population must have almost doubled.

In 1974 the Embsay with Eastby Parish Council Planning Committee made the decision that

it is considered undesirable there be any further extension and consolidation of the residential use of land which occupies a relatively open position in an area of wholly natural landscape of high scenic quality and unrelated to any recognisable community.

This halted the building of individual residences in natural landscapes outside the villages but didn't stop the creation of new estates inside village boundaries.

From then on the Planning Registers list numerous applications for groups of new buildings:

1975 – Erection of 30 semi-detached and 5 detached bungalows on land to the north of Brackenley Lane
1976 – Extension of existing residential development west of Dales Avenue for 44 houses and/or bungalows
1976 -Erection of 46 dwellings comprising 21 terrace houses, 4 semi-detached and 21 detached in Shires Lane
1977 – Erection of 9 bungalows and 35 houses on land at Hill Top Close/Millholme Rise
1978 – Erection of 17 detached houses and 2 pairs of semi-detached houses at Millholme Rise

1978 – *32 bungalows on Shires Lane/Low Lane*
1979 – *Residential development of land at Brackenley Lane to provide 34 detached houses*
1979 – *Erection of 10 detached dwellings on land adjacent to Sawley Close[iii]*

From 1980 onwards more planning applications were being refused and those that were passed were for smaller numbers of buildings – probably because there was less land available by then. But what did become more obvious in the early 1980s was planning permission being applied for holiday flats and cottages. Whether Sidney supported all the new development or not is unknown but he would have made his opinion known whatever he felt about the issue.

Hidden away in the applications for the large developments was one in January 1980 for the *erection of an extension for a sun lounge at 26 Skipton Road* with a note attached that *Councillor Waterfall declared an interest.[iv]* This enabled Sidney and Frankie to extend their living area into the garden and provide a light, sunny area for Frankie to work at her crafts of lace-making and decoupage.

Other national events that had an impact on Council during Sidney's tenure would have been Britain's entry into the European Economic Commission (EEC), decimalisation and the introduction of Value Added Tax (VAT).

Decimalisation was noted in the Parish Council Accounts of Receipts and Payments by the change of one payment on 15 February 1971 from £326 -11-9 to £326 – 59p. The introduction of VAT in 1976, prior to entering the EEC, meant the use of new accounts books with two extra columns. Next to the 'Total Receipts' and 'Total Payments' columns was a VAT column, listing the percentage rate (mostly 8%) and the amount involved.[v] Entry into the EEC seemed to have had no influence during Sidney's time on Council but in later documents the opportunities available for EEC grants was mentioned.

294

*

At the shop, after the extensions of 1958, the Greetings Card Department moved downstairs to the rear and doubled in size. The centre of the shop became a large Toy Department and the Stationery Department moved here as well. The front of the shop nearest the street remained the Book, Magazine and Newspaper Department with a large new Paperback section along one wall. The Artist's Supplies section also doubled in size

During the 60s the whole family got involved in the shop at 10 Sheep Street. Frankie helped out at busy periods, particularly at Christmas and the children did the same once they turned fifteen. Sonia had a Saturday job there for two years, a vacation job for 6 weeks in 1969 and helped out at Christmas every year until 1971 usually working in the Greetings Card Department. John worked there at Christmas several times and did the occasional Saturday, normally working in the Toy and Stationery Department in the centre of the shop. Fran worked mainly in the backroom folding wrapping paper, pricing cards and matching envelopes. The three teenagers were all paid 'under the counter' and were glad of the extra pocket money.

Roger, Arnold's son, started working part-time for the business once he left Ackworth School in 1963, working as a travel courier in summer and for the business in winter. He would later move into the travel business full time becoming a travel agent in premises adjoining 10 Sheep Street. Thus the Waterfall name continued in another line of business even after *J.J.Waterfall's* was sold in 1978.[vi]

In 1963 he had became responsible for the paperback section . Paperbacks had been part of the stock since the beginning of the war and Arnold remembered encouraging his father to stock the very first Penguin books. Penguin always remembered that *J.J Waterfall's* was one of their very first customers and sent a special message of thanks to the two brothers when they retired in 1978.

In the 1940s the order was for six of each title as they were published but once Roger took over and extended the collection, he was buying bins of fifty of a title. When D.H.Lawrence's 'Sons and Lovers' was going through the court case to decide whether it was pornographic or not, Roger had five bins of fifty ready to go on sale once it was settled. Arnold's comment was

Of course, with all that publicity, we still had to order more.[vii]

*

The climbing, walking and sometimes pot holing continued on into the 1960s. (For place names see the maps on pages 50,60 and 66)

John Gott, another friend of Sid's and a member of the Wednesday Nighters wrote an article entitled *'Days on the tops, 1960'* for the CPC Journal beginning with following statement:

I write these notes with a certain diffidence. No news here of new depths plumbed or vast heights scaled, just an account of how a small number of club members have enjoyed themselves on the hills over the past year.

He covers the December 1959 Climbers Meet and Dinner on a day of *steady drizzle and persistent mist* when half the party arrived on the summit of Simon's Seat wondering where the other half were. They met up back down at Howgill and after that

no further mistakes were made in the vital task of navigating to 'The Angel' [at Hetton] *in the gathering gloom.*

A dozen members had *two grand days of crisp sunny weather* at Low Hall Garth in February when climbers were busy on Dow Crag in Langdale and as far afield as Borrowdale.

Wednesday evenings in May and June had good weather and *climbing was enjoyed at Brandreth, Simon's Seat, Hebden Gill, Crookrise, Rylstone and Widdop. The last weekend in May saw one more of those intriguing rushes round the Moor starting at Embsay and finishing very necessarily at the Mason's Arms, Eastby. The general air of urgency on such occasions is very much out of character but if that walk did nothing else it helped to get the grouse fit for August the 12th.*

Rain and more rain prevented anything except short walks from July onwards except for

a brilliant first ascent of Pendle Hill. Unfortunately the weather prevented us from seeing the delectable Lancashire countryside to advantage. Black clouds straight out of the Lancashire Witches Cauldron drove us to more convivial surroundings.[viii]

*

In 1961 Sid was back with *'On and off the rocks'* and started by saying that this was

a brief resume of the doings of a small group of members (mainly of the older variety) who spend as much time together each year, amongst the hills, as their wives etc will allow.

He continues by saying

The high regard these friends of mine have for my mountaineering prowess might be gathered from the suggestion they have made that I should title my article, not as 'Off and on the rocks' but as 'In and out of the water'. This leads me onto one of my pet theories, a theory that most people who know me are fully, and sometimes painfully, aware of and that is that the true mountaineer should not only be familiar with the crags and summits of our mountainous areas but should also be equally familiar and have a closer acquaintance with its streams and swimming pools. My crusade in this direction, I am happy to announce, appears to be bearing fruit, as for the past year or two I have even persuaded my companions to spend one or two of our Wednesday night outings in the Wharfe at Appletreewick rather than on the summit of Simon's Seat.

He then moves on to the activities of the past year. Starting in October 1960 with a meet at Low Hall Garth where they explored the Tilberthwaite and Hodge Close slate quarries. He mentions a chamber known as the 'Hall of Silence', which, he says

is a fantastic place. Illuminated by a window high up in one wall, it has a deep wide pool along one side and in the centre there is a great stone pillar from floor to roof.

On the after-dinner meet they spent *a day of glorious autumn sunshine on Great Wolfrey Crag – one of those days that photographers dream about.* (See the map on page 66).

The December meet which was also the Climbers Dinner Meet was held on Penyghent

and after doing a couple of the easier climbs on the crag we proceeded over the summit and down and over the shoulder of Fountains Fell to the Craven Heifer at Stainforth where 18 members and friends sat down to a welcome meal.

That year, for the first time, Sid mentions the Whitsuntide Meet in Scotland when six CPC members attended the YRC meet at Loch Coruisk on Skye and had nine days of absolutely perfect weather with only one rain shower.

Unbelievable weather for Skye as most people will agree. Our expeditions were as successful as the weather, parties out on the ridge or on Blaven all day and every day – three parties accomplishing the full circuit of the Main Ridge. On the Friday whilst we were experiencing our shower of rain, the ridge was having a snow storm and on the Saturday as we sailed away from the Island the view of the Cuillins was unforgettable – the snow-capped peaks shining so brilliantly in the bright sunshine. I am sure the Kodak combine will be able to issue a special interim dividend this year solely on account of the amount of film that was used by the twenty-three members attending on that short two hour voyage back to the Mainland.

He continues to say that the Wednesday Night meets during the summer of 1961 have had good weather although not as well attended as in other years.

However the five or six regulars have visited all the usual crags – Crookrise, Rylstone, Simon's Seat, Brandrith, Almacliffe, Widdop, Cowling, Deer Gallows, Eastby and Haw Bank Quarry (See map on page 66) – needless to say we have also visited all the usual hostelries to quench our after-climbing thirst.[ix]

*

In *'Another Year Passes By -1963'* a mention is made of F.Smith being elected President and S.Waterfall becoming President-Designate.

At the end of March that year Sidney led the Lake District meet which was held at Low Hall Garth as usual.

On the Saturday, a party went up Mosedale on to Scafell, over Scafell Pike to Esk Hause and returned via Bow Fell and Crinkle Crags. On the Sunday the Coniston Slate Quarries and the Yewdale Fells were visited.[x]

In November 1963 Sidney succeeded to the Presidency and on the following day the President's Meet was held at Malham.

In wet and windy weather Pikedaw Calamine Cave was visited and appetites were sharpened for an excellent ham and egg meal at the Victoria, Kirby Malham, that evening.

*

On 12 January 1964 Sid, as President, led another meet, this time at Rylstone.

As it was cold and misty the greater part of the day was spent

299

walking but in the afternoon two climbs were undertaken. The party of 15 were then in good form for the meal that had been arranged at The Angel at Hetton.

Again on the 26 January, Sid, as President, was in charge of Keighley Night at the Wellington Hotel

where a most enjoyable evening was spent seeing an excellent collection of slides that Tim Smith had taken on climbing holidays in England, the Alps, Corsica and Alaska.[xi]

*

In 1965, Keighley Night changed to Ladies Night and at the first one held at the Unicorn Hotel, Skipton, 71 people sat down to dinner, Sid and Frankie amongst them. We also learn that Sidney led a party of climbers to Great Wolfrey Crag on the first meet of the year in 1965.[xii]

Also in 1965, Sid wrote of some new climbs he'd found on Eastby Crag. In the introduction to the descriptions of the climbs he says

Finding something completely new on gritstone, these days, is by way of being something like a miracle. ... How the climbs in question had escaped notice for so long is a complete mystery. Another amazing thing is that; unlike most of the recent discoveries on gritstone, the climbs are not of the "exceptionally severe, only for tigers" class, but range through "difficult" to "severe" and taken in conjunction with the main crag make Eastby well worth a visit both for the beginner and the aforementioned "tiger".

Accompanying the article is a sketch of the area drawn by Sid's elder daughter Sonia.[xiii]

*

In 1966, it's certain that Sid would have been one of the party of ten who, led by John Wilson, met at Barden Bridge on the 9th

January.

The weather being fine and frosty it was no day for the rocks and instead a round trip was made of the Strid, the Valley of Desolation, Simon's Seat and Howgill. The meal that followed at the Mason's Arms, Eastby, is still talked about.[xiv]

In 1967 came another contribution by Sid to the Journal – this time about the first meet of the year held at Widdop (see map on page 66) on 8 January.

The first meet of the year has traditionally become the annual 'nosh-up' meet of the climbing section of the Club. It was probably the best day of the winter with crisply frozen snow underfoot and brilliant sunshine above. The attendance was slightly down on previous years as only ten members turned out, but the counter attractions of skiing may have accounted for one or two others who usually attend. The party met at Widdop reservoir and walked over Gorple Moors, up onto the Black Hambleton (1,574 ft.) and back past Upper Gorple reservoir over Black Moss to Widdop – some 10 or 11 miles. In the evening was enjoyed the usual ham, eggs and chips at the Sutcliffe Guest House at Slack, a village above Hebden Bridge It was truly a day that will live in the memory of all who attended[xv]

By this time he was approaching his 50th birthday and this article was the last item that Sid wrote for the Journal of the Craven Pothole Club. No doubt he thought it was time for the next generation to take over. From then on the journal was a lesser publication without Sid's particular brand of humour, his emotional response to his surroundings and the descriptions of the natural world he so loved being a part of.

*

However, even though he wasn't writing or climbing any longer, he was still walking and camping. The Wednesday Nighters were going from strength to strength with the next generation joining Sid and the old stalwarts on these evening outings once a week.

In the early 1960s Tom Petit, Arthur Smith and Graham Jones joined Sid, John Wilson, Brian Hartley and Andy Anderson. David Handley started teaching at Aireville School in 1966 and joined via Tom Petit, another Aireville teacher. George Spensley was also a teacher at Aireville and Sid knew him through the YRC. Michael Jackson and Albert Chapman met Sid through David Handley. The Lancashire group, some of them members of YRC, included David Smith, Harry Robinson and DerekBush. Tim Smith, George Burfitt, Arthur Smith and John Gott, also YRC members, became part of the group towards the end of the 60s.[xvi] John also joined his father and the group for around five years before he left home to go to university. Michael Donald (Sid's neighbour on Brackenley Drive who had gone to school with Sid's three children) became part of the group in later years.

Very rarely did they all walk together but they all considered themselves as part of the Wednesday Nighters,[xvii] described by David Handley as an informal group of CPC and YRC members who quartered the Dales and East Lancashire for around 45 years. David went on to say that it was

on these forays that I began to appreciate [Sid's] *prodigious knowledge of every nook and cranny of the Dales' landscape.* [Many of his friends appreciated his skills]*of navigation in the pitch black on winter nights and experienced with him the pure pleasure of swimming in remote Dales' beck holes on midsummer evenings. He read maps with the same intensity that others might read books and had perfect recall of the topography no matter how complex the terrain.[xviii]*

Sidney was seen as the *Senior statesman of the group*[xix] and did most of the organising, then a telephone tree passed on the details of where they would meet each week and what the plan was for a particular night. The three children remember Wednesday evenings as being non-stop phone calls – all for Sid.

The Whit Meets, starting with the one to Skye in 1961, continued for several decades. Each year Sid *and his happy band escaped to remotest Scotland where the Blacks Niger tent was erected for the duration.*[xx] This was the same tent that Sid and Frankie had bought in 1956 for family camping holidays and it was still in use in the 1990s. Some years, as the group aged, they rented large houses in beautiful spots and did their own catering. Arran and Applecross stand out where these later trips are concerned. The most usual members of this *happy band* were David Handley, Albert Chapman, Graham Jones, John Wilson, John Gott (until the accident on Wetherlam that killed him in 1983), Tom Petit (until his death in 1988) and occasionally Michael Jackson.

Sid was never a Monro 'bagger' but completed a good few, usually in the company of one or other of the Wednesday Nighters. The group explored Taransay, a tiny island off the coast of Harris, a decade before the BBC programme 'Castaway' discovered its beauty.

Many Irish peaks were also added on what became known as 'breakaway meets'. David Handley remembers climbing *Brandon, the McKilleycuddies Reaks, Crogh Patrick and, sensationally, the Skelligs.*

As he got older Sid still went on the Whit meets but quite often took days off from walking and stayed in camp usually spending the day tidying up so that when the others returned in the evening it was immaculate.[xxi]

In 1976, the year before his 60th birthday he achieved a long-held ambition by completing the Grand Tour of Mont Blanc with Michael Jackson, Grahan Jones, David Handley and Albert Chapman. David remembers them taking a sleeper from Paris to Chamonix and doing the walk in 16 days which he said was a lot quicker than many others younger than themselves.

David also remembered that shortly after this achievement, Sid went on to spend a couple of weeks with Graham Jones on the GR20 in Corsica, described as 'one of the top trails in the world' and running 180 kms across the island from north to south.[xxii]

Another year they all went to the Picos Europa, a mountain range extending for about twenty kilometres and forming part of the Cantabrian Mountains in northern Spain.[xxiii].By this time Sid was well into his sixties and had retired[xxiv]

*

Meanwhile, back in the 1960s, he had spent time with his children trying to pass on his skills as a rock climber. John remembers climbing with him and being given the advice *'don't use your knees'* and Sonia and Frances remember Sid taking them to the old quarry at Rock Line or the rock slab on the way up to Crookrise.

He climbed with them, telling them where to put their hands and then showing them where the next foothold was. His reassuring and encouraging presence made them try harder to get to the top. They both enjoyed these sessions with their father and felt a sense of achievement afterwards but neither of them continued climbing once they left home.

John was the only one of the three who continued climbing into the 1970s but gave up after the unnerving experience of falling off a rock face when climbing in Llanberis in Snowdonia in 1974.

*

In the late 50s and throughout the 60s all three children were involved in Brownies and Cubs, followed by Scouts and Guides. For Sid this was a way of encouraging them to become self-sufficient and learn the skills they would need to succeed in the future both working with other people and surviving in the great outdoors.

In 1962 Sid joined them and became a member of the committee for the South Craven Scouting Association. In 1968 he became the District Activities Adviser for the South Craven District and in 1977-79 he became Chairman. He resigned from the Chair in November 1979 and in 1980 the Chief Scout awarded him the Medal of Merit for his

distinguished services to Scouting in South Craven district over many years.

In the same letter that accompanied this news, the County Commissioner, Allen Warren, went on to say that it was clear to him that

you have been a tower of strength to successive District Commissioners. .... South Craven certainly owes you a great deal. Thank you for all that you have done and are continuing to do for Scouting in the area.[xxv]

This suggests that he may have continued to support scouting in some other position but as Sidney and Frankie were about to start travelling, it would have had to be less of a commitment and more part-time.

*

By the end of the 1960s all three children had flown the nest, Sonia and John to university and Frances to college though at this stage they hadn't completely left home as they returned for weekends and vacations.

Sonia left for the University of East Anglia in Norwich in 1965, moved to Newcastle in 1967 where she got her B.A, had a gap year then completed her education, an M.A. in Librarianship at | Sheffield in 1970-71. John attended Nottingham University in 1966 for two years, returned home to Skipton to work in 1968, then joined the Civil Service working for DVLA, in 1971. Frances attended Bradford College from 1967 to 1968, then worked at Ingleborough Hall School for a year, finally completing three years of teacher training at Alnwick College ending in 1971

The 1970s began with two weddings in 1971 – Frances to Duncan Elson in June and Sonia to Terry Sumner in November. John married Anne Jones four years later in 1975. This was the end of family life for Sidney and Frankie as the three young couples created their own lives, Frances and Duncan in Northumberland, Sonia and Terry in New Zealand and John and Anne in South Wales before moving to Hastings in East Sussex. With the coming of grandchildren in the 1980s, the family expanded again but in a different way.

*

The last big event of these two decades came in 1978 with the sale of *J.J. Waterfall*'s at 10 Sheep Street Skipton.

The brothers saw it coming early in the 1970s with the tightening of laws relating to employment and then the introduction of VAT. The latter involved a large outlay for new electrical tills so that every sale could be divided into two columns: goods sold with VAT and none taxable goods with each column being totalled up separately at the end of the day. A big expense just to keep the Tax Inspectors happy.

Arnold foresaw huge changes on high streets up and down the country.:

From a personal service to the customer, it has become a service to the community, individuality has been lost, the supermarkets have become supreme. The future of shops in general, will be that the multiples will take over the High Street shops and the small family specialist businesses will be found in the cheaper rented premises, with no employees except family. They will be able to pay more attention to customers' needs and
306

less time to PAYE returns and restrictive staff clauses. Where staff have to be taken on, it will be on a part-time basis.[xxvi]

How right he was!

So when a fellow business man from Leeds asked if they wanted to sell out, Arnold was keen though Sid was diffident. They sent their agent round to value it but the offer they made wasn't realistsic.

Arnold then wrote to W.H.Smiths and four valuers arrived to have a good look round. Their opinion was that it was too big for Skipton, having only looked at the population statistics for Skipton (13,000) instead of recognising the hinterland and visitor population totalling over 40,000.

Then the brothers got a query from Preedy's of Birmingham, a family company. They were keen from the start and accepted the price that Arnold and Sidney asked and the deal was done.[xxvii] They agreed on a completion date of 1 September 1978 and that was the end of a family business that had started in 1885 when Edmund Hargreaves, an uncle of Arnold and Sidney's mother, had moved into the premises at 10 Sheep Street.

93 years since it became the family business and 71 years since it became *J.J. Waterfall's.*

*

Left: Family group, Sonia & Terry's wedding, Skipton Registry Office,November 1971. L-R: Terry, Sonia, Sidney, Frankie, John, Duncan, Fran

Sidney and Frankie, 'Lyndhurst', Skipton Road, Embsay, 1972

Above: Sidney with his two girls, Fran & Duncan's wedding, Embsay Methodist Chapel, June 1971

Right: Family group, John & Anne's wedding, South Wales, 1975. L-R: Duncan, Fran, John, Frankie, Anne, Sidney, Sonia, Terry

Left: Sid and Frankie at Sid's retirement event, 1978

Right: J.J.Waterfall's, 10 Sheep Street, Skipton, prior to selling, September 1978

Left: Sidney and Arnold, at the front counter, J.J.Waterfall's, prior to selling, September 1978

Right: Sidney in the map room, J.J.Waterfall's, prior to selling, September 1978

Left: Mont Blanc trek, July 1976. L-R: David Handley, Albert Chapman, Sid and Graham Jones

i   Waterfall, Sonia. Choices and opportunities: memories of a baby boomer. Feedaread, 2019.

ii   Embsay with Eastby Parish Council. Tree Planting Committee. Minutes. 1977-1985

iii Embsay with Eastby Parish Council. Planning Register, 1974-1982.

iv Embsay with Eastby Parish Council. Planning Register. 1980.

v   Embsay with Eastby Parish Council. Accounts of receipts and payments , 1964-1976

vi Craven Herald. 15 September 1978. p14.

vii Waterfall, Arnold. Life at 10 Sheep Street. [unpublished]

viiiGott, John. Journal of the Craven Pothole Club. 1960 2(6) pp344-345.

ix Waterfall, Sidney. On and off the rocks. Journal of the Craven Pothole Club, 1961. 3(1) pp27-29.

x   Anonymous. Another year passes by – 1963. Journal of the Craven Pothole Club, 1963. 3(3) pp159-160.

xi Anonymous. Another year passes by – 1964. Journal of the Craven Pothole Club, 1964 1(4) p194.

xii Anonymous. Another year passes by – 1965. Journal of the Craven Pothole Club, 1965. 3(5) p249.

xiiiWaterfall, Sidney. Recent developments at Eastby. Journal of the Craven Pothole Club, 1965. 3(5) pp232-233.

xiv Anonymous. Another year passes by – 1966. Journal of the craven Pothole Club, 1966. 3(6) p295

xv Waterfall, Sidney. Widdop January 8 1967. Journal of the Craven Pothole Club, 1967 4(1) p42.

xvi Interviews with David Handley and Albert Chapman by Sonia Waterfall. Various dates, 2017

xviiInterviews with David Handley, Albert Chapman and John Wilson by Sonia Waterfall. Various dates, 2017.

xviiiHandley, David. Obituary: Sidney Waterfall. Yorkshire Rambler 2004 (21) p37-38

xix Handley, David. Interview with Sonia Waterfall. 2017

xx Handley, David. Op cit endnote xvii.

xxi Op cit endnote xix

xxiihttps://en.wikipedia.org/wiki/GR20 . Accessed 25 February 2020.

xxiiihttps://en.wikipedia.org/wiki/Picos_de_Europa . Accessed 25 February 2020

xxivOp cit endnotes xvii and xviii

xxvLetter from Dr Allen Warren to Sidney Waterfall, dated 13 June 1980.

xxviWaterfall, Arnold. Op cit endnote vii pp11-12.

xxviiWaterfall, Arnold. Op cit endnote vii

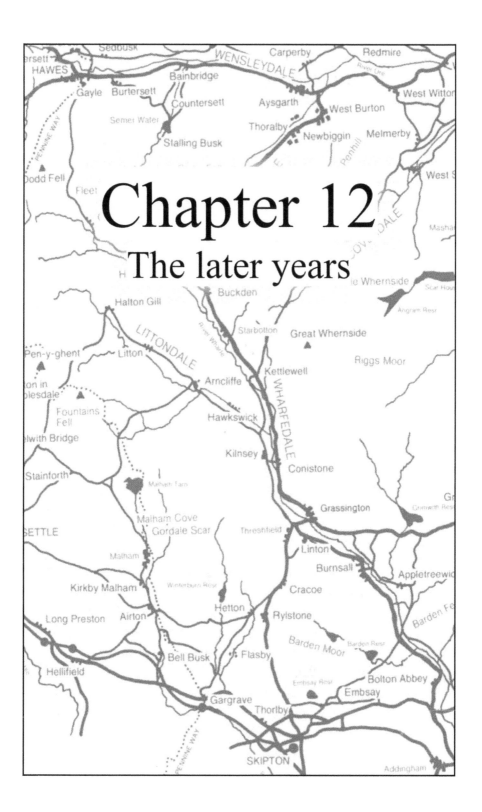

Chapter 12
The later years

Chapter 12

The later years

Retirement really came too early for Sidney, aged 61 but Arnold, being three years older at 64 was ready for a more relaxed lifestyle.

Both brothers planned to travel, Arnold planning a trip to Austria to see his daughter Brendalyn and her family and Sidney planning a trip to see his sister Barbara and her family.[i]

But first there was the retirement party, a gathering of friends, family and staff past and present from *J.J. Waterfalls*. Sidney was presented with a beautiful slate clock which stood on their mantle-piece at 'Lyndhurst' from then on.

Sidney and Frankie almost immediately went over to Canada and had a good time in the snow and on snowmobiles. By this time Barbara had been diagnosed with Multiple Sclerosis so this would be the last time Sid would see his sister who died in 1988 after a long period in hospital.

*

Next on the list was an extended four-month trip to New Zealand to visit Sonia and Terry. They left England on 1 December 1980 an had a four-day stay in Singapore where the highlight for Sidney was when he went for a stroll one evening and got invited to go to a massage parlour or hire the services of a prostitute but, as Frankie wrote in her diary, *he had no money so came straight back to the hotel.*[ii] They landed in |Auckland on 5 December, flew on Christchurch where Sonia was waiting for them. They took two days to get to Denniston, Frankie describing the road up to the plateau as *a spectacular mountain road which winds upwards in sharp S bends.*

She was not so enthusiastic about Terry and Sonia's house and says

The shock at the living conditions was nearly too much for me and it did not help that the house was freezing cold. They made a brave attempt to make everything as comfy and nice as possible but everything is terribly primitive and shabby. This first night I cried myself to sleep. I was so cold and miserable. Even Sidney found it hard to take.[iii]

Her opinion of the house never changed but Sidney learnt the art of keeping the fire going in their bedroom so that they always had somewhere warm to retire to if necessary. Terry also built her a windshield to sit behind outside when it was sunny and she spent many days outside busy with her lace or crochet. Luckily it was a fine summer but this also had its downside as water was an issue at Denniston as it was provided by water tanks which caught the run-off from the roof. Unfortunately they ran out of water and at that time there was no pump to get the water from the lower tank to the upper tank so Terry had to go up a ladder to the upper tank and everyone else filled buckets from the lower tank and passed them to him to empty into the upper tank. It took a full day to fill the tank, lots of friends came to help and had a hilarious day including getting wet through in the process. Sidney worked along with everyone else while Frankie took photos but wasn't impressed.

Despite the challenges of Denniston, they loved New Zealand and saw a lot of it during the three months they were there. Before Christmas Sonia took them up the West Coast to Karamea and the beginning of the Heaphy Track where they went paddling on the beach and had a chat with the warden. Then on 13 December they left on the first of many trips heading via Nelson to the most northerly tip of the South Island, first staying with friends Pat and Andrew in Nelson then driving up onto the Tasman Peninsula, staying at Marahau, Pohara Bay and Collingwood. They did the Farewell Spit Safari Trip and saw an amazing number of birds. Wherever they went they

316

stopped to pick fruit and sometimes vegetables which Frankie said was *very exhausting but great fun!!!*

Christmas Day passed in the usual way with presents in the morning and a traditional meal in the evening. Sonia and Terry's neighbours, Fred and Marie, came over for a drink and the meal in the evening. They just took short day trips until New Year when, together with Fred and Marie and Chris, their grandson, they had a bonfire and barbeque outside until midnight when they let off fireworks and toasted each other. Frankie wrote:

It was the best New Years Eve celebrations Sidney and I ever had.

On 3 January all four of them went down to Punakaiki for a few days, Sonia and Terry camping on the campsite there and Sidney and Frankie staying in a lovely cabin nearby. They 'did' all the usual sights as far south as Hokitika but the highlight for Sidney was a 'walk' up the bluff behind the settlement with Terry. According to Frankie's diary

they found that there wasn't a track so they 'bush-bashed' their way up the 1500 foot cliff. It meant walking on the top of Kiki trees which are like a small palm tree. Very hard and dirty work by the looks of them on their return.

Back to Denniston for two days then Sonia took them on a trip up the Buller valley to Murchison first, then into the Nelson Lakes National Park with swims in the Buller River and the lakes and a drive up to the ski-field below Mt Robert for the views. Back again to Denniston for four days then they set off in Sonia and Terry's car for Christchurch to pick up a campervan and set off on their trip round the southern half of the South Island on 22 January 1981.

They went down the east coast then across country to the Hermitage and Mt Cook. Frankie describes the scenic flight they went on.

We flew up the right hand side of the Tasman Glacier and over the Tasman Hut and then across the Main Divide by the Graham Saddle.and dropped right down the Franz Josef Glacier to the Franz Josef airstrip. Whilst we were there the pilot was told that there were two more climbers at the Fox Glacier airstrip who needed flying back to Mt Cook airstrip. So we took off and flew over Lake Matheson to land at Fox Glacier. After having taken on our two passengers we returned to the Franz Josef Glacier and flew over the Fritz Range and then re-crossed the Graham Saddle and landed on the snowfield at the head of the Tasman Glacier. After ten minutes on the glacier we took off again and flew down the west side of the Tasman Glacier. Over the Delabeche and Haast Huts into the Hochstotter Icefall and over the Grand Plateau before returning to Mt Cook airfield. It was a unique experience for me to see those huge ice-fields and glaciers in brilliant sunshine and with beautiful blue skies. Although as we crossed the Great Divide we flew through thick clouds which made all the tops look formidable....What a marvellous day!!![iv]

From there they went on down the Clutha River (a swim for Sidney and a paddle for Frankie) to Queenstown where they spent their 36th wedding anniversary with a meal up the mountain after a trip up in the Gondola. They went with another couple to Skippers Canyon and the following day Sidney walked with them up Ben Lomond while Frankie booked herself on a cruise on Lake Wakatipu to a sheep station. After this they moved on to visit Bob and Pauline (friends of Sonia and Terry) on their small holding at St Bathans.

We experienced another example of the alternative lifestyle. Everything was just as dirty and untidy but they had goats, a horse and lots of cats and their vegetables were flourishing.

From St Bathans they drove to Dunedin, visited the Albatross Colony, Lanarch Castle and Glenfalloch Gardens. From Dunedin it was on to Te Anau where they booked three trips for the next three days – Doubtful Sound, Te-Ana-Au Caves and Milford Sound, the last day ending with a swim in the lake – *So ended another perfect day,* wrote Frankie.

Then it was back to Queenstown and on to Wanaka for the night, over the Haast Pass in pouring rain to the Fox Glacier campsite for the next night. The weather was still poor so they continued on along the coast road (where Frankie said '*I had to negotiate a 'wash out')* as far as Hokitika. From there it was over Arthurs Pass to Christchurch, where they handed in the van, picked up the car, had two days exploring Christchurch then drove back to Denniston – *and so we are back again in dirt and discomfort,* wrote Frankie – arriving back on 16 February 1981.

Sixteen days later on 5 March they left Denniston for the last time. The car took four people, all their luggage and two bikes over to Christchurch where they picked up the campervan and drove north along the coast to Blenheim. Terry rode his bike and Sonia drove the car to Nelson to leave it with Pat and Andrew until they returned on their way home. They all met up again at Pelorus Bridge, the bikes were loaded into the van and it was off to Picton for their last night in the South Island.

After the crossing which Frankie described as *rather uneventful and boring* they drove on to Masterton for the night. Then it was on to Wanganui and then the Tongariro National Park. They drove up to the snow fields of Ruapehu, which Frankie described as *quite an amazing place as it is the crater of an extinct volcano.* The next day was their first experience of hot springs and thermal baths. Frankie described the hot springs as

a weird but fascinating sight seeing steam rising off the water and hot mud bubbling out of the ground.

Then it was on to Taupo, Sonia and Terry cycling and camping and Sidney and Frankie driving. Sonia remembers these last three weeks as an uncomfortable experience after almost three months of living together and says that

the option for us to bike during the day was the only thing that kept us all sane during these last three weeks.[v]

319

After two days in Taupo, it was on to Napier, where Sidney and Frankie explored the town, (Frankie in her wheelchair) and had a trip out to Cape Kidnappers to see the gannet colony there. Frankie records

What a sight!! Hundreds of beautiful birds allowing us to watch them from very close by, There were also lots of young ones. We stayed there for 50 minutes and could have stayed for hours. A truly unique experience.

The next day it was on to Urewera National Park and Waikaremoana campsite via Tutira Lake where they fed the swans and *Dad was chased by a black swan.* They explored the sights next day and drove on to Rotorua where they had another *very welcome hot bath and swim* at the campsite.

By this time Frankie writes that she *is getting so weary and tired that half the enjoyment has gone out of this trip.*[vi]

This was the last entry in Frankie's diary and the last seven days is described briefly by Sonia.

From Rotorua we went on to the Bay of Plenty and Mt. Manganui, across to Hamilton to show Mum and Dad where we had lived for our first two years in New Zealand. Then up the Coromandel Peninsula, across to Auckland, then north to the Bay of Islands and Cape Reinga, then back down through the Kauri forests with a last night north of Auckland.

The next day was the drive out to the airport, where Sonia and Terry loaded all their gear onto their bikes and Sidney and Frankie handed back their campervan.[vii]

Frankie and Sidney flew out of Auckland Airport while Sonia and Terry began the long cycle trip home to Denniston.

*

Sid basking in the sun c.1980

Above: Denniston, New Zealand, 1981. Frankie and Sidney in the front garden, Fred and Marie's cottage behind.

Right:: Denniston, 1981. L-R: Frankie, Fred with Ben the dog, Sidney behind and Terry up the ladder refilling the tank after running out of water.

Left: Christmas dinner, 1985. L-R: Frankie, Duncan, Chris, Sidney and Sonia

Over the coming years Sidney and Frankie would also go to Kenya, the Gambia, Crete, Corsica, and several times to Madeira as they loved it there.

*

The late 1970s saw the first of their grandchildren born. Nicola was born to John and Anne in November 1977, followed by Kim in October 1981 and Lisa two years later in October 1983. Chris was born to Frances and Duncan in November 1980 and Heather a few years later in May 1982.

This gave Frankie and Sidney an excuse to spend Christmas at opposite ends of the country, travelling down to Hastings one year then up to Northumberland the next. John remembers bringing the Waterfall family up to Embsay at least once a year, usually during the summer holidays and Frankie and Sidney often made the trip down south during the summer months as well.[viii] Fran and Duncan and family, being closer, saw them more often and spending Mothers Day together became a habit – quite often at halfway points between the two households at places such as Barnard Castle, Rievaux Abbey and Blanchland. Trips to Skipton by the Elson family were also a regular occurrence.[ix]

*

Once the business closed, Sidney had to find other ways of filling his time.

The 'Wednesday Nighters' continued although rock climbing was no longer on the agenda for the older members and the walks may have become shorter over time. They still ended their nights out at a local pub for a meal and a drink and this part of the proceedings may have become longer as the walks became shorter. Even during the last couple of years of his life, Sid still enjoyed a short walk, his favourite being around Embsay Reservoir followed by a drink at the Elm Tree pub.

Above: The 'Wednesday Nighters', Yorkshire Dales, mid 1980s. L-R: Arthur, David, Albert, John, Sid, Brian, Graham

Right: The 'Wednesday Nighters', Lake District, mid 1980s. Rear L-R: Sid, Arthur, Brian, Graham. Front L-R: John, Albert, David

Whitsuntide camping trip, Skye 1980s: L-R: Tom Petit, Arthur Smith, Albert Chapman, David, Handley, Graham Jones, Sid

The Whit Bank Holiday meets continued also – right through the 80s and into the 90s although camping meets may have become fewer and renting a house and self-catering may have become more the norm.

In the last few years of his life, Sidney's activities may have been a bit curtailed but his interest in who was doing what in the hills both at home and abroad was undiminished

*

Having Arnold (a well-known philatelist and an expert on Tibetan postal history) as a brother, it was inevitable that Sid should become a serious stamp collector. Being Sid, it was also inevitable that this should become a detailed and extensive map-themed collection built up over the last twenty years of his life.

In fact, it is a six-volume work of art. Each country has a page of introductory information, giving a brief statement of history, a location map and/or detailed map, the name of the capital, when the first stamp was produced and the currency.

It even contains details of countries that once were independent and produced their own stamps but no longer exist. One of the most interesting pages belongs to Tuva

A province of Central Asia, formerly known as North Mongolia and Tanna Tuva. Incorporated into the USSR on 11 October 1944. Now uses Russian stamps.

The map shows it sandwiched between Russia and Mongolia not far from Lake Baikal. There is only one stamp on this page – a 1927 Definitive Issue showing a map of Tuva.

The whole collection is, indeed, a thing of beauty and shows Sid's curiosity about the world, his neatness and organisational skills and, above all, his love of maps which first became evident during his walks with his father and at Ackworth School in the 1920s and 30s.

He also inherited a George VI stamp collection which he developed extensively over many years. He continued working on both collections right up until a few days before his death

*

Sid and Frankie started playing croquet in the 1980s and in the 1990s Sidney played carpet bowls on a weekly basis at Embsay Village Institute both of them being social activities as well as a form of gentle exercise. He also became a regular supporter of the Upper Wharfedale Rugby Union Club and could be found on the sidelines shouting them on at every home game they played.

*

Arnold died in April 1990 after a six-month battle against pancreatic cancer. Even though they hadn't seen each other as often since retirement it was a blow for Sidney as a lot of his early memories of childhood and teenage life were closely tied to his brother as was his post-war working life. When talking about Arnold's death at a later period, he said that one of the last things that Arnold said to him was *"We had some good times, Sid, didn't we"*. Arnold's funeral service was held at the Quaker Meeting House in Airton where Arnold and Phyllis and their children had lived for many years during their time as caretakers there. He is also buried there in the Quaker graveyard

*

During the late 1970s Frankie started having problems with her left leg which became painful and stopped her walking any distance. This became most obvious during a holiday to Crete when her lack of mobility halted their plans to repeat Sidney's walk down the gorge to Sphakia which he had done after the fall of Crete and before he was captured by the Germans in June 1941.

Over the next months Frankie underwent numerous tests and

325

was eventually diagnosed with *Arteriosclerosis* as a result of a lifetime of smoking. She had to give up smoking immediately which she did but it was too late for her leg which continued deteriorating until it was decided that the only way to prolong her life was to amputate it below the knee. She underwent the operation in January 1991 and as soon as she returned to 'Lyndhurst' it became obvious that she wouldn't be able to continue living there for any length of time.

At the beginning of 1994 her leg was deteriorating again and the specialist advised her to let them operate again and amputate above the knee. Frankie, with Sidney's support, bravely refused this option even though she knew that this decision could endanger her life. She'd had enough of hospitals and operations and accepted whatever the future held for her.

*

Meanwhile, the house was put on the market during the summer of 1991. Halifax Property Services who had an office at 6 Sheep Street, Skipton were the estate agents and it was offered for sale at *Offers in the region of £89,500.*

After turning down several offers, Sid decided to sell to Brian and Sue Swales, mainly because Brian was a rock climber who had pioneered many recent routes on Crookrise in the 1970s and 80s (and continued to do so into the 1990s when he named one of his new climbs 'Lyndhurst' after the house). There were other links as well. Sue's Aunt and Uncle, Edgar and Irene Horner were friends of Sidney and Frankie, Sidney and Edgar having played together as children when both sets of their parents had businesses on Sheep Street. On Brian's side, his sister Stephanie had worked at *J.J.Waterfalls* for many years when it was still owned by Arnold and Sidney.

So it seemed like a sale that would suit both sides. Brian and Sue made a couple of offers and the price that was finally agreed on was £87,000. The exchange of contracts was on 28 October 1991 and Brian and Sue moved in on 30 October.[x]

This was the end of another era, the Waterfall family having lived at 'Lyndhurst' for 52 years.

*

While the sale was proceeding, Sidney and Frankie had been looking for a new place to live and after investigating a few Park Home sites around the Dales, had settled on the one at Overdale, at the top of Cross Bank, halfway between Skipton and Embsay. So in the end, they only moved about half a mile.

The home they chose was all on one level for Frankie with a small garden that Sidney could quite easily cope with. Most important of all, there was a view of Embsay Crag and Crookrise from the bedroom windows in winter when there were no leaves on the trees. In summer it was a mass of greenery and home to numerous species of small birds. The bird table in the back garden was a source of continuous delight to bird-watcher Sidney and he enjoyed sitting in bed watching the endless activity there right up until the end of his life.

The following year they had a sunroom/workroom built on for Frankie to continue working at her craft and once this was done they had the perfect place to live.

So 1991 was a year of huge changes for Sidney and Frankie but despite the worry about Frankie's health and the possible regret at having to sell the family home, both of them must have realised that downsizing was a step in the right direction in their mid-seventies and for the rest of their lives.

*

Frankie had been selling her craft at craft fairs throughout the Dales since the beginning of the 1980s together with a friend and fellow craftswoman, Ruth Lawson. As they ventured further afield in the late 80s and early 90s, Sidney became the driver for the two women allowing them to concentrate on the making and

Right: Family group, Christmas 1991. Rear L-R: Lisa, John, Anne, Fran. Middle L-R: Frankie, Sidney, Chris, Nicola. Front L-R: Kim, Heather

Left: 'Lyndhurst' Embsay, October 1991. Heather, Sidney and Fran in the garden prior to selling.

Right: No 84, Overdale Park, Ocober 1991, prior to moving

Left: Sidney with Frankie in hospital after the operation to have her leg amputated, January 1991

Above: Family Group the day after Frankie's funeral, The Strid, Bolton Abbey, September 1994. Rear L-R: Heather, Lisa, Kim. Middle row L-R: Duncan, Anne, John, Nicola, Chris. Front: Sidney, Sonia, Fran

Above: Fran and Sidney scattering Frankie's ashes on Kilnsey Crag, September 1994

Above: Sonia, Sidney and Fran, Barrier Reef, Australia, March,1995

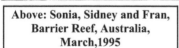

Right: Sidney, Sonia and Fran, Cairns, Australia, March 1995

selling.

Neither of the two women made a fortune but it was something they enjoyed doing and an outlet for their creativity. It was also a social outing as they got to know their fellow crafters who exhibited at the fairs and spent a lot of time talking to potential customers who were interested in what they produced. As well as that, they were both independent women and enjoyed the sense of freedom that a small amount of self-earned income provided them with.

It was at a craft fair in the village hall at Grassington in August 1994 that Frankie complained of a bad headache and went to lie down in a room off the hall. When Sidney went to find her after half an hour, he found her almost delirious with pain and decided to call an ambulance. By the time the ambulance had got her to Airedale Hospital, she had lost consciousness and never recovered it.

Sidney called Fran and Duncan and John and Anne and luckily Fran and Dncan could come down and sit with him and Frankie through the night until they made the decision to turn off her life-support, knowing the odds against her ever recovering the life she had. Her death certificate says she died of a stroke.

Then they had to phone Sonia in Australia and let her know. She flew home the following day and the family were together again but this time with a big hole where Frankie used to be. The funeral service was at Embsay Methodist Chapel where Frankie and Sidney had been members of the congregation for the last few years. This was followed by cremation at Waltonwrays Crematorium at Skipton and the wake at the Elm Tree pub in Embsay.

Fran and Duncan later helped Sidney scatter Frankie's ashes – half on the top of Kilnsey Crag, her favourite spot in the Dales and half on the top of Crookrise where Sidney planned to have his ashes scattered on his death.

One precious memory of this period was Sidney and the three siblings walking across the moors on Black Park above Eastby on a glorious autumn afternoon, picking heather to place on Frankie's coffin the next day. This was a moment of peace for the four of them before facing the funeral and the mass of people who attended.

Once the funeral was over, Sidney and Sonia went up to Rothbury with Fran and Duncan for a few days before returning to Skipton where Sonia caught the bus to London and Heathrow and the flight back to Australia. Sonia remembers waving goodbye to a very lonely looking Sidney from the bus as it left Skipton Bus Station.

Frankie's sister Anita (known as Anni) died in Rotterdam a couple of months after her towards the end of 1994. Luckily, Anni had managed to come over to England and spend time with her sister earlier in the year.

*

Three weeks before Frankie died, she and Sidney had phoned Sonia in Australia to tell her that they had booked a flight out to see her the following March in 1995. After she died, Sidney decided that he would like to carry on with their plans and invited Fran to join him.

Once they arrived at the beginning of March they had a couple of weeks exploring the Sunshine Coast region which was where Sonia was living at the time. She had three weeks leave booked and had organised a three-centre trip designed to introduce them to as much of possible of the East coast of Australia as was possible in that amount of time.

First they flew down to Sydney, picked up their hire car and drove up into the Blue Mountains for two nights. The weather was terrible so no views but a trip to Jenolan caves made up for that. Next day it was on to Lithgow, west to Cowra for the Japanese Garden, then south to Kosciusko National Park for three nights.

Fran and Sonia climbed Mt Kosciusko in deteriorating weather while Sydney had a rest day. The next day was fine so they went on to Jindabyne, Perisher and Charlotte's Pass for a walk amongst the snow gums and alpine scenery. The next day they headed north again and as the weather forecast was good for the following day they decided to spend their last night in the Blue Mountains and 'do' the sights and take the photos before heading down to Sydney airport for the flight to Alice Springs.

Sonia had hired a 'Britz' motorhome for their six nights in Central Australia. The first day was spent in Alice Springs, seeing the sights and doing shopping for the next few days. The second day was a trip into the West MacDonnells National Park where they walked the tracks into the waterholes and gorges, topped off, on the way back to Alice, by a flash of green and yellow streaks as a flock of budgerigars flew across the front of the vehicle.

The next day they drove down to Yulara and had three nights in the caravan park there. They did the sunset viewing the first evening and next day Fran and Sonia climbed Uluru while Sidney had a guided walk at the base then met his daughters back in the National Park Centre. The next day was Katajuta where Fran and Sid did a short walk into the gorge while Sonia stayed with the vehicle. After lunch, Fran and Sonia went off for a longer walk where they soon discovered they weren't carrying enough water. They quickly became dehydrated but eventually got to a water point, filled their water bottles and made it back. It made them realise how easy it would be to die in the desert.

Next day they drove back to Alice Springs and took their mid-afternoon flight to Cairns and their two-bedroomed apartment which they'd booked for six nights. The first day was a rest day when they picked up their hire car, did shopping and watched the waders along the sea front. After that they had a day up on the Atherton Tablelands with a swim in Lake Barrine, another day when they travelled up the coast to Port Douglas, the Mossman

Gorge and Daintree where they took a river trip and saw some huge crocodiles plus fruit bat colonies and several tropical birds. A third trip was out to the Barrier Reef where they snorkelled and Fran got sun burnt. The last day was a rest day for Sidney who stayed in Cairns while Fran and Sonia went white-water-rafting up the Tully River, a day of beautiful scenery and an exciting river-ride.

That was the end of their holiday – a trip that included the city, gorges and mountains of New South Wales, the red desert sands, desert shrubs, gorges and monoliths of Central Australia and the lush tropical scenery and seacoast of the Cairns region. The next day they flew back to Brisbane, had a couple of days at home then Fran and Sidney flew out back to the UK and Sonia went back to work.

*

After Frankie's death, Sidney worked out routines to keep himself busy. He got a paper delivered every day and spent an hour every morning completing the crossword. He continued working on his stamp collections, continued with his weekly carpet bowls sessions and continued going out with the Wednesday Nighters. John Wilson visited him once a week and other friends also called in at regular intervals.

He continued his visits to John and Anne in Hastings and Fran and Dumcan in Northumberland but no longer tried to drive the long distances – instead taking a bus to either London or Newcastle, from where either John or Fran would pick him up and take him to their homes.

He spent time with three women friends: Dorothy Holmes (his friend Geoff's widow) who lived in Skipton, Amy, his pre-war fiancee who lived in Blackburn and Rene, a friend from Embsay who had also worked at the shop for many years and still lived in the village. He took them out for drives in the country, for meals and on short holidays.

*

1997 was to be Sidney's 80th birthday and unbeknownst to him, the family had organised a surprise party for him in Embsay Village Hall. Fran sent out the invites, booked the hall and organised the food. Sonia arrived in the country in early June for a month and John and family came up for the big event. As far as Sidney knew they were just going to have a meal out with immediate family and a few friends at the Mason's Arms at Eastby.

They were expecting around eighty people who had come from all over the country to be there and Fran and John and their families were at the village hall to welcome them all. Sonia drove Sidney up through the village and he was a bit nonplussed when they stopped at the village hall. But he did as he was told and followed Sonia into the hall to be greeted by a large crowd of family and friends all singing 'Happy Birthday'.

Sidney was a bit dazed for a time but in the end he really enjoyed the night and laughed along with everyone else when his friends got up to tell tales about him.

The Wednesday Nighters bought Sidney a voucher for a balloon ride. Sonia tried to organise this before she had to return to Australia but it was too windy on the day and Sidney wasn't too enthusiastic about the idea anyway so he let the voucher lapse.

Sidney and Frankie's friends from Leicester, with whom they had done a lot of travelling, gave him the gift of a holiday of his choice. Sidney chose to go to the Orkneys and the three of them had a week there the following year in 1998. This was to be the last of Sidney's holidays except for trips to see family.

The next day a group met for lunch at the Strid Cafe by the River Wharfe at Bolton Abbey – mainly close family and anyone who had travelled from away to be there. It was a fitting end to a special birthday for a wonderful and well-loved man.

2002 brought Sidney's 85th birthday, a smaller affair this time. The family had invited a number of his friends to join them for lunch at one of his favourite pubs up the Dales at Linton. Including the family there were about twenty-five people and a room had been booked for the event. It was a good meal in good company and everyone sat around in the sun outside for more drinks and coffees That evening there was a family gathering at Sidney's home at Overdale before everyone went their separate ways.

*

For the previous few years Sidney's health had been deteriorating and he had been diagnosed with angina, had started having to use an inhaler if he tried to walk too far and had also started to lose weight.

During April 2004 he managed to see all the family: John and Anne came north to see him over Easter; shortly afterwards, Sonia arrived home from Australia for a couple of months and during the following two weeks she and Sidney had a few drives around the Dales and the Lake District and she also drove him up to Rothbury to see Fran and Duncan and family. On 1 May Sonia, Fran, Duncan and the two dogs said goodbye to Sidney in Yorkshire, drove over to Manchester Airport to pick up Vaina then on to Nantwich where they were to start a three-week trip on a narrowboat, *Pimpernel*.

On Friday 7 May 2004 Sidney had been visiting Amy and began to feel unwell. She told him to go to the doctor, but instead he drove back to Embsay, called in at the village shop for a couple of items and then went to visit Rene. She also told him he should go to the doctor, so, to stop the nagging, he drove down to Skipton to see his doctor.

The doctor was worried and sent Sidney to Airedale General Hospital by ambulance. Once there he was diagnosed as having had a mild heart attack and was admitted for further tests. On the

Left: Sid and Amy, Gargrave, 2002

Below: Sid and Rene, Cragside, Northumberland, 2001

Below: Sid and Andy at Sid's 85th birthday celebrations, Linton, 2002

Right: Sid and Sonia, Gargrave, April 2004

Family group, Sid's 80th birthday celebrations, 1997. Rear L-R: Chris, ?, John Pennington, John, Terry Pennington, Roger, Isobel, Jenny, Nicola, Nadina Hooper Middle L-R: Toby Pennington, Kim, Heather, Fran, Sonia, Lisa, Anne. Front L-R: Duncan, Gillian Preston, Shiela Preston, Tony Hooper, Sid, Hazel Pennington, Phyllis Waterfall, Ian Hooper with Hani

Sunday he was allowed visitors and they reported him to be in good spirits and expecting to be discharged the following day. This didn't happen, as at eight o'clock in the morning on Monday 10 May, he had a huge heart attack and the doctors and nurses at the hospital were unable to save him.

John and Anne were first on the scene and had to organise the funeral with the help of Sidney's friend, John Wilson, who was a funeral director. Sonia, Vaina, Fran and Duncan had to organise somewhere to leave the boat in Birmingham to be collected later, pick up the car from Nantwich and get themselves back to Yorkshire.

Sidney's funeral service was held on Friday 14 May at Embsay Methodist Chapel followed by a cremation at Waltonwrays Crematorium in Skipton and a wake at the Elm Tree Pub in Embsay. Most of Sidney's ashes were scattered on Crookrise the following Monday at the same spot as Frankie's ashes ten years previously. Another, smaller amount was scattered around the old oak tree on the Storiths Road near Bolton Abbey.

*

Sidney's friend, David Handley, wrote the following tribute as part of a longer obituary which appeared in the Yorkshire Rambler's Club Journal:

Sidney was a quiet unassuming man with endless reserves of patience which he frequently exercised with the more outrageous of our group [The Wednesday Nighters']. *His calm cooperative nature cemented endless friendships. He was without malice. guile or anger and will be remembered with warmth and affection.*

*

Two years later a memorial seat for both Frankie and Sidney was erected at Embsay Reservoir, next to the path that had become one of Sid's favourite walks in his later years.

i   Craven Herald. 15 September 1978 p14.

ii   Waterfall, Frankie. Holiday diary. [unpublished] 1980.

iii Ibid endnote ii

iv   Ibid endnote ii

v   Waterfall, Sonia. Choices and Opportunities: memories of a baby boomer. Feedaread, 2019 p.212.

vi   Waterfall, Frankie. Op cit endnote ii

vii Waterfall, Sonia. Op cit endnote v p.212.

viii Waterfall, John. Email to Sonia Waterfall, dated 20 February 2020.

ix   Waterfall, Frances. Email to Sonia Waterfall, dated 27 February 2020.

x   Swales, Sue. Email to Sonia Waterfall, dated 29 February 2020.

Afterword

Sid left behind three children, Sonia, John and Frances, and five grandchildren, Nicola, Chris, Kim, Lisa and Heather. Sixteen years after his death five great-grandchildren have been added to the mix, Chloe, Archie, Dylan, Isla and Frankie.

We have all moved away from Yorkshire nowadays but visit when we can. Whenever we get the chance to return to Sid's beloved Yorkshire Dales, the memorial seat at Embsay Reservoir and the old oak tree on the Storiths Road near Bolton Abbey are places of pilgrimage where we can feel closest to our roots.

None of us identify as Quakers and I believe Sid lost his faith during the war years. However we all grew up loving maps and the outdoors, roaming the hills, watching the birds, noticing the wild flowers as they appeared each year and picking the 'fruits of the forest' when they were in season. We all believe in walking gently on this earth.

This is Sid's legacy to us, his family.

Above: Scattering Sid's ashes, Crookrise, 2004. L-R: John, Fran, Heather, Sonia, Vaina, Lisa

In Loving Memory Of
SIDNEY
and
FRANKIE WATERFALL
They Loved The Dales
The purple headed mountain
The river running by
The sunset and the morning
That brightens up the sky

Above: the plaque on the memorial seat at Embsay Reservoir.

Appendix 1

Names and addresses from Sid's Wartime Log

ADKINS. J	3 Newton Road, Sunny Bank, Clydach, Swansea
ANDERSON, R.H	'Somerset', Ladies Mile, Hollywood, Belfast
ARTHUR, R.J.	Exchange Street, Upper Hutt, Wellington. NZ
ASCOTT, F	14 Park Avenue, Handsworth, Birmingham
AULD, A	14 Park Avenue, Handsworth, Birmingham
BALDWIN, F	1 North Street, Lumb, Rossendale, Lancs
BARRY,P	297 Palmerston Road, Gisburn, NZ
BENZIES, P	
BILSON, S	68 Wilford Road, Meadows, Nottingham
BOOTH, F.L	4 New Bryn Gwyn Street, Newbridge, Monmouthshire
BOWNESS, Harry (Les)	38 North Road, Egremont, Cumberland
BRADBURY, V.V	3 Staff Cottages, Weston Road, Bury (?)
BRUNT, M	250 Springfield Road, St Albans, Christchurch, NZ
BULMAN, S	1 Thornhill Drive, Gaisby Lane, Shipley
CASSON, S.M	5 Argyle Terrace, Workington, Cumberland
CHAPMAN, J.K	49 Nearcliffe Road, Heaton, Bradford
CHEW	165 London Road, Biggeswade, Beds (Yoredale, Askrigg)

CLARKE, W.J	103 Salisbury Road, Welwyn Garden City, Herts.
CLAYTON, D.T	25 Orchard Street, Great Harwood, Blackburn
COWPERTHWAITE, J.E	Dalts Farm, Gaisgill, Tebay, Westmoreland
CURTIN, W	c/o GPO, Waitoa, Te Aroha, Auckland, NZ
DIGGS, I	20 Denby Street, St Albans, Christchurch, NZ
DITTMER, F	Laudvale, Tamananui, NZ
DOWNING, J.D	7 Harrington Street, Pear Tree, Derby
FREEMAN, H	69 Jubilee Road, Romford, Essex
GRIME, F.W	8 Liddell Grove, West Denby, Liverpool 12
HARRISON, V.A	84 Park Street, Heannor, Notts.
HORNER, F.(32612)	
HUNTER, T.W	15 Front Street, Corbridge, Northumberland
KANE, W (Sugar)	67 Suffolk Street, Guelph, Ontario
KELLY, B.J (24083) E543	'Rosslane', 1 Hazel Grove, Bishop Auckland, Co.Durham (24083) E543
KEMP, D.H	30 Buckingham Street, Wolverton, Bletchley, Bucks
KENNEDY, A	Helenbank, Cardenden, Kirkaldy

LAMBERT, H.R	'The Forge' Bentley, Near Farnham, Kent.
MACEY, F.S	20 Church Street, Weedon, Northants
MALE, W.B	69, Nunts Park Road, Exhall, Coventry
MARTIN, W	11 Modden Terrace, Armley, Leeds 12
MEAD, T	41 Neil Street, Fulwell, Sunderland, Co.Durham
NORRIS, F	235 Grangehill Road, Eltham, London SE 9
O'CALLAGHAN, W	27 Colston Road, Easton, Bristol 5
O'DONNELL, P	24 St. Phillips House, Lloyd Baker Street, London W.C.1
O'ROURKE, E.J	Beaver Road, Blenheim, NZ
PALMER, G.H	61 Field Drive, Shinebrook, Notts.
PERRY, J	34 Fenswood Road, Long Ashton, Bristol
RITCHIE, S.W (21301)	53 Helena Street, Dunedin, NZ (21301)
ROBINSON, G.W	C/o 36 The Green, West Comfort, Ferryhill, Co Durham
SAUNDERS, W	18 Reservoir Road, Church Hill, Hedensford, Staffs.
SHAND, H.G	'Springfield', Budleigh Salterton, Devon.
STEWART, G.D	Foxhill, Nelson, NZ

TOYE, F	73 Kilmalcolm Road, Greenock, Scotland
WATSON, G,E	9 Grange Cottages, College Road, Ashworth, Aldershot
WELCH, H	1 Barony Terrace, Nantwich, Cheshire
WRIGHTSON, A	9 Station Lane, Gilesgate, Durham City

Appendix 2

Elisabeth Wieland came into Sid's life during the period he was a POW at Tost Reserve Lazarett in 1944.

After the war he received three letters and a card from her (all in German) between October 1945 and November 1946. They told of her experiences as a German civilian during the final days of the war in 1945 and on into 1946 and give an alternative view of what was happening in Germany at that time.

The translations (by Janine Hogben) are included here because it is sometimes too easy to forget what a tragedy the war was for the majority of the German population.

*

Elisabeth Wieland, Berlin, 2 October 1945

2 October 1945

Dear Mr Waterfall,

Now that the terrible war is over and I've survived and although everything weighed on me like a terrible dream, I will keep my promise and send you a greeting from my present homeland. And I hope I greet you in your dear home in full health and surrounded by your beloved family.. Before I actually begin the letter I must thank you most heartily for all your love and kindness which you showed to me, especially in **Cosel**.

With our departure from **Cosel** suddenly about to take place, it wasn't possible for me to say a last farewell to you. At midday when I came out of the Keglerheim [?] my boss who was the manager Dr Kauff, said that we would stay a few more days in

349

Cosel but in the evening we got a sudden order from the manager to depart immediately because of the Russian advance.

So, various people, me included, set off in our truck [LKV}. We spent the night in a barracks where the windows and doors were partly missing. The day before a bomb had done its work well. Our first destination was **Neisse** [Nysa?] where we arrived at 2am and spent the night in another barracks. The next day we went on to **Reichenbach** and here we had decent quarters and were well looked after.

In Reichenbach we stayed 2 days for we female employees were supposed to take up our work again in the hospital [Lazarett] which didn't happen because Reichenbach had also received orders to evacuate. We received orders to report to the Doctor in charge of the Military Area in **Hirschberg** who would be in charge of us.

Unfortunately in Reichenbach our lorry was taken away from us so we had to discover how to continue. The trains were hardly running any more. After we'd stood in the station for 2 hours and were nicely frozen through an army transport train arrived which took us to Hirschberg. We arrived on Sunday night at midnight. To our misfortune, we learnt that the barracks we were supposed to spend the night in was 1 hour's walk away.

So we set off in violent driving snow and freezing temperatures and when we came to the first barracks we weren't accepted because it was already overfull with refugees. We were pointed to a second barracks 20 minutes walk away and here we weren't accepted either and when we arrived at the third lot of barracks and didn't have any success, I wanted to lie down in the snow and leave everything to fate. But finally I pulled myself together and found shelter in the 4th lot of barracks.

Next day we introduced ourselves to the army doctor in charge of the Hirschberg area. He wanted to send us to the anti-aircraft unit in **Altenburg, Turingen.** I didn't want to gamble my life at the last moment (for it was already forseeable that the war

350

would be coming to an end) and I asked for a travel permit to Berlin.

On **31 January 1945** I arrived in the evening with Fraulein Langsch at my relatives in Berlin. I had no great desire to be in Berlin but as most of my relatives were in O/S [Ober Silesia], those in Berlin remained to me my only refuge. I didn't stay here very long. On **3rd February** the North American bombers attacked Berlin in a heavy raid. Berlin was bombed for 3 hours constantly and the area of my relatives flat was very badly hit.

Berlin burned for almost a week and one couldn't go out on the street without a wet cloth over one's mouth or a pair of protective glasses. On the **26th February** a second attack took place that was even worse and in spite of everything one was glad to go back to the flat after the attacks.

The happiness I found in finding a second home with my relatives wasn't to last very long because on **28 February** the British bombers landed a heavy night attack on Berlin whereby the flat of my relatives was changed into a heap of rubble by the bombing. It was an unparalleled inferno and it was here that I thought my last hour had come because the air-raid shelter partly collapsed and only with a lot of difficulty were we rescued.. Soon after I had a nervous breakdown.

The attacks on Berlin became more frequent and worse. The sirens didn't stop and in pure fear I just did not know where I should run to. So on **26 March** on the invitation of Frau Gerischer, the wife of Walter Gerischer that you know from Tost, I went to **Rodewisch** in **Vogtland**. But here I didn't have peace for very long for first of all the town had been attacked from low-flying aircraft and as the Front came nearer and nearer, the town suffered from artillery fire as well.

You can imagine I was glad when the Armistice came. But I was so homesick that I couldn't stay in Rodewisch any longer. So on **13 June** I set off for Upper Silesia for I wanted to look for my mother and brothers and sisters. Unfortunately I only got as far as **Gorlitz** for the Poles were there and wouldn't let anyone over the border.

Finally I succeeded one day in getting across but the Poles saw us and took away all my things. When I at least wanted to save my satchel (for I had in it my fur coat, 2 dresses, 2 pairs of shoes ana pullover which you kindly gave to me in Cosel). The Pole hit me with his gun to such an extent that I was glad when I was back on German soil again. In Gorlitz I stayed for 6 weeks because I still believed that the border would open but as this wasn't the case and I couldn't stand it any more because I was starving (I didn't have any food ration tickets). In Gorlitz my home was a ditch by the side of the road, I still had dysentery and I could only find potato peelings and nettles to eat.

At the **end of July** I took myself off to Berlin. When I arrived in Berlin I didn't know where I should go for my relatives had fled shortly before the Russians took over the city. I wandered around for 2 days on the street and had no roof for my head. I met by chance a student friend of my brother's who got me a room at a film director's place and here I worked in the household. From my mother and brothers and sisters I hadn't heard anything yet and the letters to my husband were all returned. Life is so bitter, hard and difficult and often I think I cannot bear it any longer. If I didn't have a belief in my faith in God then I would have brought my life to an end a long time ago.

I've put up with all the bombing attacks in Berlin and was glad that I'd survived. Now I would be glad when a bomb would hit me – what should become of me now I don't know. Overnight I had become homeless and as poor as a beggar. I possess only that which I have on my body. Some of the things I lost between Tost and Cosel, the second lot of things I lost when my relative's flat was bombed in Berlin and the rest the Poles stole from me. Unfortunately, I put some of my cash in the satchel which was stolen from me by the Poles.

I hope everything is good for you Mr Waterfall, better than it is for me. I wish it from my whole heart.

Often I have asked myself what I have done to deserve so hard a destiny. When I lie down at night I wish that I could sleep forever.

If you come to Germany I would be pleased if you would visit me – couldn't you come on a fast RAF plane then you would be here soon – but please no bombs as I have had enough of them.

Krista Dank, who you knew from Tost, died in Leipzig from lung disease. The family, wife and 2 children of Sergeant Tietz, the officer in charge of the Revier [at Tost], died in the bombing of Berlin.

The war has left behind the suffering and misery and the innocent have to atone for all this. Hopefully, the sun will shine for us once again. Excuse me that I haven't got any more joyful news for you but after the above events you will understand that I need someone to whom I can open up my heart and complain about the suffering because I seem to stand alone in the wide world.

In my satchel I had your picture which you gave to me at Christmas. I would like to ask you and would be very grateful if you could send me a memento of yourself.

*

Elisabeth Wieland, Vahrholz, 2 April 1946

My previous letter was taken by a US soldier of the American Command in Berlin because there were no postal services at the time. I don't know if you received it so I will send a copy of that first letter.

Now thank God the block on the post has been lifted so this

letter is a dear greeting for you from me. From my first letter you will understand that fate knocked me for six and thing's really haven't got any better. Only the one difference is that I found my family. On **31 December 1945,** by chance, I found my mother and 2 sisters and it was through a family I knew in Berlin. The joy was huge – over the moon – because for a year I hadn't heard anything from my family although I had gone to a great deal of trouble to try and find them.

As my mother told me, the Russian take-over of Upper Silesia was very bad and I'm happy that at that time I fled with the staff of the Tost Reserve Hospital although I regretted it when I was alone there for such a long time.

There was a ‚lot of plundering in Upper Silesia and ‚many dear friends were murdered, amongst them a very close relative of ours. Our town had about 10,000 inhabitants and every day a hundred dead were noted. The women, without consideration of age or health, were raped. To be sure, on my flight, I was subjected to great danger from the Russians but God held his hand protectively over me. In **January 1945** my mother didn't flee but stayed to try and keep a home going for us children. But all her sacrifices were in vain for on **6 July 1945** when the Poles took possession of Silesia all German citizens from the Reich were expelled. On the 7 July at 3.30 am 10 soldiers from the Polish police arrived and my mother and two sisters had to leave within 10 minutes without being able to take anything with them. The house was immediately locked up and my family left with only what they were wearing. Not until they were on the road did friends give them clothes to wear. And even if they'd had anything with them they would have lost it.

During the Russian time, before the end of the war, a Russian general lived in our home and my mother was allowed to live in one room although articles of clothing and crockery had been taken

When the Poles came in, a large lorry drove up to the front of the house and upholstery was taken out first and afterwards the rest of the furniture. My mother, who used to be so kind and helpful was now as poor as a beggar – as indeed was the whole family. When I saw my mother again in **January 1946** I didn't recognise her at all. Because of the difficult time and above all, because she had been expelled from her homeland, she had aged 10 years and she was also suffering mentally which was understandable.

Here in the village where we are living, we are existing in the most primitive conditions. The village has 100 inhabitants. To live here permanently is naturally not what I want. I can't bear to be in this wilderness for much longer, as well as there being no prospect for a job but for the moment it is better here in the country than in the town so that's why I've transferred here from Berlin, even though I had the prospect of a nice job in an office in Berlin. At present I work now and again for some farmers but only for food because hunger is terrible. I have never been so hungry in my life as during those terrible years of 1945 and 1946. In Tost I was given Russian KGF food but it always troubled me when I saw that the poor ill people there (patients?) weren't given anything sensible to eat. If today, I had the food that I gave to the Russians then I wouldn't need to go hungry today. In the village I am supposed to be taking over the running of a kindergarten but my nerves are shattered at the moment and I can't take on this duty at present.

Dear Mr Waterfall, I hope you are very well after your 4-year imprisonment and have been allowed to spend some time with your dear family. Unfortunately that won't be the case with my brothers as we don't know if they're alive and if they're alive we won't be able to find each other because they won't suspect that we are in this small village.

How was the getaway when I left you in Cosel. I would be very pleased if I could hear from you. If your path should bring you to Germany I would be pleased to see you. If I was to get to England (not much likelihood as I've no relatives there) I would love to come and see you. Now I've received an invitation from my former landlady in Berlin who now lives in Vevey and is married to a diplomat, Moreover, she is alone and I could go there as her house-daughter

I would like to do this as in the present circumstances in Germany, one loses the courage to live. Unfortunately, it's not yet allowed to be able to travel abroad. What the Nazis have committed, we innocent people have to carry the can.

Dear Mr Waterfall, 25 June is your birthday so I am sending my good wishes for a happy birthday. May the coming year give you a lot of joy and happiness and may your efforts be crowned with success.

She sent a brief card also from Vahrholz, dated 28 June 1946, mentioning the 3 letters and asking if Sid had received them.

*

Elisabeth Wieland, Wolfenbuttel, 26 November 1

I've already written 3 letters and a card.

Two years have gone by since we said goodbye in Tost, that is to say, in Cosel. Those were nice times in Tost and I often think back to that time when my typewriter had to be repaired and I rang up the English Revier [surgery office] and asked for your help. This often happened when I was alone in the main Business Centre. The remembrances are the only paradise from which we cannot be driven.

Since this glorious time a lot has happened. If you have received my letters you will see fate has hit me hard. At the moment I possess 1 summer coat, 1 dress and light shoes. I fear the coming winter and it is already cold and I have nothing to put on. The only thing to do is to hibernate for the winter.

[Here she repeats letter 2]

In August I was in Berlin and went to a social office because I wanted to do a state exam to qualify as a young person's carer but at present I am not in a position to do this as I have no money. So I have applied for a scholarship which I hope will be successful and I'll get a grant.

From Cosel you no doubt had all sorts of difficulties to deal with.

When we stopped between Tost and Cosel with the car, I was observed taking something into the car by Deputy Director Reinhardt and I wasn't allowed to do it. He informed on me to the boss and I was seen as a spy by our officers. Just because I was trying to do someone a favour. For me it was, on one side an advantage that everything went topsy-turvy because otherwise I should have had to appear before a War Tribunal.

_____

She mentions a Major Thomas

Mentions Christmas 2 years ago (1944) when they had to send 'Liebespaketan' – love packages secretly – using someone else as a go-between.

*

Appendix 3

A transcript of the handwritten daily record of march from Stalag VIIIC Sagan to Stalag IXB Bad Orb as provided by Arthur Pattinson, a patient at Tost Reserve Lazarett.

07/02/45		Sagan	
08/02/45		Wiesau	22 kms
09/02/45		Birktmare	23 kms
10/02/45		Gleisnau	15 kms
11/02/45		Spremberg	18 kms
12/02/45		Leiske	20 kms
13/02/45	Via Senftenberg	Ruhland	25 kms
14/02/45	Arthur's birthday	Blochwitz	19 kms
15/02/45	Via Grossenhian	Weissig	21 kms
16/02/45	Via Riesa	Oschatz	26 kms
17/02/45		Gottwitz	17 kms
18/02/45		Grimma	18 kms
19/02/45	Changed guard	Oelzschau	15 kms
20/02/45	near Leipzig	Wiederoda	24 kms
21/02/45	Via Bohlen	Bunthal	18 kms
22/02/45		Grossjena	28 kms
23/02/45	Stalag IXC	Bad Sulsa	16 kms
24/02/45	Via Apolda	Kapellendorf	18 kms
25/02/45		Linderbach	28 kms
26/02/45	Via Erfurt	Siebleben	25 kms
27/02/45		Mechterstadt	16 lms
28/02/45	Eisenach	Stedtfeld	20 kms
01/03/45	Via Gerstungen	Obersuhl	25 kms

359

02/03/45		Heimboldhausen	13 kms
03/03/45	Rested for 1 day		
04/03/45	Via Vacha	Grossebach	32 kms
05/03/45		Ruckers	7 kms
06/03/45	Rested for 1 day		
07/03/45	Via Fulda	Neuhof	27 kms
08/03/45	Schluctern	Steinau	25 kms
9/3/45 – 13/3/45	Rested in a barn		
14/03/45	Stalag IXB	Near Bad Orb	16 kms
02/04/45	Released by Yanks		
04/04/45	Moved to Field Hospital		
06/04/45	Flight to Paris		
07/04/45	Train to St Val		
10/04/45	RAF to England		

Acknowledgements

Organisations

Skipton Public Library where I spent many hours accessing their material in a comfortable work space.

Yorkshire Ramblers Club Library where I spent an interesting afternoon

Craven Pothole Club Library which I never visited but accessed through its librarian, Pat Halliwell

North Yorkshire County Record Office, Northallerton where I spent two days

Stalag VIIIB Museum at Lambinowice, Poland which I was planning to visit in person in March 2020 but was prevented by the COVID lockdown. Thanks to the staff and volunteers, both Polish and English, who answered my online queries and created an incredibly informative website, www.lamsdorf.com and Facebook Group (Stalag VIIIB/344 Lamsdorf Prisoners of War).

Individuals

Firstly the family:

Duncan Elson, my brother-in-law, whom I have to thank for the maps, for working his magic on many of the photos and most particularly, for the cover design. Once again, thank you for your patience Duncan especially when dealing with a picky sister-in-law.

John Waterfall and Fran Elson, my siblings, for your ongoing encouragement and support.

Nicola Waterfall, my niece, for whose research skills I am

eternally grateful and who has built (and is still building), with help from her father John, a brilliant website www.waterfall.name. Nicola was also the person who introduced me to the Stalag VIIIB/344 Lamsdorf Facebook Group.

Jenny Waterfall, my cousin Roger's wife who allowed me to borrow her copy of Arnold Waterfall's unpublished autobiography. I could then get it scanned and distribute a digital copy to other members of the family.

Brendalyn Horl, my cousin in Austria who scanned for me some pages from Arnold's autobiography that were missing from Jenny's copy.

Jane Dewhurst, my cousin in Canada who produced a veritable cache of family photos, many of which family on this side of the Atlantic had not seen before and some of which were used in the book.

Next, friends and acquaintances:

David Handley, Albert Chapman and John and Marion Wilson for their memories of Sid from the 1950s onwards. Albert also for allowing me access to the Yorkshire Ramblers' Club Library

Stephen Craven in South Africa for the search he did for publications relating to the Waterfall brothers in local (Yorkshire) publications.

Pat and Ric Halliwell for the copies of photos from the Craven Pothole Club Journals and their generousity in copying these free of charge.

Beverley Breare, a volunteer at Skipton Library and an old friend from Embsay, for her hstorical research on Skipton and environs

Sue & Brian Swales for documents relating to 'Lyndhurst' 26

Skipton Road, Embsay.

Jane Shawcross for the photos of Crete 1941, taken by her father Leslie Vickers.

Ros Lomas for the photos of Stalag VIIIB from her father, Hilary Jarvis's papers.

Robin Kay for the Long March route from her father-in-law, Arthur Pattinson's papers also for information about Tost Reserve Lazarett.

David Walmsley for the photo of the Tost medics from his father's papers.

Next, my Readers

These were the people who scoured chapters for spelling, punctuation and grammatical mistakes. Also frequently suggesting improvements in expression or organisation, what was 'over the top' and needed to be removed or extras that needed be included.

They are: John Waterfall, Fran Waterfall, Chris Harrison, Sheena Carter, Janine Hogben, all in the UK, Laurel Henry and Peter Walton in Australia and Terry Sumner in New Zealand.

Thanks for your patience with my questions and your interest which meant you agreed to 'one more chapter'. The result was that every chapter was read and commented on by at least two people. Whether I took their advice was my decision and the end result is solely my responsibility.

*

Finally, my ex-partner, Vaina Ioane, who helped keep me sane during the COVID pandemic with his regular phone calls. His was the friendly voice on the end of the phone who asked me what I was going to be doing that day and I replied 'working on the book'.

*

Author Profile

Sonia Waterfall was born and bred in the Yorkshire Dales before leaving home for university in Norwich, Newcastle and finally Sheffield where she gained an MA in Librarianship .

She emigrated to New Zealand with her husband in 1972 and spent the next fifteen years there, living and working in both the North and South Islands.

In 1987 she went as a volunteer to Tokelau, a New Zealand dependency in the South Pacific, where she worked for two years after which she moved to Australia with her new partner and lived there for almost thirty years.

Sonia retired in 2007 and after ten years of spending half the year in the UK and half in Australia, she settled permanently near her sister in Rothbury, Northumberland.

She started writing on retirement and has self-published two previous books, *Escape to Auschwitz: Hulda's story,* an account of her grandmother's life and death during World War II and *Choices and Opportunities: memories of a Baby Boomer,* her memoir.

All her books are available online from the publisher FeedARead at www.feedaread.com.

Lightning Source UK Ltd.
Milton Keynes UK
UKHW012014180821
389072UK00001B/17

Sonia Waterfall
8 Addycombe Cottages
Rothbury, Morpeth, NE65 7PD
Ph: 01669 838394
waterfallsonia@gmail.com

9 781839 458408